# Gone at 3:17

## Related Titles from Potomac Books

*Crucible of Fire: Nineteenth-Century Urban Fires and the Making of the Modern Fire Service*—Bruce Hensler

*Battleground New York City: Countering Spies, Saboteurs, and Terrorists since 1861*—Thomas A. Reppetto

*Rubble: How the 9/11 Families Rebuilt Their Lives and Inspired America*—Bob Kemper

# Gone at 3:17

The Untold Story of the
Worst School Disaster
in American History

David M. Brown and Michael Wereschagin

Potomac Books
Washington, D.C.

*The prose and poetry of Carolyn Jones Frei is used with her permission.*

**Library of Congress Cataloging-in-Publication Data**
Brown, David M. (David Mark), 1948–
  Gone at 3:17 : the untold story of the worst school disaster in American history / David M. Brown and Michael Wereschagin. — 1st ed.
    p. cm.
  Includes bibliographical references and index.
  ISBN 978-1-61234-153-8 (hardcover: alk. paper)
  ISBN 978-1-61234-154-5 (electronic edition)
  1. Consolidated School (New London, Tex.)—History—20th century. 2. Explosions—Texas—New London—History—20th century. 3. Disasters—Texas—New London—History—20th century. 4. High schools—Texas—New London—History—20th century. 5. Disaster victims—Texas—New London—Biography. 6. New London (Tex.)—Biography. 7. New London (Tex.)—History—20th century. I. Wereschagin, Michael. II. Title.
  LD7501.N4662B76 2012
  373.764'185—dc23

                                                        2011023365

Printed in the United States of America on acid-free paper that meets the American National Standards Institute Z39-48 Standard.

Potomac Books
22841 Quicksilver Drive
Dulles, Virginia 20166

First Edition

10 9 8 7 6 5 4 3 2

*Gone at 3:17* is dedicated to preserving the memory of the events of March 18, 1937, in honor of the many victims who perished and those who survived to courageously carry on for the sake of all of us.

*It is also dedicated with much appreciation to Clyde Williams, a great teacher and friend.*

In the darkness with a great bundle of grief
the people march.

In the night, and overhead a shovel of stars for keeps,
the people march:

"Where to? what next?"

—CARL SANDBURG, THE PEOPLE, YES

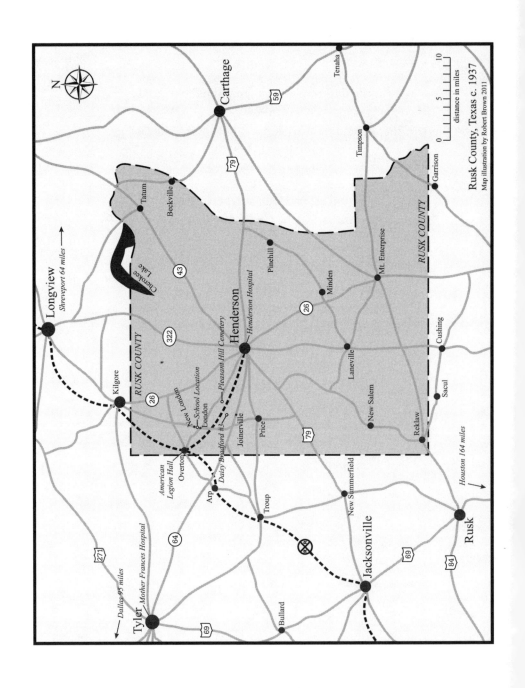

Rusk County, Texas c. 1937

Map illustration by Robert Brown 2011

# Contents

## Part III. **Aftermath, March 20–29**

## Part IV. **Epilogue**

# Acknowledgments

The authors wish to thank, first and foremost, their wives, Mary Brown and Neva German, without whom this and so much else in their lives would not be possible. These two women have shepherded this project, steered our writing, reeled us in, and lifted us up. It is for them that we write.

Mary Brown took on the additional responsibility of managing the book project in its various phases. She maintained a list of people who were interested in the book and kept them updated with e-mail newsletters. She spent painstaking hours putting together the victims list that appears in the "In Memoriam" section, gleaning information from archival records, statements by family members, and tombstones in various cemeteries. Mary also gets credit for the book's poignant title.

So many others helped, directly and indirectly, with making *Gone at 3:17* a reality that naming them runs the risk of leaving some out. Please accept our apology for any oversights in advance.

Hilary Claggett, senior editor at Potomac Books, cannot be thanked enough for believing that the manuscript she received from us contained a powerful story that needed to be told in a book. We also appreciate the skill and hard work put into improving the book by Amanda Irle, assistant production editor at Potomac Books, and copyeditor Julie Kimmel. David Fugate, our agent at LaunchBooks, showed the kind of determination in finding a good publisher for this work that makes him a champion in our hearts.

David and Mary's children—Anita and Ina Brown, Dallas Hallam, and Mackenzie, Blair, and Ted Trunzo—were of priceless assistance.

Michael would like to give thanks for years of support from Laura and Michael and from John. He is also grateful to Joshua, Alexis, Barrett, Nikolai, and Elyana for showing what can be. Finally, he wishes to acknowledge his parents—all of them—for the unconditional and the inexpressible. Mom, Dad, Mary Jo, and Victor, thank you.

Thanks also to Dr. William Hirsch for calculating the power of the monster.

Those who read successive versions of the manuscript, offering editing advice and catching t's that were not crossed and other errors, received many hugs and handshakes for that sometimes tedious work. Thanks go to Bill Thompson, Carolyn Jones Frei, John Davidson, Miles Toler, Peggy O'Leary, Joyce Lynch, Carmen Gentile, Bob Del Greco, Steve Lydick, Martha Schroeder, Mary Schroeder, and Brad Bumsted.

Special thanks to B. J. and Agust Gudmundsson—B. J. for creating our wonderful book trailers and Agust for his enduring friendship and solid advice. Special thanks, too, for Druva, who created the hauntingly beautiful music for the first book trailer.

We've thanked Rob Pratte of KDKA Radio in Pittsburgh in person many times and now give him a formal thank-you for showing strong early interest in the book and going the extra mile to let us talk about *Gone at 3:17* on the air while interviewing survivors of that terrible disaster.

Thanks to Jo Ann Gosnell for the good work she did in cleaning up some of the archival photos used in the book, and special thanks to Anita Brown for re-creating all the photos in the book from very old and weathered snapshots.

Thanks to Robert Brown, Amy McCarty, and the staff at Inhouse Associates for creating and maintaining the book's website. Thanks also to Robert for creating the map of Rusk County, Texas, in 1937.

We also are grateful to have gained insights and knowledge from the groundbreaking works of Lorine Zylks Bright and Robert L. Jackson.

# Preface

Meander along the back roads of Rusk County, Texas, into a countryside rolling with gentle hills, and you come upon a rustic cemetery.

The sun fires hazy shafts sideways through the branches of tall pines on Pleasant Hill. Near the graveyard's entrance a marker quickly catches your eye. Black stains creeping down the face of the stone show its age.

JAMES W. HARRIS

June 19, 1924

March 18, 1937

GONE, BUT NOT FORGOTTEN

Near James's plot, surrounded by white wildflowers in the spring of any given year, is the angled headstone of Sammie Lee Shoemate, born November 28, 1925, died March 18, 1937. Behind her is another, and another behind that, markers with one date in common. Turn, and there are more.

When the sun slips behind the pines, and the wind stirs softly through lush green grass covering the long-ago scars of a calamity, it is possible to imagine that you hear the whisper of voices. This is sacred ground.

March 18, 1937, has been called the day a town lost its future, the day a generation perished, the day when angels cried.

In this world there are monsters, inhuman forces that devour the innocent and the foolish, the beautiful and the shy, the strong and the weak.

They are sometimes born of the carelessness of familiarity. We surround ourselves with dangerous elements, and the more we use them, the less we think of their danger. But the substance of their danger does not change.

*Gone at 3:17* is a factual account of the worst school disaster in American history, told in the words and recollections of survivors and witnesses. It is also a cautionary tale of what can happen when we lose sight of dangers inherent in nature and gamble against their predictability.

# 1
# 3:16 p.m.

A sandy-haired, blue-eyed boy named Bill Thompson squirmed sideways, shoved his legs free of the desktop, and sat still for a moment, pondering his next move.

It was a beautiful day in East Texas, sunny and clear, the kind of balmy weather that made being cooped up inside a schoolhouse all the more tedious.[1] The afternoon had grown warm, nearing seventy degrees, and the teacher, Miss Ann Wright, instructed a student to open the windows. A breeze stirred through the classroom, lifting strands of hair on the heads of students nearest the long row of windows. Bill felt the air brush his cheeks. The day even smelled pleasant, carrying a hint of earthiness signaling the arrival of spring. Miss Wright gave permission for the students to talk among themselves, in low voices, for the last few minutes of class.

Bill was twelve years old and smitten. He wanted desperately to flirt with a pretty girl two desks away named Billie Sue Hall. Whenever they met in the halls or the cafeteria and talked, something seemed special between them—at least that's how the boy felt, and he was pretty sure she felt it too.

Bill leaned toward Ethel Dorsey, the quiet, sweet girl between them, and whispered a fifth grader's plea: "Switch seats with me?" Ethel smiled impishly and agreed.[2]

On a ground-floor wing of London Junior-Senior High School, often simply referred to as the New London school, Carolyn Jones had followed a teacher, Mrs. C. R. Sory, and her classmate Barbara Moore into a vacant room where Mrs. Sory could help the girls prepare for a spelling contest. The girls were the finalists who would represent their school in a county-wide interscholastic match the next day. Mrs. Sory, a fifth-grade teacher, had taken Carolyn and Barbara out of their regular fifth-grade classes so they could practice.

Carolyn felt good about her young life for the first time in a long while. Her family had moved out of the garage located a few hundred feet from the Old London Baptist Church and even closer to an oil derrick. They had shared the garage with another family; only a hung blanket separated them. The Joneses moved into a house newly built with green lumber and tucked into a stand of trees near London. The location provided more privacy, and the dwelling offered more room than the garage had. The new house had a bedroom on one side, a lean-to on the other, and a gas refriger-ator and range in the kitchen. The move delighted Carolyn's mother, who could now make ice cubes for their tea and serve special dishes and des-serts to them on trays—"oven roasts and towering lemon meringue pies," Carolyn remembered. She watched her mother cook, her "pale tapering fingers, lightly dusted with freckles like cinnamon gracing baked custard, whipping and stirring, dismembering a fryer, cutting skillfully through the joints. I looked at my own hands, small and square like my Welsh carpen-ter father's, the nails on my stubby fingers chewed to the quick." When they finished their feasts, Carolyn stood on an apple box or a chair beside the sink to wash their dishes. Some of the locals, those who'd moved to this corner of East Texas, which had been quiet before oil was discovered beneath it, called Carolyn's family "oil-field trash." Such derision mattered little to the workers and their families, a transient crowd robbed of their roots by the Great Depression. "All they wanted was to eke out a living until they could return to their previous homes and lives, to avoid the trek to California or to the fruit fields or logging camps of the Northwest," Caro-lyn recalled. "I was happy. After so many moves, so much time as a lonely stranger, I had found home in our small unpainted house, in school and in the redbrick church. I thought I could live forever in that familiar place, withstanding the biting cold and the baking heat, trading what others might see as poverty for the wealth of optimism and the warmth of shelter."

Only nine years old, Carolyn had lived all over Oklahoma and Texas. She had been pulled into and out of schools as her roughneck stepfather chased jobs on wooden derricks. The East Texas oil boom that drew her family to New London in 1934 was still going strong and expected to last for years to come.

Mrs. Sory, wife of the school's band director, was Carolyn's homeroom teacher. She was "a soft-spoken young woman in her late twenties with kind brown eyes behind rimless glasses," Carolyn recalled. "Her hair was finger-waved in the latest style, her dress simple and modest as the school board and the community would require. She was slightly round."[3]

Carolyn and the students of New London had been raised against the backdrop of the Great Depression. By 1937 those hard times finally appeared to be receding.

Hundreds of other students, teachers, and visitors—honeycombed inside the sprawling two-story centerpiece of the richest rural school district in America—grew restless as the final class period drew short. Fidgeting children slid their pants seats and dresses over smooth chairs. Elbows leaned on durable wooden desktops. The final moments crawled inside this sanctuary of solid walls and scuffed floors, sturdy doors and tall windows, stairwells built to be filled with galloping students, and ceilings planed to echo the stampeding footfall of an exodus into a bright, budding Thursday afternoon. The school day was nearly history.

Friday had been declared a holiday for the Interscholastic League contests taking place in Henderson, the county seat about ten miles to the southeast. The school bells, silent but set to ring in less than fifteen minutes, would signal more than the end of another tiresome day in class. They were to herald that glorious, giddy prize of childhood—the three-day weekend.

Young eyes glanced at the thin second hands gliding in measured fits around moon-faced clocks. Minds drifted, paper rustled, and seven thousand cubic feet of natural gas whispered into the darkness below.

Superintendent William Chesley Shaw left his office with D. C. Saxon, the janitor, and Frank Hodges, the contractor. Shaw strolled toward the exit, the others in tow, to monitor the progress of school buses being loaded with students from the elementary school two hundred yards away. He pushed open the heavy door near the northwest corner of the high school, and he squinted into the light. The superintendent's round spectacles glinted in the sunshine.

Could Hodges finish the job in time, Shaw wanted to know. "Tomorrow, Saturday the latest," Hodges said. As much as any man, he'd built Shaw this magnificent school. A grease trap for the cafeteria would be a snap.

"So long as it's done by Monday," Shaw said.[4]

James Henry Phillips, a four-year-old handful, darted toward the high school, missing the trio by inches. James's mother, waiting outside, had given the child permission to go to his older brother's classroom so James could walk out with his hero when the bell rang.[5]

The Parent-Teacher Association (PTA) meeting was winding down in the gymnasium a short distance behind the junior-senior high school. Bobby Joe Phillips, seven, was acting up, running about like an unleashed puppy, so his mother sent him to wait in the car. Felton Waggoner, junior high school principal, ducked out of the meeting and strode west toward the high school. He would help clear the halls after the bell rang and corral students onto their homeward-bound buses. But first Waggoner was on a brief mission for the PTA mothers. They needed a few more sheets of blank paper to use for ballots in the election of new officers. Waggoner was heading to his office in the high school.

Lonnie Barber sat behind the steering wheel of one of the idling rigs parked in the roundabout, while young children, elementary students whose classes were dismissed a few minutes earlier than those in the high school, clambered into seats in the bus trailer. Barber's four children, three sons and one daughter, were in classes in the junior-senior high school. Students in the fifth through eleventh grades were assigned to the high school. The first through fourth grades attended the adjacent grammar school. A twelfth grade was not customary at the time, nor was kindergarten.

For a lucky, unwatched few, the weekend had begun. A business teacher had gone early to a match in Henderson. She left her class supervised only by the memory of her instructions: to spend the period copying an exercise ten times. "Yes, ma'am," her students told her; she must have known what they meant.

"The girls and boys were cutting up, naturally, and we were only about half through with our work," recalled Catherine Hughes. Hughes had permission to go to the gym before the PTA meeting concluded, and she was waiting for the teacher who was going to escort her. When the math teacher, J. H. Bunch finally arrived, they walked together out of the building toward the gymnasium.[6]

Bill Griggs, a fifth grader, jumped at the chance to do an errand for his teacher. Asked to empty a trash can, Bill complied gladly. He grabbed the can and headed to a trash bin out back. The chore gave him an early sampling of the bright afternoon, perfumed with the smell of spring, just outside the school's doors.[7]

Lillian Anderson, a seventh grader, hurried toward the high school. She and other girls were playing softball on the practice diamond behind the school during their physical education class. As the afternoon sun bore down, heating the air and the dirt across the open field, Lillian's throat became parched. She had decided to slip away from the practice long enough to get a drink of water. It was almost time, anyway, for her to meet her sister, Allene, a sixth grader, when classes let out. Lillian was fourteen and had the job of shepherding Allene and Billie, their first-grade sister, onto the school bus each afternoon. A big, wide field of stubble grass and knee-high brush lay between the bus stop and their house, and their mother insisted that Lillian always accompany the younger girls across the lonesome meadow.

Billie Anderson had just gotten out of class in the grammar school and was heading toward the high school to meet her sisters. A friend caught up with her and asked Billie to play a game of jacks. Billie, six, figured there was time at least for one game, but afterward she would need to hurry. Her mother was strict about rules. If Billie failed to meet Lillian and Allene on time, they had orders to come looking for her, and they might all miss the bus.

"Just a quick game," Billie told her friend, and they both dropped to their knees and scattered jacks on the concrete walkway.

Allene Anderson sat in her classroom longing for the bell to ring. The day was so pretty she couldn't wait to get outside. None of the sisters had wanted to catch the bus that morning. When they learned their mother was planning to go shopping at Montgomery Ward in Tyler, the three girls begged her to let them skip school and accompany her to the city. Going to Tyler was always an adventure. Lola Anderson, their mother, smiled at the silly question. School came first. She reminded the older girls to watch after Billie when they were crossing the long field. She kissed them good-bye.

Now Billie scooped up the last of the jacks when the ball bounced high. "I won! Got to go." But her friend squealed that quitting after just one game wasn't fair. She pleaded with Billie to give her one more chance.

In a fifth-grade classroom, Zana Jo Curry recited her book report on *Rip Van Winkle.* Her copper-colored hair lay in a half-bowl shape around her soft features and oval face. Zana had been nervous, as always, having to speak in front of her classmates. It didn't matter how well prepared she was, apprehension swelled in her chest until Zana felt her heart pounding at the base of her throat and her temples flushing with heat. She had carefully written the report and practiced it over and over, before the mirror in her bedroom at home and several more times in front of her mother, who was very active in the PTA. Her mother praised the work and told Zana she would do an excellent job reciting it. And sure enough, as soon as the child opened her mouth and the first few words fluttered out, the anxiety popped like a balloon, leaving Zana perfectly calm. Now the words flowed as smoothly as a stream trickling over a stone. "Rip Van Winkle was a quaint man who lived in a quaint time, and one afternoon he fell fast asleep, thinking it was just a nap."[8]

Students in a nearby classroom were finishing a test on *Treasure Island,* the adventure story by Robert Louis Stevenson. Another class discussed the life of poet and storyteller Edgar Allan Poe.

Girls in home economics class baked cookies, cut cloth, and threaded needles. Boys in the manual training shop sawed planks, hammered nails, and stained nearly finished cabinets. One of them needed the electric sander.

Second-grader Marie Beard slipped into the empty hallway and stepped toward her sister's class. Her footfalls sounded amplified and hollowed by smooth walls and right angles. She and Helen had permission to leave school a few minutes early. The sisters were planning to walk out together.[9]

The typing room ticked softly. Absent was the clack and clatter of a roomful of students hammering upon every machine. Only a few pupils, pecking gingerly at the keys, remained in the room. Most of the class and the teacher, Miss Hazel Shaw, the superintendent's daughter, had already made the journey to Henderson High School to compete in the contest's early rounds.

Carroll Freeman Evans had finished teaching his last class for the day. He had lingered a while after the bell, talking with Willie Tate, who used the same classroom for teaching the final-period science class. Evans gave Tate a couple of pointers about covering a lesson on phases of the moon in an entertaining way. Evans, the school's former football and basketball coach, had confiscated six basketballs and shaded them with white paint to represent various moon phases. The all-white ball was the full moon. The unpainted one was the new moon. The others were shaded with waxing and waning phases. Tate thanked Evans for the demonstration, and Evans headed home.

At a small white house, only a short distance from the school's rear, Evans now stood beside the clothesline on his lawn and looked for his toddler. The schoolteacher spotted him playing nearby, between the wooden home and the school's beige brick wall. Evans stepped back inside, to the ironing board, and tapped the iron's metal with the tip of his middle finger to test its heat. He looked out the window once more and watched his son for a long moment. Worried the boy would totter inside without anyone noticing, Evans pulled the iron's cord out of the wall so his child would not be burned.[10]

Music teacher Mattie Queen Price was explaining a piano recital piece to one of her pupils and the child's mother. The trio stood just outside the door of Miss Price's classroom, while several of her piano students worked through a lesson inside the room.

Queen, as she was known to everyone, had hoped to finish a few minutes early and drive the four miles to her apartment in Overton before her brother Bud got there. Bud Price managed the Overton Chamber of Commerce. When he and Queen met for breakfast that morning at an Overton café, she asked him to drop by the apartment in the afternoon. She had something important to tell him—a surprise. She wouldn't give him even a hint at the café.[11] Queen told Bud she expected to arrive home early because of the PTA meeting. Classes usually were dismissed an hour early on the afternoon the PTA met. But today the school administration decided to hold the students for the full school day because of the long weekend to come. Now it looked as though Queen wouldn't be able to leave until at least 3:30, and she hoped Bud hadn't already come and gone.

As she chatted with Mrs. Euda Alice Walker and her daughter, Lucille, about the recital, the music teacher was surprised to see Eddie Herman Gauthreaux padding through the hall toward her. The third grader was one of Queen's special students. Eddie stuttered at times. Queen's training as a voice teacher included methods to help children overcome stammering. Queen had finished a lesson with Eddie during the last period, and she was puzzled to see him back at her class. The boy explained that he had forgotten his jacket. Miss Price told Eddie to get the jacket. "Hurry so you don't miss your ride," she said.

On the lower level of the school, shop teacher Lemmie Butler plugged in an electric sander. He lifted the power switch. Metal neared charged metal. A blue spark flashed.[12]

# Part I. **Calm**

# 2
# Daybreak, March 18

Jolted to consciousness by a dream, Joseph Wheeler Davidson awoke in the dark stillness well before dawn. He stared at his bedroom ceiling, its white paint reflecting midnight blue, and drew in a deep breath.

Sweat had moistened the bottom sheet, and it clung to the curve of his back, a warm dampness against his skin and muscle. He remained still, hoping not to wake his wife. The bedroom doors of their oil-patch home all were open, and he heard one of his four children stir, then sink back into rest. In these solitary moments, his nightmare continued to flash its vivid menace. He had dreamed of the oil field, of one of his men, of death.

He had envisioned a young man perched high on a drilling derrick. His crew's derrick man, Dewey Deer, was clinging to the wooden tower with one gloved hand, while his other hand coiled wire cables to keep them clear of the churning machinery as another slimy section of drill stem rose from the well. Deer slipped and seemed for a moment to hang suspended in the air. Gravity took hold. Momentum followed. The big, rawboned country boy, accelerating as he fell, arms and legs swinging awkwardly in every direction, twisted in space as his hat shot away from his head. In the final moment, he seemed little more than a blur. Davidson watched the body slam against the wood planks at the derrick's base and heard the sickening cracks.[1]

The derrick was a dangerous place with a dangerous history. The very structure borrowed its name from Thomas Derrick, an Elizabethan-era hangman who invented a more efficient gallows that relied on crane-like wooden beams and pulleys rather than the crude setup of a rope tossed over a plank or branch. Everything had a past and a purpose, and Davidson, a man of reason above all else, believed reality governed every step a man was fated to take. He counted on no stories from a book to elevate his life to heaven, and hell was all around in the chaos of the natural world. The wolf lurking in the storybook forest can hurt no one; the real beast has sharper teeth, keener eyes. Red Riding Hood never had a chance. For Davidson, mystery did not succumb to mysticism. His hard shell had shielded him through the Great War and the Great Depression to New London, an oil boomtown churning inside a bent and muddied country.[2]

On this morning, though, logic offered no solace. The ethereal vision of tragedy gripped him, yet lying in his bed he himself could find nothing of which to take hold. Inaction was a palpable fear; better to keep a grip on a 10-pound pipe wrench. Davidson found this feeling unfamiliar, and the unfamiliarity added to his anxiety. He was haunted by the vague whisper of death.

Though Davidson spurned superstitions and myth, mysticism bore responsibility for the roughneck and his young family coming to East Texas in the first place. Not ten years before, the Louisiana-born Davidson and his wife, Mary, a Pennsylvania native, would have found no reason to venture into the farm country of this region. But for a precipitant wildcatter, a broken drilling rig, and a snake-oil geologist with lunatic methodology, the Black Giant might have remained locked two-thirds of a mile below ground in its vast, 65-million-year-old chamber. The wealth that created jobs for Davidson and his contemporaries was found in East Texas not by reason but by eccentricity and blind luck that aimed a drill into the largest oil field known then to exist.

The last great oil boom in America originated in an Ardmore, Oklahoma, home nearly a decade before the first gusher was struck. The home belonged to Columbus Marion Joiner, a real estate prospector who had made and lost millions of dollars by selling land and mineral leases—sometimes to several people at once. On a night long before Davidson's nightmare, Joiner had leaned over his lamp-lit table and frowned.[3]

A short man, already bent at the waist from a bout of rheumatic fever, Joiner wanted a closer look at what his partner had just told him was a treasure map to their next fortune.[4] *Fortune.* The word alone powered more of Joiner's life than any other thing. He was among the last of the Wild West entrepreneurs, half man of confidence and half proprietor of dreams. How a person remembered him depended on how their deal worked out—and at the time it was made, rarely did the buyer or Joiner really know where it was headed. Yet even to those who despised him, he would one day become known as Dad, for being the undisputed father of the East Texas oil rush.

Standing in his sparse dining room, early in the 1920s, Joiner found no hint of the vast wealth he was destined to find in the puzzling map his partner had unfolded on the table in front of him. In fact, the map gave no hint of anything, as far as Joiner could tell. The furrows in his brow deepened.

The big man standing next to him uncorked a jug of corn whiskey and poured a couple of fingers into his glass. He ached to know what Joiner thought. The lamp cast both of their shadows against the wall behind them—Joiner's stooped and narrow as he leaned over the table, A. D. "Doc" Lloyd's bulky and bearish as he tossed back his head and downed the whiskey in a single gulp.[5]

The pair had been friends for years, a yin and yang within the world of quick-money schemes. What Joiner finessed his way around, Lloyd, with 320 powerful pounds on his six-foot frame, bulldozed through with jovial explosions of energy. He would make patently absurd statements—"This scar on my head? Got it in a fight with Pancho Villa, that son of a bitch!"—in ways that made listeners want desperately to believe him. Supposedly he'd once been a physician and pharmacist in Ohio. He boasted of six marriages and innumerable children. Born Joseph Idelbert Durham, he once traveled across the South as a salesman under the guise of "Dr. Alonzo Durham's Great Medicine Show." Shortly thereafter he changed his name to A. D. Lloyd to avoid being found by several of his previous wives. He wore khaki clothes; tall, laced boots; and a sombrero over steel-gray hair. He had mined for gold, studied medicine, and practiced as a veterinarian with dubious credentials.[6] Lately, he'd begun to fancy himself a geologist. He was a cunning self-promoter, an audacious peddler of absurdities, and—if you didn't buy what he was selling—one hell of a good time. Joiner, a sweet talker with a calming demeanor, was much more reserved in his approach.

Columbus Joiner was born March 12, 1860, in Lauderdale County, Alabama, not long before his father, Confederate corporal James M. Joiner, marched away from his farm to fight in the Civil War. Corporal Joiner was killed in 1864 during a battle in Mississippi. Columbus's mother, Lucy, died when he was a little boy. It was a wonder his hardscrabble life went anywhere. After being raised by an older sister, who taught him to read by using the Bible, Joiner set out on his own at seventeen and picked cotton long enough to realize there had to be an easier way to make a living. He became a politician, studied law in Tennessee, and was elected to the state legislature. Eventually he met back up with his sister in Ardmore, Oklahoma, where she had married a Choctaw man and was living with the tribe. Joiner, who didn't drink, smoke, or curse, became a land dealer by helping the Native Americans lease tribal property.[7] He decided to try his hand as an oil wildcatter after talking it over with Doc Lloyd.

The map Lloyd had laid on his friend's table showed the United States. A network of carefully drawn lines overlaid its surface, crisscrossing and diverging in bizarre patterns. Where each of the lines intersected, forming an apex, a new line spun away like a strand of spider's silk until it crossed another line and created a new apex. The web of pencil markings skewed westward across the Mississippi River and drew to a center near the eastern boundary of Texas.

"Okay," Joiner murmured, "what am I looking at?"

Lloyd's fleshy face twisted into a sly grin. He had expected Joiner to be mystified. Now he had to be delighted to see a quizzical frown appear on the old wildcatter's face. Lloyd jabbed a long index finger at one point on the map.

All the main lines, Lloyd explained, were drawn between the major oil discoveries in the United States. Joiner, who knew the existing terrain of oil country as well as any living person, immediately perceived what his friend had done with the map. Using a straight edge and sharp pencil, the self-proclaimed geologist had connected America's oil fields in much the same way a child would follow the numbered dots in a picture puzzle. Only this was a puzzle without a picture. Some of the lines were short and others crossed the entire continent.[8]

Edwin Drake's famous 1859 discovery in Titusville, Pennsylvania, tied into the mammoth Seminole field of Oklahoma, which connected to Spindletop in Texas—the great gusher that on January 10, 1901, proclaimed the twentieth century the Age of Petroleum. California's crude oil fields linked to fields in other states. The maze of pencil lines converged at a spot in East Texas, about midway between Dallas and the Louisiana state line.

Lloyd called that spot on the map the "apex of apexes." He told Joiner his best bet was to drill for oil precisely there. Joiner knew the area well. He had passed through it often. The tracings on the map suggested a spot in a piney woods region a couple of miles from the sleepy community of London, Texas. The region's nickname was Poverty Flat.

Joiner was skeptical. The major oil companies had explored the area and had come up empty-handed. And he knew Lloyd was no more a doctor of geology than Joiner was a guru of oil and gas. It was a gamble, but Joiner knew too that every now and then a lucky strike could send a spout of incredible wealth shooting from the earth. Joiner had spent his life, and several of his life's fortunes, on gambles such as this. He was ready to bet everything he possessed to win the prize.

Joiner had given up on Lloyd's hunch once before, and it had cost him. Although Lloyd had never even taken a formal course in geology, he told Joiner, "I've studied the earth more, and know more about it, than any professional geologist now alive will ever know." The surveys Lloyd furnished his friend and client through the years were so filled with mistakes that other oil-field surveyors dismissed them as works of fiction.[9] Yet, had Joiner drilled eighteen feet deeper in the spot where Lloyd had told him years earlier to "punch a hole" in Oklahoma, the wildcatter would have tapped into the heart of the great Seminole oil field, which was ultimately left for others to discover. Following another tip from Lloyd, Joiner would have discovered the great Cement field in Oklahoma had he continued to drill about two hundred feet. Using his peculiar chart of circles and lines on the U.S. map, Lloyd now had pinpointed for Joiner where to drill in East Texas.

Lloyd clapped his friend on the back and poured himself another shot. Joiner never touched the stuff. "I will never quit a well without drilling eighteen feet deeper," Joiner quipped.[10]

Despite Doc Lloyd's boasting and Joiner's later pleas to lease land on widows' farmland, neither man imagined the enormity of what awaited them. In a quiet corner of a country parched of wealth, they would tap an enormous black reservoir, covering three hundred square miles and at some points as thick as seventy-five feet. With the gushing oil came a flood of roughnecks, squeezed southward by hard times into a muddy stew of prosperity. Historians described it as "the California gold rush, the Klondike, the Oklahoma land rush, and the wildest of past oil booms all rolled into one."[11] The population of Kilgore, near the heart of the Black Giant, ballooned in just days from a village of a few hundred townsfolk to a sprawling town with thousands of newcomers. As the months rolled by, villages of canvas and cardboard dwellings transformed, plot by plot, into towns called Joinerville, Pistol Hill, and New London.

With industry and broad backs, they pulled from the earth the fuel of an American era. The great locomotives and steamships of the Industrial Revolution met their end in these verdant hills, undone by pockets of workers looking for something more. Towers rose tall and narrow like forests of Italian cypress. They sprouted from backyards, farm fields, and church lots. Lumbering machines ground holes through the earth. Drill stems toppled onto men. Pressure pockets pushed up around drill holes, swallowing whole derrick crews into bubbling, black sinkholes. For all this, the pay wouldn't make a man rich, but the work kept him too busy to know the curse of quiet, desperate hours in a soup line. The roughnecks' skin did what it could. It creased and set to accommodate habit and motion, sacrificed softness to sun and wind and dust, and turned their palms to rock.

The foolish or careless seldom lasted long enough to become supervisors like Joe Davidson. When Joiner's discovery well came in a gusher in October 1930, Joe and Mary Davidson were raising four children in a rented house near West Columbia, Texas, about thirty miles from the Brazos River's outlet into the Gulf of Mexico.[12] They had lived there since about 1918, the year the twenty-square-mile oil field was discovered in the salt domes near the gulf. A frenzy of drilling that year brought in the heavy operations of oil-field giants like the Texas Company—later known as Texaco—and Gulf Production Company. At the field's peak in 1921, West Columbia wells pumped 12.5 million barrels of oil.[13] On July 21 of that year, the Davidsons' baby boy, Joseph Wheeler Davidson Jr., was born. The couple's other children, all girls, came along shortly after: Marilla in 1923; Helen in 1924; and finally, Anna in 1926.

Production had fallen steeply in West Columbia by the time the stock market crash of 1929 unleashed the Great Depression. The major oil companies slashed production operations in the field, and within less than two years the town's population plummeted from nearly 2,500 to just 1,000.[14]

Joe and Mary Davidson joined the exodus. They packed all their belongings, tied mattresses and boxes to the roof of their car, and, with their children, headed north toward New London and the Black Giant. Word of Joiner's extraordinary discovery, and the wealth of jobs it had created, proved irresistible to the Davidsons. There they found something more permanent, a new bounty of backbreaking labor and full dinner tables.

On the morning of March 18, 1937, Joe Davidson rose quietly from his bed and walked to the window. His life had been a constant challenge, from an upbringing in poverty-stricken Cajun country to the carnage of war-torn Europe to the oil fields. He had guarded his soul behind bars of clenched teeth. What gentility he preserved belonged to his family. The rest of life was work. This morning he had plenty of time before he needed to prepare for his day, but the nightmare was still too fresh for rest or peace. It was barely above fifty degrees, but soon crickets would be chirping in bushes outside the house. The forecasters called for clear skies and calm winds, with temperatures warming. This countryside of low, rolling hills and fields dotted with growing towns and rural hamlets generally enjoyed pleasant weather this time of year. It tempted people in the prediction business to imagine consistency where none existed. Tornadoes could snap from the bellies of storm clouds, snatching metal and flesh from the ground, and rarely would the forecasters predict it. Even on this day, the weather seemed calm, yet hundreds of miles from East Texas, a towering, violent storm was moving slowly northward from the Gulf of Mexico. The pressure in New London was falling, the gases in the air expanding.[15]

Davidson pushed back against the ghost of his dream. He began to dress as his wife and children stirred from their sleep. Beneath him and for three hundred square miles around, the Black Giant sprawled with monstrous, pent-up power.

# 3

# The Superintendent

William Chesley Shaw sat at his desk in his home on the school's campus and was bothered by other people's headaches. For more than a week he'd been investigating recurring complaints from students and teachers about strange headaches occurring during class in various parts of the high school. Others reported irritated eyes.[1] So far, the source was a mystery. He had the janitors check for a gas leak, and they found none—although one of them had wiggled into the crawl space one day and, right under the gas line, lit a match so he could see better.[2] The memory made Shaw push up his round glasses and massage the bridge of his nose. Today he would meet several school directors for a walk-through of the building to check again for the source of the problem.[3]

The headaches were one item on a lengthy agenda requiring Shaw's attention this day. The monthly meeting of the Parent-Teacher Association at the high school was the highlight.

The medium-height, trim superintendent of the sprawling school district—serving more than twelve hundred students—had begun his career thirty-seven years earlier, teaching a dozen children inside a rural one-room schoolhouse near Jacksonville, Texas.[4] Shaw had come a long way since then. The London Consolidated School District had risen rapidly on the region's fortunes and was considered now to be the wealthiest rural district in the nation, some said the world.[5] This had little to do with the parents' wealth. Most of them, like Joe Davidson, were oil-field workers who generally struggled to make ends meet. Any money left after paying for rent, food, clothes, and the car was doled out for rare luxuries—a trip to an ice cream parlor or a movie over the weekend—or saved for a new appliance or the family's first radio. Other parents operated family farms, and many of the farmers were forced to take jobs on the side to supplement income from farming.

Chesley Shaw was born and raised on a family farm about two miles from "Old" London, the original hamlet that gave rise to New London. Hard times shaped much of his life, even before the Depression hit. Although he was superintendent of a school district awash in oil money, Shaw remained tightfisted when it came to expenditures he considered frivolous, ever aware as a student of history that bad times followed good. Only a fool loses sight of this, Shaw thought. The nation's economy sputtered slowly toward a recovery, but nobody could guarantee the bottom wouldn't fall out again—even in East Texas.

Around Superintendent Shaw's white-walled home, a dozen wells chugged away throughout the day and night, drawing barrels of money from the Black Giant. The families who followed the East Texas oil boom—transients and displaced workers seeking shelter from the Depression—brought with them the need for schools, and New London had commissioned a masterpiece three years earlier. The junior-senior high school—a two-story, 250-foot-long, E-shaped building—sat at the district's center, a jewel of beige brick and red Spanish tile. To run it, they hired Shaw, now sixty-one, an educator whose accomplishments at New London echoed across the country in educational journals and news stories. The oil money flowing in allowed the district luxuries no school had ever acquired. A crew erected towers around their football field crowned with floodlights, among the first Friday night lights in a state that would one day become famous for them. Shaw had opposed the lights but was outmaneuvered by the football coach, Carroll Evans, a wily and garrulous man whose block-like noggin begat the nickname Boxhead. Shaw thought the lights garish and extravagant. Boxhead thought they were a hoot.

Shaw's renown made him one of the region's most prestigious figures; PTA meetings like the one coming this afternoon never passed without a stream of mothers looking for a quick word with him. He spoke to each of them, and they loved him for it, but the exercise was time-consuming and required a measure of diplomacy that could be difficult to muster after a long day in a building filled with adolescents. Because of this demand on him and his teachers, he normally declared early dismissals on days the PTA met. Today he had made an exception. The district's athletes and top students would spend the next two days competing against their rivals in nearby Henderson. Shaw declared Friday a holiday so the students not participating could cheer on their classmates. With no school the next day, he decided to keep the children in class today until their normal dismissal time of 3:30 p.m.

Shaw stood in front of his bedroom mirror and examined himself. His large, inquisitive eyes peered at his reflection from behind the round lenses of wire-framed glasses. Some students considered his eyes owlish and wise. Others saw them as forbidding and stern. If you were quick enough, you could catch a glint of humor, flash of approval, spark of kindness, or shadow of doubt.

Shaw carefully combed his hair and inspected his clothes, head to toe, in the dressing mirror. He wore his hair short on the sides, trimmed neatly up around his ears, and longish on the top. He shaved with a straight-razor.

The sun crested the horizon at 6:24 a.m. Shaw gathered his papers into a neat pile and looked up from his desk, through the window, toward his school. The pink glow from the sunrise washed over the building's red-tiled roof. He heard his wife pad into the kitchen and his children—a grown daughter and teenage son—begin to shuffle sleepily in their rooms. Two other sons were grown and gone from home, and another daughter was living at a teaching academy in nearby Tyler.

Although his father had been a Confederate soldier during the Civil War, Shaw thought of himself a modern man who embraced change when clear reasoning supported it. Electric lights around a football field seemed a foolish way to spend good money, regardless of the school district's wealth. The lightbulb burning in his study, though, obviously brightened his life with a convenience undreamed of when he was a farm boy squinting to read by the flickering fireplace and coal oil lamps. The house the school district provided to the superintendent also had the luxury of gas heaters and a gas-burning stove for his wife, Leila. The same gas line that fed the heaters in the high school and burners in the chemistry lab made it possible for Shaw and his family to take hot baths without the fuss and bother of building a fire and hauling kettles to the tub.

When he was a young man, a cold March morning like this meant Shaw would have to stoke up a blaze in the fireplace to take the chill off the house. Now, he had only to strike a match and light a heater. Amazing, the changes he'd seen in a lifetime. The superintendent stood with his back to the heater, soaking in the warmth and listening contentedly to the soft, evenly spaced whisper of flames in the grates.

# 4

# Sweet Chariot

Lonnie Barber stepped outside onto the porch and stood still a few moments, taking in the morning. He always got started a little before daybreak, no matter the day of the week. His home was swept around by rural landscape the farmer held dear. Roosters crowed in every farmhouse yard. Here and there, a cowbell jangled, hogs grunted, a car door slammed. Whip-poor-wills whistled in the meadows.

Mixed in with ordinary sounds, the chugging resonance of oil-well pumps had by then become a mechanical rhythm so prevalent throughout the region that it no longer seemed disharmonious. By 1937 the droning pumps and steam whistles of locomotives and factories had become as commonplace as church bells on Sunday.

Barber left his home and drove his car down the same gravel and dirt roads he would be following shortly in the school bus—his part-time job. He saw oil lamps burning in the windows of his neighbors' homes. Lanterns, carried by farmers and farm boys, swung along paths between the houses and barns.[1] The morning's most distinctive smell—an odor of smoke from fireplaces and kitchen stoves—traveled over rooftops throughout the scattered communities making up the school district. When Barber reached the campus, the high school and elementary school were still dark, but electric lights gleamed in the windows of Superintendent Shaw's house, called the Teacherage.

Barber parked beside the bus barn and went about inspecting his bus. The school district owned a new fleet of tractor-trailer rigs for transporting more than a thousand students to the adjacent schoolhouses.

Other drivers arrived. Most, like Barber, were farmers supplementing their income by driving part-time for the school district. Barber poured a cup of coffee from his thermos and walked the full distance around his rig to make sure the tires were inflated properly. He checked the engine oil, cleaned the windshield, and took a look at the coupling between the truck and trailer. He glanced at his watch. It was about time to start his route, which included a swing back past his own house to pick up his sons, Arden, Burton, and L. V., and his daughter, Pearl. One of the first stops all the drivers made was at the house of a conductor assigned to the bus. Conductors were teachers who rode in the trailer, which was designed like a rail car. They supervised students' conduct on trips to and from school. Conductors had to be firm because bus rides inspired more devilment than the schoolhouse, where teachers and principals kept their paddles handy. Two of the best conductors were math teachers John Propes and Lena Hunt, both forty-nine years old and strict disciplinarians. Propes's reputation as a stickler for order and accuracy was so respected by his neighbors that he routinely was chosen to count votes after an election.[2]

Barber stepped on the crank button that started the engine, shifted into low gear, and pulled out onto the road. The sunrise, painting a wider expanse of sky now, gave promise of a magnificent day.

For children on the buses, the ride to school was a long and bouncy journey across rough roads that crisscrossed throughout the school district. Drilling derricks and oil wells dotted the countryside at every bend in the road. Sporadic, slender towers stood in what had once been cornfields or watermelon patches. Flames licked from their tops, burning constantly, devouring the fumes of waste gas produced while refining oil into gasoline.

The young travelers knew the flares as markers for whatever part of the sprawling oil field they were passing through because refineries, large and small, were located at strategic points along the pipelines to cash in on some of the enormous quantity of oil flowing up from the earth each day. Some of the children could see the flares at night from their bedroom windows.

Carolyn Jones saw something repulsive dancing in these fiery lights. They reminded her of the red glare that fanned the sky when a well burned out of control. Every child growing up in the oil patch knew of such fires—"hell with the lid off," roughnecks called them. Several, each announced with an earth-shaking explosion, had occurred in New London. The fires would burn for weeks. Men died.

Men were always dying in the oil fields. Carolyn remembered a young man who came to her stepfather one night, hat in hand, to ask him for a job. Barely more than a boy, he'd married the previous year. The derrick man's job posed risks, he knew, but he had a family now, the young man told Ervin Lowe. Ervin hired him. A few weeks later, the man fell to his death, on his first wedding anniversary. The aftermath—hushed, sorrowful conversations among the grown-ups, the mortal lessons, the risks these men would take the next morning—remained with Carolyn the rest of her life. She saw as heroes these men who faced forces they did not fully understand and came home exhausted and filthy with a modest paycheck in hand.[3]

The newspaper carried stories of roughnecks dying in odd ways: a thick wire cable snapped and its powerful backlash struck a roughneck like lightning; a pipe wrench accidentally slipped from a derrick worker's hand and his friend working below the derrick was killed instantly when the 5-pound tool cracked his skull; a man operating a bulldozer backed the massive machine over another worker who had carelessly stepped into its path.

A few poor creatures actually drowned in the sludge pits at the base of the huge empty storage tanks. These men, the tank cleaners, worked on crude scaffolds just above the surface of the deep tar pools, painstakingly shoveling the sludge into buckets and removing it from the tanks. If a man's foot slipped and he plunged into the pit, he would sink slowly into gluey sludge as thick as quicksand.[4]

Fire claimed the largest toll. Boilers blew. Dynamite blasted prematurely. Explosive chemicals were handled roughly. A stray spark could ignite a well, letting loose a thunderous roar.

One of the worst of these detonations struck New London early in the boom. Nearly everybody heard it. People ran from their homes and gazed at the sky. A column of brownish-black smoke towered over the community, and the smell of burning oil quickly filled the air. Men jumped into their trucks and cars and hurried toward the site of the explosion. The first to arrive discovered that the owner of the well, Paul Vitek, and three of his employees had been blown to pieces.[5] Firefighters struggled for weeks to control the monstrous blaze. Ash and soot littered the air and settled on the rooftops and lawns. They extinguished the fire, but reminders of its ferocity lingered day and night in the gas-burning flares.

# 5

# Pleasant Hill

The morning light shone like bronze mist on hillsides and tops of pines. White, yellow, and pink wildflowers stirred in sandy beds along the roadside as the yellow school buses zoomed past. A haze lingered in the air just above the cemetery grass. The chilly morning relinquished the last of its dew as the sun bore down. The buses were rolling now, heading in both directions on the road that passed Pleasant Hill Cemetery.

The hilltop once belonged to Capt. Robert W. Smith, a veteran of the Texas Revolution. A marker shows his life spanned from 1814 to 1851—just thirty-seven years. Captain Smith rode with Sam Houston at the Battle of San Jacinto in April 1836, when Smith was twenty-two years old. General Houston's victory there, some 180 miles south of the graveyard where Smith is buried, gave Texas independence from Mexico. The cemetery first served the Pleasant Hill Cumberland Presbyterian Church, a one-room building on the pine- and oak-covered hilltop, starting with the burial of Dewitt Smith in 1850. Beside Captain Smith's grave lay buried warriors from the Civil War and the Great War.[1]

This region, this hill, once served as the gateway to Texas, a pocket of the promised land, the untamed West. Through it passed Stephen F. Austin and Sam Houston, Thomas Jefferson Rusk and J. Pinckney Henderson, Jim Bowie and Davy Crockett, the dreamers and adventurers, the ambitious and daring, the restless, rambling horde, pioneers all. Many left signs

[27]

tacked to their doors back home in North Carolina, Georgia, Tennessee, Ohio, Pennsylvania, or Maryland. Scrawled in large hand-printed letters, they read, "G.T.T." (Gone to Texas).[2]

The pioneers came in crude boats down the rivers of the North or in canoes up the winding passage of the Sabine River at the eastern boundary of Texas. They came over land in rattling wooden wagons trailing a cloud of thick yellow dust across the center of America. After crossing the river on ferry boats, they fanned out in every direction—cutting timber, clearing woods, plowing up the earth, building cabins, and founding small villages at each spot along the trail with a captivating view or reliable source of water or certain peculiarity that reminded them of the homes they left behind.

They came into the wilderness belonging to Mexico, not intending to leave the American dream behind them on the Louisiana side of the Sabine, but determined to push it forward into a rich new frontier. Just a few short decades would lapse before a new flag of stars and stripes flew over the vast land of the new state of Texas.

Heading north out of the old mission town of Nacogdoches, the pioneers' road reaches hill country. It rises weakly up one side of a low ridge and then descends lazily through wooded ravines and vine-choked hollows. Along the highest points, vistas open on broad expanses of lowlands sweeping away toward a distant plateau. Here lies the upper extreme of a forested area known as the Big Thicket. The great hardwood forest begins to give way to patches of pine, the countryside rolling beneath the cover of mixed timber. In the spring, the whole land is shades of chartreuse flecked with purplish-pink redbud trees, stark white dogwoods, and lavender wisteria. In the summer, a deep, luscious green overcomes all. The drier fall brings dusty tints to the green. Autumn colors come late, the bright red and yellow briefly painting the hills before turning them russet brown. Even in winter, bands of dark green remain where the pines stand slender at the base of the hills or bunched in thick colonies along their summits.

Students on the buses opened some of the windows, welcoming the spring-like coda to what had been a harsh winter. In mid-January, a sleet storm swept across parts of Rusk County, including Overton and New London.

Ice grew thick on the trees, bending the smallest until they touched the ground. In ramshackle homes not built for harsh winters, children huddled close to their fireplaces, their fronts burning, their backs freezing. The chill reached inside, as a string of twenty-one January days passed without a glimpse of the sun. On the 22nd day, the clouds split at noon, and the sun shone for scant minutes. On February 2, snow fell for about an hour.[3]

Helen Smoot, a seventeen-year-old senior at New London, wrote a poem about the surprise snowfall. After the sky cleared as the sun went down, she watched the moon rise. On the ground outside her window the snow reflected "like a thousand tiny diamonds."[4]

Cold remained beyond its season, with sleet and snow in the Texas panhandle and near freezing temperatures in East Texas, until the warm spell on March 18. The good weather reminded the children of festivals to come. Each year since Pleasant Hill became a cemetery, the church grounds served as the location of a festive summer picnic that drew hundreds of people from all the nearby communities. The adults used the event to perform maintenance chores throughout the cemetery—plucking weeds from around headstones, mowing, raking up leaves and fallen tree branches, restoring order and sanctity to the grounds. The children played among the trees, picked wildflowers, frolicked across the cemetery with careful and respectful steps as their parents and other adults had instructed, though with a litheness of spirit that governs the physics of childhood on a bright summer day.

As the last bus passed on the way to the New London school, dew still glistened on blades of grass in the cemetery. Although Pleasant Hill Cemetery had been in use for eighty-six years, relatively few graves were scattered about the generous portion of land that Captain Smith had donated. The landscape looked more like a green meadow than a graveyard.

# 6
# American Dreams

Lemmie Butler and Carroll Evans frequently said good morning from their adjacent porches and often chatted while strolling the short distance from their homes on Teachers' Row to their jobs in the high school.

The pair of teachers and their wives, Mary Butler and Mildred Evans, grew close during their years as next-door neighbors. The couples were both in their mid- to late twenties. Lemmie taught industrial arts and science in the school's shop, sharing with students his fondness for tinkering, carpentry, and the beauty of precision. Whenever he left his house, whether to go to work or church or to run an errand, Butler carried with him his prized pocket watch. He cherished it, both as an intricate machine and a family heirloom.

Carroll taught high school science. Mildred Evans was a teacher in the new grammar school located two hundred yards from the high school, on the downward side of a gentle slope.

Lemmie typically went outside early to get a sense of the weather so he would know how to dress. He likely saw the Evanses' little black dog curled up on the porch next door. All the homes along Teachers' Row were modest dwellings—cracker-box houses that previously sat on oil leases around the area, shelter for roughnecks and their families. Such houses were built by the thousands during the early years of the boom. Later, many of them were sold at a bargain price to people willing to jack them up off their foundations, load them on trailers, and transport them to different locations. Moving buildings became a side industry to the oil boom.

Most people tried their best to let nothing go to waste in those times. They didn't have to look far beyond their own doorsteps to see the gaunt faces of those in desperate need.

During the early part of the Great Depression—after the stock market crashed in 1929 and the jobless rate began to soar across the United States—the future understandably looked bleak to many Americans.

A caseworker for the California State Unemployment Commission jotted notes from a conversation with an octogenarian who was seeking relief in 1932. The old man told the caseworker, "Years ago Horace Greeley made a statement, 'Young man, go West and grow up with the country.' Were he living today, he would make the statement, 'Go West, young man, and drown yourself in the Pacific Ocean.'"[1]

Between 1930 and 1932 hundreds of national banks failed and thousands of state banks went broke. Their failures erased futures, wiped out savings, and devastated farmers who depended on loans to seed their fields each spring. Lives tumbled. Americans bought far fewer electric appliances. Furniture sales plummeted. Many families gave up their telephones to cut expenses. Restaurant business and jewelry sales plunged. By early 1933 banks and mortgage companies were repossessing an estimated thousand homes a day. The suicide rate jumped to an all-time high.[2]

When people on a sidewalk in New York City spotted a man outside a window high up on a skyscraper one day, a rumor spread quickly that another stockbroker was about to jump. A crowd of several thousand gathered before it came to light that the supposed jumper was actually a window washer.[3]

When John Maynard Keynes was asked if there had ever been anything like the Depression, the renowned economist replied, "Yes. It was called the Dark Ages and it lasted four hundred years."[4]

As the economy hit bottom, nearly one in four Americans couldn't find a job. The unemployment rate soared even higher in some cities.

At least twenty-nine Americans starved to death in 1933. In 1934 the official count of starvation deaths rose to 110 nationally; most of this number were children.[5] Hunger accounted for substantially more deaths than reported, especially in Southern states. The cash crops that supported the farming communities of East Texas—like the hamlets where Carroll Evans's and Mildred Jones's families lived—shriveled up well before the Depression hit Main Street USA. The boll weevil, cotton blight, and cattle tick fever made hard times a way of life for many Texans early in the twentieth century.

Even so, it was as good a time as any to fall in love. Carroll and Mildred didn't worry much about bankers and brokers running amuck on Wall Street. They invested in each other. Their romance was intoxicating and their dreams were vivid, built from scratch.

Carroll Evans borrowed a hundred dollars to start college at Sam Houston State Teachers College in Huntsville. Charlie Goodman, a family friend, took the money from his Bible and gave it to Carroll. The teenager from Spring Prairie, a village north of Houston, promised to repay the loan from his first teaching job.[6]

Mildred was born and raised in Laneville, a hamlet twelve miles south of Henderson. As a little girl on her family's plot, she churned butter, collected eggs from the hen house, and scrubbed the smoky globes of her home's oil lamps. Her brother Luther, her best friend, died when he was twelve and she was ten. Mildred turned to education to try to fill the space he'd left.

Laneville had three churches—Southern Baptist, Missionary Baptist, and Methodist—four little stores, a telephone office, and a cotton gin across the road from the school. The school was a two-story structure with a belfry. Mildred and other students in grades one through ten took turns pulling the rope that rang the bell for the start of classes, lunchtime, and dismissal.

Carroll fell for Mildred the first time he saw her. She was standing with two other girls on the steps of a building at Sam Houston State Teachers College. "I picked out the middle-sized one to be my girl," Carroll liked to quip with a wink toward Mildred.

Their commonality stretched from their upbringing in rural parts of Texas to the future they both wanted as teachers. Both came from families with seven children. Carroll's study of agriculture and science was leavened with a passion for sports, particularly football, which he wanted one day to coach. Mildred's ambition, which arose when she was in elementary school, focused on teaching elementary-age children.

Whereas Mildred was reserved, quiet, and introspective, her husband romped through each day like a broncobuster itching for his next adventure. From the time he was a teenager, Carroll's sense of humor bordered on light-hearted havoc. Late one night he and a buddy returned to the Evanses' home after dropping off their dates. Relatives visiting for a family reunion were sleeping on pallets throughout the house. Seizing the opportunity, Carroll and his friend grabbed a harness from the barn and ran through the house, slapping the harness and yelling, "Whoa! Whoa!" Nearly everyone in the house jumped up and dashed out into the night, screaming their lungs out. Neighbors came running to see if the house had caught fire.

Grandma Evans, who was hard of hearing, came out last, waddling onto the porch. "Do some of the children have colic?" she ventured.

Mildred and Carroll married on August 21, 1930, barely a year into the Depression. Mildred was eighteen and Carroll was twenty-one. In the fall of 1931 they landed jobs at a school in Pennington, Trinity County.

They bought a used Buick and took a trip to Carlsbad Caverns in New Mexico. The smoking old Buick later transported the young lovers all the way to Niagara Falls. Carroll had to jack up the car twelve times between Texas and New York to fix flat tires.[7]

They later bought a new Chevrolet with a radio. Because they couldn't afford the luxury of a radio at home, they would park the car outside their bedroom window with the radio playing. But the Depression deepened, and in 1932 the school in Pennington ran out of cash.

The East Texas oil boom rescued them. "People were just about starved to death," Mildred said. "If it hadn't been for the oil fields some of them would have starved to death."

Carroll was hired in 1933 as a coach and teacher at New London High School. "Not only did he coach everything, but he drove a bus and would take all of the football boys home after practice," Mildred said. "And not only that, they came over to the house every Saturday and washed their football uniforms in my washing machine."

The boys loved Carroll—and who wouldn't, Mildred added—because he took a genuine interest in their lives. Even though he was grown, Carroll was no less of a ham. To prove to his students he was in top form, the coach let the strongest of them punch him in the stomach any time they felt a need to hit somebody. Carroll never flinched. And he still had tricks up his sleeve. Once he hid a wooden washboard beneath his shirt and dared one of his athletes to slam him in the stomach with a sledgehammer.

"I'm not going to do that. I might hurt you," the student said.

"Go ahead," the coach insisted.

After he took a full swing, the boy's face screwed into an alarmed grimace. It sounded as if he'd cracked every rib in the coach's body.

Carroll and Mildred bought their first home, a small two-room house at the edge of the campus, in New London.

"New London was a wonderful place to be," Mildred said.

Boxhead and Troy Duran, the senior high principal, became fishing partners. The Shaws—Chesley and Leila—welcomed the new teachers, though Chesley and Boxhead Evans would clash over spending for the athletic program. Evans saw a school flush with cash, and opportunities for luxuries such as lights around the football field and twelve basketballs to allow more rapid drills. Shaw saw frivolities. More often than not, Evans won out.

"Mrs. Shaw? A very retiring lady," Mildred Evans recalled many years later. "Bess Truman reminded me of her. You know, Mr. Shaw was a little itty-bitty go-getter, like Harry Truman. Mrs. Shaw was a very retiring, quiet little woman. Well, not very little. She was kinda large."

Carroll and Mildred eventually saved enough money to invest in a side business with his father—the Tip-Top Tourist Court in Belton, Texas—to tap into the growing market of car travel and motor hotels. Keeping a dozen cabins in operable condition was more than his father could handle alone, so Carroll frequently traveled to Belton on weekends to help with upkeep.

Carroll's last class on this Thursday ended at 2:30. If all went smoothly today, he figured he could be ready to strike out for Belton before the sun went down.

# 7
# Wildcats' Pep Rally

"Let us pray now," Reverend Robert L. Jackson, pastor of the London Methodist Church, said in a clear voice that carried through a sound system out across the high school auditorium.

Sunshine streamed from tall windows into the building. Students bowed their heads and listened, or at least appeared to, while the preacher asked the Maker to bless them and be their constant guide through this day. Jackson thanked the Almighty for the blessings already bestowed on the school, its students and teachers, the people and communities of East Texas, and the United States of America. The preacher was well known for his flowery, upbeat sermons. He was a zestful booster for all London Wildcat activities.

Jackson frequently served as quasi-official school chaplain at assemblies in the auditorium and sporting events on the field and in the gym. If no other minister was appointed or volunteered to do an invocation or benediction, Jackson suddenly appeared on stage with a warm smile and lifted hand. This Thursday morning's event was not a full assembly, but a rally of many of the students who were taking part in the interscholastic contests. Jackson and school officials wanted to get in a last-minute dose of inspiration.

"London students, we are for you!" the preacher exclaimed, raising a fist for emphasis.[1]

An American flag stood on the right side of the broad stage, and a Texas flag occupied the left. The colors in the flags—red, white, and blue in both Old Glory and the Lone Star banner—blazed against the majestic backdrop of the auditorium's sapphire stage curtains.

Superintendent Chesley Shaw and Junior High Principal Felton Waggoner spoke briefly, ramping up the students' spirits. On this day, the chief focus must be preparing to excel in the contests, Shaw said. As a student at the old London School in the 1880s and 1890s, Shaw himself participated in the annual games, and the experience helped him succeed in life, he told them. The athletic events in those times were held in a wide bed of sand piled in the middle of the Henderson town square, around which men on horses and families in mule-drawn wagons cheered on contenders from their various schools.[2] Nowadays, the contests were much more sophisticated.

Six championship trophies, 80 pennants, and 150 ribbons awaited the top finishers of the games in Henderson, the county seat, always the site of the final events of the Interscholastic League competition. A ball tournament, tennis playoff, and one-act play contests had taken place Tuesday. Today's matches included typing and shorthand. Athletic events and literary competitions were set for Friday and Saturday.[3]

New London Senior High Principal Troy Duran traveled to Henderson that morning, and there he and Henderson High School Principal Earl Adams measured off the staging area on the football field for track and field events.

Reverend Jackson gazed across the auditorium, into the faces of so many children. He would carry the memory of that moment for the rest of his life. "They saw no storm clouds ahead," he later wrote.[4]

Alvin Gerdes's thoughts circled an arena of sports topics, from techniques he needed to perfect in tomorrow's javelin throw—in practice, he had hurled the javelin farther than last year's first-place finisher—to the exhilarating and increasingly likely possibility of going to college on an athletic scholarship.[5] As long as he stayed healthy, Alvin could choose between several good schools and also whether to play football or baseball. During the past season as a halfback for the London Wildcats, Gerdes led his team to a district championship. Tall, trim, powerfully built, and quick as a jackrabbit, he was a threat to score on just about any play. He passed, kicked, and carried the ball with equal skill. It usually took more than one tackler to bring him down.

*After the dust settles slowly downward, the grunts and groans subside, and the striped-shirted official sorts through the sprawling pile of bodies, an announcer on the public address system calls the play:*

*"Gerdes carries for twelve. First down Wildcats!"*

*A burst of applause and wild cheering comes from one side of the grandstand, while the opposite side hoots and boos. The teams huddle. They break with a clap of hands and form lines opposing each other. A lanky, freckle-faced quarterback, standing directly behind the center, calls the signal. One, two, hut! The pigskin snaps into his hands. Two quick steps backward. He hands the ball to one back who deftly switches it to Gerdes. Gerdes secures it, sprinting in a reverse sweep away from the flow of runners. The stiff-arm comes up, wham! A big boy in a grass-stained red jersey and worn leather helmet tumbles down. Clumps of sod and grass fly away from the runner's cleats. He gallops. Another quick stiff-arm. Wham! Another big boy in a red jersey hits the ground. Then a collision of bodies near the sidelines raises a cloud of yellow dust. A shrill whistle pierces the crisp October air. Blood glistens. The announcer, truly excited now, calls the play:*

*"Number 47 Alvin Gerdes for a spectacular carry of twenty-two yards! What speed! That boy's faster than greased lightning! First down London Wildcats!"*

*New London cheerleaders pipe in from the sidelines: "Cigarettes, cigarettes, rolled in cotton, the Gaston Red Devils sure are rotten!"[6]*

*The Wildcat band, resplendent in blue and gold caps and capes, rushes into a drum-and-bugle fight song to prep the team for the next play.*

*Gaston's fifty-member pep squad, outfitted in maroon gabardine belted jackets with three rows of gold braid on front and on each sleeve, join the Red Devil cheerleaders in an urgent chorus: "Locomotive, locomotive, steam, steam, steam! Pull together, pull together, team, team, team!"[7]*

*Cheers rise high into the big Texas sky and then fade as the dust settles once more and the ritual closes on another Friday afternoon.[8]*

Gerdes gained local fame with game-winning scores in the closing seconds of critical matches. Many of the Wildcats' fans felt the star likely could have made the difference in the bidistrict championship game, which London had lost to the Center Rough Riders in December.

Gerdes, yelling encouragement to his teammates until his throat was hoarse, had been forced to watch the game from the bench, as the Wildcats and Rough Riders battled back and forth across a muddy gridiron. When it seemed London might score, Alvin jumped up and cheered, only to receive a painful reminder of why he wasn't playing. Two weeks before, when pushing through the winning touchdown in the district championship game against the Gaston Red Devils, a Gaston defender plowed into Gerdes. Gerdes's strength and momentum carried him into the end zone, but his shoulder began throbbing from a deep-tissue injury in his upper chest. Playing in pain, he finished the game, but it turned out to be his last of the season.[9]

If Gerdes's injury wasn't enough to alert Texas football fans that boys playing the brutal sport needed thicker pads and headgear—helmets were made from cowhide and had no face protection—that alarm was sounded from another football field at Terrell, a town east of Dallas. On the same day Gerdes was injured, an eighteen-year-old member of the Crandall High School football team received a fatal head injury during a game against Terrell. Thomas Curtis Lowe, knocked unconscious, died one week later of a massive brain hemorrhage.[10] Lowe's death shocked the state and delivered to the students of New London an unwelcome lesson in their mortality.

Nursing his shoulder, Alvin Gerdes watched his team lose the bidistrict championship to the Center Rough Riders, 6 to 0.[11]

Gerdes's parents didn't have the money to send their children to college. John Gerdes, a German immigrant, had driven trucks for a living in the West Texas oil fields near Crane in the late 1920s and early 1930s; and his wife, Mary, a native Texan, took in laundry to help support the family.[12] Their children—Ruby, the oldest, then Alvin and their sixteen-year-old brother Allen—were born in Texas. The family migrated to New London soon after the East Texas oil boom gained steam.

Gerdes's injury healed quickly. By January 1937 he had joined the basketball team and again displayed his athletic heroics to the cheers of his many local fans.[13] An eighteen-year-old senior, he would graduate from high school in May, and college football scouts were already courting him. Alvin Gerdes was nearly certain he wanted to accept a football scholarship. The highlights of his life had occurred on the gridiron. Sometimes he replayed them from memory, scene by scene, a motion picture of himself and his teammates in action.

Except when it rained and turned the contest into a muddy scrum, the fields were always a little dusty.

After the pep rally, Reverend Jackson dropped by the superintendent's office to let the secretary know that he was returning to the school in the afternoon. Jackson needed help on a mailing he was preparing, and several students volunteered to do some typing for the minister, using the project for practice on the keyboard. In case anybody was looking for him, Jackson said, he would be in the typing room from around 3:00 until school let out at 3:30 p.m.

# 8
# Farmer's Boy

Like all his fifth-grade classmates that day, Bill Thompson was restless for school to be out for the weekend. Bill and his friends, in fact, already were counting down the days until summer vacation. Judging by this day's warmth, winter had finally passed.[1]

The past summer had been one of the best, though it was one of the hottest summers on record across the United States.[2] Bill and his friends spent much of their free time swimming, splashing, and clowning in local streams. They discovered their ideal swimming hole on Caney Creek, a smooth stream about a mile from the farm where Bill and his family lived.

As his buddies set off down the road raising a cloud of dust behind their bicycles, Bill would climb astride his pet calf, Tony, and prod him toward woods lining the creek. The born-and-bred country boy had faith his animal would get him to the water ahead of the others. The calf was better in bushy terrain, while the bikers had to stay on the road and a path through the woods. Bill named his calf Tony after the horse ridden by Tom Mix, the most popular hero in Western movies at the time.

It was a summer rich in those qualities that make life thrilling when you are a boy and free for a season from the rigors and containment of a classroom. The landscape was a luscious green and smelled of honeysuckle and wildflowers. The sky was clear most days—so wide and blue the beauty and enormity of it just stopped your thoughts and washed away petty annoyances like stickers in the grass and mosquitoes buzzing near your ears. The days were sultry but filled with rare adventures for Bill and his best friends, Joe Busby, Leo Warren, and Randall Rodgers. The boys carried firecrackers and cherry bombs, gleaned from stockpiles left over from the Fourth of July, in the pockets of their jeans. They liked putting a firecracker inside a tin can and packing it into the sandy soil before lighting the fuse. The explosion shot the can, a wobbling, spinning rocket, high into the air.

Bill had three sisters and a brother. Another brother, Oren, had died of diphtheria at age two, shortly before Bill was born. Alvin and Bonnie Thompson, his parents, felt harrowing grief over the loss of their child, but Bill's arrival a few months later helped dispel some of the sorrow. The timing of his birth put him in a special category with his parents. He'd taken the place of a brother he never knew.

His older sisters teased him about being pampered by his mom and dad. Nadine, the oldest, told Bill she had one hip lower than the other because she lugged him around so much as a baby.

Bill was born on May 2, 1924, in the same farmhouse where his father had been born in 1893. Paint never touched the house's exterior. It was roomy enough: living room, kitchen, dining room, and three bedrooms with two beds each where the children slept. A screened porch extended across the front of the house.

Alvin Thompson inherited a hundred acres or so from his father, William Thompson, a prominent local politician and farmer. William, known as Uncle Billy throughout the region, had migrated from his native Georgia to Texas after the Civil War, looking for fertile soil to till. He and his wife, Sarah, a Mississippian, acquired a spread of good cotton and corn land near a community called Jacobs in north-central Rusk County. Uncle Billy's neighbors held his work ethic and judgment in such esteem that many encouraged him to run for the county board of commissioners. As a commissioner, his main job would be making sure the county's dirt roads remained passable, a daunting task during rainy spells but vital for farming communities. The roads led to churches, stores, cotton gins, railroad stations, and the county courthouse in Henderson, and provided the essential links for transporting farm goods to market. In 1900, the year William Thompson was elected commissioner, all the roads in the county were just dirt lanes, widened, cleared, and smoothed enough to be useful. The roads were fine for mules pulling wagons, even when downpours turned them into sloppy bogs. When one of the few motorized vehicles out and about at that time sank to its axles in the mud, farmers made a little side money by using their mules to pull the cars out of the muck.

Bill Thompson's grandfather served as a commissioner until about 1915, when he retired from politics at sixty-eight and began parceling land among his six children. William "Uncle Billy" Thompson died in February 1922, two years before Bill was born. Even so, Bill grew up feeling his prominent grandfather's presence. On a mantel in the Thompson home, William Thompson stared from a framed photograph taken of him when he was in his sixties; he looked distinguished and rather pensive with a silver, walrus-style mustache, white shirt, charcoal coat, and black bowtie. He came across as the kind of man who won more battles than he lost, yet a glint of tenderness showed in his bold eyes.

Alvin Thompson enjoyed a few successful years farming his part of the land until the Depression hit in 1929. Fortunately, he got a job working in a new state program trying to eradicate the infamous Texas cattle tick that spread a deadly fever in livestock. As an enforcement officer for the program, he rode a horse to all the farms and ranches in the area to make sure neighbors and strangers alike were dipping their herds in a solution to kill the ticks. The job didn't endear Alvin to those Texans who felt the government should stay out of their business, but the work paid.

An amiable man, Alvin Thompson remained generally well liked in the community. He felt inclined to follow his father's political instincts and decided to run for the commission post his father had held for fifteen years. He lost two attempts to win the post by slim margins. Though the defeats stung, his children remember no bitterness in the man.

Alvin's laid-back nature translated to leniency with his children. Their mother, more particular and structured, served as their disciplinarian. Conservative in values and liberal with a switch, she ran the house.

Bonnie Thompson roused the family early each Sunday morning for services at the Baptist church in Grandview, between New London and Henderson. Alvin would cut the hair of whoever was waiting on the porch that morning—his skill with a pair of scissors meant there was always someone—while Bonnie dressed Bill in a shirt and tie or, when the weather turned cold, a manly little suit.

The year he started first grade Bill gave his parents a terrible scare. He fell gravely ill with diphtheria, the same dreaded respiratory disease that had killed Oren Thompson. A doctor in Henderson and his mother at home gradually nursed him back to health, although he missed so much school he had to start first grade again the next year.

After talk started about prospectors drilling for oil around the London community, Alvin Thompson put forth a plan to swap his sizable farm, farmhouse and all, for a seventeen-acre parcel with a shack on it near London. The owner thought it was a great trade and was ready to sign the papers before Alvin told Bonnie about the deal. She reacted angrily and said she wasn't about to abandon the farm for a ramshackle home on a patch of dead clay. The two bickered, Bonnie's conservatism versus Alvin's speculation. Bonnie won. Sort of. By the end of that next year, the oil boom was on, and at one time there were seventeen productive wells on the scabby seventeen acres Alvin Thompson failed to buy.

Alvin never mentioned it again, even after his job with the state ended and he found himself looking for work. He took a job selling cars at a new Oldsmobile dealership in Henderson. His friendly nature boosted his sales. As a perk, he got to drive a new Olds as a demonstrator. The family's own car was put in storage in the barn, jacked up on blocks to keep the tires from rotting.

There was a reminder in the house, however, of what might have been. Alvin Thompson had a souvenir he brought home after witnessing Dad Joiner's well hit pay dirt. It was a Coca-Cola bottle filled with crude oil that shot up out of the ground when Daisy Bradford No. 3 first tapped the field that soon became known as the Black Giant.

The Thompson family and several thousand other local residents went to the well site on the morning Joiner anticipated he would strike oil. Bill was six. His father drove their car across a wide, bumpy field to the drilling rig. Although it was early autumn, the land remained white with unpicked cotton. The farmer figured on quick riches from oil and just left the crop in the field. He and the landowners around him had never seen oil rig operations, with their churning machinery, towering derricks, and spinning drill stems carving through the black unknown beneath them. The lives they'd known paled in the derrick's shadow; the farmwork they'd performed began to seem quaint, even naïve, to some of them. The stem bore ever deeper, and the anticipation welled into a festival to honor what might come. Around the derrick, the entrepreneurs had already begun work, setting up stands to sell hamburgers and cold drinks to the crowds who gathered daily to watch the crew of roughnecks.

The boom arrived as a sound to Bill Thompson and the rest who stood on that piney knoll on October 3, 1930. A low rumble grew beneath them, its volume rising toward an explosive roar. The ground shook.

# 9

# The Black Giant

The crowd of onlookers eagerly waiting to see if Joiner's gamble was finally going to pay off stood at nearly five thousand on the morning of October 3, 1930. Mud pumped up from the rig had been streaked with oil since early September.

"Joiner was glassy-eyed with fatigue and strain," according to one description.[1] He was seventy years old and in declining health.

A teenager named Jim Miller, Daisy Bradford's nephew, sold sandwiches and iced soft drinks from a makeshift stand in a clump of trees. Vendors, busy as opening day at the county fair, hawked popcorn, candy, and balloons. A couple of bootleggers meandered among the throng of people, peddling pint jars of white lightning. All morning and into the afternoon, spectators plodded toward the clearing on horses and in buggies, wagons, cars, and trucks that trailed clouds of yellow dust from every direction. The throng swelled to nearly ten thousand.[2] Many in the crowd had some stake in the well.

Joiner's financing plan involved selling $25 certificates that gave the purchaser a miniscule interest in the project and a share of the syndicate that owned mineral rights on five hundred acres surrounding the well. Joiner peddled the certificates to everybody he met. For groceries, drilling supplies, and other needs, he signed scraps of paper that were pledged against "future production" at the well. "Dad [Joiner] issued so much scrip for supplies and services that storekeepers and customers alike circulated it as real money," wrote oil-field historian Ruth Sheldon Knowles.[3]

[45]

By this time, Joiner was so near to being flat broke that his drilling crew was burning brush and old tires to fuel the rig's boiler. The odor of burning rubber wafted across the clearing. "The poorest of poor boy operations," wrote historians Roger and Diana Olien. "His rig was a dilapidated affair composed of various secondhand parts and worn machinery."[4]

Late that afternoon, the prospectors lowered into the hole a "swabbing" device made of steel and rubber. The contraption created suction at the bottom. The crew brought up more sand and mud, but now it was streaked heavily with oil. Deep down, a gurgle vibrated up into the boards and pipes of the rig.

"Douse the boiler!" the driller shouted.

The crowd grew hushed for a moment as the ground began to tremble, and a faint rumble grew louder and louder until it became a deafening roar. Somebody shouted wildly, "Put out all the cigarettes!"

A silky, black spout breached the wellhead and touched sunlight for the first time in sixty-five million years. It crashed skyward, bellowing, dwarfing the massive timbers of the derrick. Its colossal, unleashed pressure felt to Joiner like a freight train steaming past inches in front of his face. Trembling from the inside out as the earth quaked, Joiner looked up and could hardly believe his eyes. The thunderous fountain rose over the crown block at the top of the derrick and spread into a widening black canopy that came down as a sticky warm rain. One of the drilling crew, wild with excitement, drew his pistol and fired several shots into the sky, risking an explosion from the sparks, before bystanders wrested the gun from him.[5] Rafe Kangerga, a Henderson businessman, tapped the shoulder of the woman next to him and politely inquired, "Could that be oil?"[6]

The crowd erupted with joyous shouts and wild laughter, tears streaking down some of the faces, as Joiner's grand scheme became an awesome reality.

Men tossed their hats in the air. One man gleefully ran under the spray and took a shower. Children painted their faces with oil. Marshall Cox snapped a picture of his children, Perry Lee and Bobbie Kate, with the spouting derrick as a backdrop.[7]

Joiner, pale and shaking, was engulfed by a mob of men and women all trying to hug him and pat his stooped back at once. D. H. "Dry Hole"

Byrd, Joiner's friend and helper, gauged the flow of the gusher—6,800 barrels a day.[8] Joiner, who had drilled only dry holes for seventeen years, was stunned. "I always dreamed it, but I never believed it," he said.[9]

Nobody who witnessed the Daisy Bradford No. 3 explode with riches that day fathomed the scope of the power that had been unleashed. By early 1931 the first wave of the boom crashed across a five-county region of East Texas.

"The daring, the resourceful and the unscrupulous had caught the scent of oil and money in the spring air, and then swooped down on the five oil counties like the cavalry of Genghis Khan," James Clark and Michael Halbouty wrote. "Behind the oilmen came the opportunity seekers; unemployed workers from virtually every state; thieves and gunmen, con men, gamblers, pimps and brigades of pajama-clad prostitutes."[10]

Work-hungry families pouring into the region made do with all the resources they had or could scavenge to claim a stake, even a small one, in the boom. Many tent houses consisted of wooden floors and frames, wrapped and covered with tarpaulins that could be rolled up to let breezes blow through or lowered on stormy nights. Most had screens to keep flies and mosquitoes out.

William T. Jack grew up in Joinerville when the boom was in full swing. The house his family lived in "was hardly fit for human habitation," Jack recalled in his memoir, *Gaston High School, Joinerville, Texas, and a Boy Named Billy Jack*.[11] "But within the perimeter of the field," he added, "we were not as bad off as you might suppose. During the Depression the difference between respectability and trashiness was cleanliness."

"Joinerville became like every other place," he recalled, "except that an oil field can never be quite like any place else, at least not to the eye and nose. The derricks, jacks, tank farms, slush pits, rod lines and blazing torches made it distinctive. An oil field by its nature is dirty and smelly."

Honky-tonks vibrating with banjo and guitar music sprang up throughout the regions. Prohibition did little to discourage drinking in the oil fields. The influx from around the country brought all manner of bootleggers and bathtub distillers, the mad scientists of the working man. One brew, called Choc beer, was made with malt and various ingredients by the Choctaws. Roughnecks said a gulp of it could "raise your feet off the ground." White lightning—the classic bootlegged spirit—was always available, although there were no warnings on the jug that the contents sometimes killed the imbibers because of lethal additives or risky distilling operations at backwoods stills. Some roughnecks created a bizarre concoction by taking gelled heating fuel and squeezing it through their socks, a Texas Ranger said. The result, presumably, could either be drunk as a cocktail or used to roast marshmallows. Another oil patch drink, the Ginger Jake, caused a nervous disorder that resulted in a loss of equilibrium and a permanent inability to walk straight, a condition known as jake leg.

Such behavior and attitudes shocked the sensibilities of those whose lives were anchored in an agricultural society and deeply held biblical teachings, such as Lou Della Crim. She held tight to her priorities even as the boom spilled closer to her home and little white church.

On the last Sunday in 1930, Mrs. Crim was walking slowly toward the Presbyterian church where she had worshipped for decades when she was hailed "by a wildly excited messenger" shouting that oil was discovered on her farm near Kilgore. Nodding politely, she paused for a moment. It certainly meant she would become rich beyond anything she had ever imagined. It also would change the region she held dear. "I think the oil well will keep until churches services are over," she said, walking on.[12]

Many of the oil-field families that were religious—and many were—typically attended services conducted by itinerant preachers, including roughnecks who worked on the rigs during the day and preached at night and on Sunday.

Previously poor farmers, such as Claude Ashby, who had worked his fingers to the bone raising corn and cotton on a 170-acre tract outside of Henderson, suddenly became wealthy beyond their dreams. After nine wells struck oil on his property, a swarm of salesmen camped in Ashby's yard trying to finagle a piece of the action. "They have tried to sell me everything from needles to steamships," he said.[13] Instead, Ashby bought a diamond stickpin for the only tie he owned.

Within a month of Joiner's discovery, a rural parcel near London had become the town of New London, with two dozen businesses and more than six hundred residents. Kilgore, the center of oil-field activity, went from being a hamlet with about seven hundred residents in 1930 to a bustling town with more than four hundred businesses by the end of 1931.[14]

"Drilling in the mammoth field was frenzied," Knowles wrote. "During one week a new well was completed oftener than once an hour. . . . Not an oil mind in the country was prepared for the magnitude of the field. The Oklahoma City field had been among the nation's largest, covering 20 square miles. The East Texas field was soon producing over an area of 211 square miles. A forest of derricks stretched 43 miles long and 3 to 12 miles wide." By June 1931 a thousand wells were producing 360,000 barrels of oil a day. Two months later production had soared to 848,000 barrels a day.[15] The Black Giant was on its way to producing 1.5 billion barrels within a decade.[16]

A vast cast of characters that represented the multifaceted work entailed by every boom arrived in East Texas. The veterans had experience that recommended them as ready hands in various roles: drillers, derrick men, pipe pullers, pipeline "cats," tank builders, tank cleaners, machinists, boilermakers, carpenters, equipment operators, mechanics, welders, and cutters. The inexperienced found abundant work as laborers called roustabouts, until they had the chance to work on the rigs. Some of the toughest, strongest, and most reliable men were put to work as roughnecks, a name tailored for a specific role, though often applied generically to anyone who worked in an oil field. The roughnecks were the men on drilling rigs working directly for the driller. One of their tasks was hauling the drill pipe up from the hole to change bits, which became dull about every two hundred feet. The process could take more than two hours as roughnecks wrestled up from the ground three joints of pipe at a time, unscrewed—or "broke"—the sections, and put them on a rack on the derrick floor. As each section arose, mud would spout from the wellhead, covering the workers.

The music of their work was the clank of heavy metal, the grind of motor-driven winches, the swoosh of steam from hissing boilers, the clatter of boots on wooden drilling platforms, and the call of commands in a lingo as idiosyncratic as a foreign tongue to men unfamiliar with it, such as those who worked at desks in starched white collars.

"Take off your tails, cats, and put on the hooks. Deuce and four. Ace and three. Now all together. Hit her like you live—hard," bellowed the foreman of a crew laying a pipeline, as described in *Voices from the Oil Fields*.[17]

"Load up on them hooks, you snappers [workers always looking for light duty]. That's high. Ring her off, collar-pecker [the man who keeps time for the men who are screwing the line together, by beating on the pipe]. Up on the mops. Out, growler-board [the foundation used to support boards holding up the pipe]. Next joint. High like a tree and down to the velvet. Bounce, you cats, bounce."

By March 1937 Columbus Joiner, the man who started it all and was hoisted on men's shoulders and paraded through the streets of a village named Joinerville in his honor, was long gone from the great oil field he had lucked upon less than seven years before. He was rumored to be in a borrowed hotel room somewhere, maybe Dallas or Oklahoma City, hiding once again from creditors and dodging men who once called him a friend. Joiner always seemed either loaded with riches or down to counting pennies. Nowadays, although his worth on paper was nearly $3 million, he was out of cash and watching his riches disappear like a mirage on the Texas plains.

He had lost his fortune for the last time and was biding his time as old age transformed him, day by day, into a ghost of his former self. But his legacy was solid. He would always be Dad Joiner—a title conferred not as a tender expression a son uses for his father (Joiner's own son was a plaintiff in one of several hundred lawsuits filed against the old man claiming breach of contracts) but in a broader sense: he fathered the Black Giant. The glory of that day belonged to him as long as he lived.

# 10
## Lunchtime

A stream of students began to flow from the New London High School toward the cafeteria located a short walk from the main building. As the noon hour neared, the procession of children was flowing both ways, to and from the cafeteria, along the concrete walk between the buildings. Many students shed the sweaters and jackets they had worn to school that morning. Dozens drifted away from the cafeteria line toward the hamburger stand, which sold ice cream and other treats also, located on the campus and operated by Alf Shaw, Superintendent Shaw's nephew.

Carolyn Jones went to the cafeteria with several of her classmates. She rarely saw her older sister, Helen, although they attended class in the same building. When they did meet by chance, Helen quickly disappeared. They hadn't been close recently, but it still irritated Carolyn when Helen dodged her in the halls, as though she didn't want to be seen talking with somebody who was just nine years old. Carolyn and Helen hadn't gotten along in the years since their mother and father had divorced. Their mother, angry at their father for being too choosey about the jobs he was willing to take, took the girls from Wichita Falls, Texas, to her parents' home in Oklahoma in 1931. Carolyn and Helen's grandfather was dying of sarcoma, and their grandmother was struggling to keep their general store open. In the tumult, Helen sided with their father, Walter Jones. She and her mother, Eula, constantly clashed. Carolyn was canny enough to stay out of their fights. After their mother married Ervin Lowe, an oil-field roughneck, and the family began moving from one boomtown to the next across Oklahoma and Texas, the strained relationship between the girls did not improve. Helen left to live for a time at their grandparents' home in Ardmore, Oklahoma. Carolyn missed her sister, but Helen's absence spared Carolyn the upset and tension of witnessing arguments between Helen and her mother.

The separation wore on Carolyn, though, and she was comforted when Helen returned to live with them in New London. Later, Carolyn was happy when her seventeen-year-old uncle, Paul Greer, moved to New London from Woodford, a hamlet near Ardmore, where he attended a two-teacher rural high school with about twenty students. A senior at New London, he was the baby brother of the girls' mother. He was closer in age to Helen, fourteen, an eighth-grader, than to her little sister, Carolyn, but it was nine-year-old Carolyn who adored Paul as if he were an older brother. Paul wanted to be a doctor, like one of his older brothers, and chased his education with a rare single-mindedness. Few places in the country offered New London's educational opportunities.

Bill Thompson lunched with a couple of his fifth-grade buddies and commiserated with Perry Lee Cox over Perry's unfortunate morning. He'd tried unsuccessfully to skip school, and it backfired on his backside.

After his father left home to go open his store, Perry Lee convinced his sister, Bobbie Kate, that it would be okay for them to miss classes because nothing new was happening at school anyway. The school bus came and went, and Perry Lee and his sister were outside playing when Marshall Cox arrived back at the house for something he'd forgotten. He gave Perry Lee a hard spanking for hatching the plot, then drove his children to the New London school.

Perry Lee, red-eyed, had darted away from the car and into the high school.

Mattie Queen Price sat at a table in the cafeteria among the students and other teachers. While she ate, she looked through lesson material she had brought from her room—a scrapbook stuffed with sheet music, poems, sketches, newspaper clippings and written anecdotes she'd been saving since she was a young girl.[1] She dipped into the scrapbook almost every day for her lessons in piano, voice, dance techniques, and theater, and as a private music and poise instructor. Her homespun jokes and movie-star looks endeared her to the students.

She nearly always wore a flower pinned to her blouse, something she'd picked that morning from her garden. Queen loved flowers almost as much as she loved children. She never missed a meeting of the Overton Garden Club, where she was a founding member.

This day, she saw the father of one of her students sauntering across the cafeteria, sidestepping tables filled with students, until he reached her seat. The man handed her money for his daughter's last piano lesson, cash that he didn't have at the time Queen performed the lesson. He apologized for not getting it to her sooner. She laughed and told him she was quite confident he would pay the bill. She was not on the school's payroll, but since school officials considered her work important, she was given office space with a piano and room enough for dance lessons. Although many of her clients lived paycheck to paycheck, nearly all of them found some way to pay her before the month was out.

"You take good care of my little girl," the man said, tipping his scruffy work hat.

"I always do," Queen said.[2]

When Alvin Thompson didn't bring a lunch from home for his midday meal, he had a choice of more than two dozen restaurants and cafés in bustling Henderson. Ten were within a short walk from the downtown car dealership where Thompson worked—Quick Lunch, the Court House Café, Dan's Lunch, Cut Rate Café, Ye Lion's Den, the Randolph Hotel Coffee Shop, Wyatt's Café, and the lunch counters at the movie houses.[3]

Near the dealership, workers were setting up a traveling carnival for the weekend. It featured an arcade padded with straw dust for games like tossing darts at balloons, ringing horseshoes, and flipping coins into saucers for a chance at winning stuffed animals, trinkets, and baubles. This weekend food smells would waft through the crowded midway: popcorn, cotton candy, saltwater taffy, candied apples, corn dogs, hamburgers, and fried potatoes. Even the small carnivals at least featured a merry-go-round, bumper cars, a Ferris wheel, and a pony ride. A half-dozen tent shows with jugglers, fire-eaters, tiny people and giants, magicians, and knife throwers rounded out the show.[4]

Thompson tried to take his children to town any time a fair or circus stopped in Henderson. When he farmed, they often didn't have enough money. When he worked for the state as a cattle tick inspector, he could get the family into circuses for free because any venue with animals fell under his authority. Now that he sold cars, Thompson earned enough to splurge once in a while. He and Bonnie enjoyed it as much as the kids.

Roustabouts tacked up posters on telephone poles all around Rusk County to spread word of the carnival. One of the hired hands tested the carousel, its music spilling into the streets of Henderson.

# 11

# Fateful Afternoon

Superintendent Chesley Shaw made two unusual changes regarding the school day. First, he decided to keep students in the high school until their normal dismissal time at three thirty, instead of letting them out thirty minutes to an hour early, as he normally did when the PTA held its monthly meeting at the school. Second, he agreed to move the PTA meeting from the high school auditorium, where it had always met, to the gymnasium located behind the school.

Louise Taylor, the grammar school principal, visited Shaw after lunch and told the superintendant more elementary students would take part in a show at the start of the PTA meeting than expected. The program, called Dances of the World, needed room for the dancers. The auditorium stage would be overcrowded. Somebody suggested using the basketball court in the gym. Parents could sit in the bleachers. The PTA meeting would not interfere with activities in the gym because physical education students in the last period would be outside playing ball.

Shaw approved the move and gave instructions to post signs at each of the high school's entrance doors informing parents of the change.

Hundreds of students throughout the high school picked up copies of the latest edition of the *London Times*, the student newspaper. It normally came out each Friday. A front-page story announced why the paper was a day early: "There Will Be No School Friday."[1] But broadcast news had scooped them. Days earlier the holiday had been announced over the public address (PA) system, rousing cheers and smiles throughout the school.

The mimeographed newspaper urged all students to get behind the school's finalists in the Interscholastic League playoff competition being held in Henderson. "If Mr. Shaw thinks this event is important enough to turn out school, we should certainly lend our moral support by attending as many of these events as possible," the story read.

Today, though, came an unwelcomed announcement shortly before 2:30 p.m. The students thought they'd be dismissed early until the word came through the PA system just before the bell sounded for the day's last period: dismissal would be at the regular time. Grumbling ensued.

New London head football coach Red Moore was expecting a large turnout of boys, including several lettermen from this year's team, for the start of spring training on Monday, the *London Times* reported. Moore planned to divide the squad to compete against itself in a spring scrimmage under the lights of the football field. The London Wildcats' band would be taking part in a five-day clinic, also starting Monday, directed by Hale A. VanderCook, founder and head of the VanderCook College of Music in Chicago, the school newspaper reported. "The band is indeed fortunate to have Mr. VanderCook," said a front-page article that likely was written by New London band director C. R. Sory.

In sports news, both New London's high school and grammar school girls' softball teams took first place in the "playground division" of the county meet that had just finished, reported sports editor Elmer Rainwater, a senior and football letterman. The high school volleyball team had defeated Gaston in an early match and was favored to win the county title on Friday, another story said. But the high school track team had a miserable showing in an event the previous week.

"The Wildcats were invaded by a four cornered situation last Friday afternoon and were unsuccessful in their attempt to take first place; they, however, took fourth which was better than nothing," Rainwater reported, adding glumly that just one team finished lower than the Wildcats. Henderson won first place, Overton was second, Gaston placed third, and Carlisle High School was last. "London was fourth because they had only two men that could take a little punishment," Rainwater said.

Star athlete Alvin Gerdes was one of the two standouts. Of the nineteen points scored by New London, Gerdes won twelve. His injury from football season clearly was mended.

Students grabbing the school newspaper, then as now, were more interested in gossipy chatter and whose names were dropped, especially if they were theirs, than actual news items. In this regard, Gerdes again was a frontrunner. Besides appearing in the sports news, Alvin was mentioned prominently elsewhere. Under a column called "Believe It or Not," the item was a teaser: "Alvin Gerdes and Winifred Diamond seem to be getting friendly."

When New London math teacher J. H. Bunch left his class unattended for a few minutes during the last period, his students had begun talking, laughing, and cutting up. It got so noisy, recalled tenth-grader Arthur Shaw, that English teacher Katie Mae Watson, finishing a lesson in an adjacent classroom, sent one of her students to Bunch's class to order them to quiet down.

Sambo Clifton Shaw, Arthur's cousin and close friend, sat at a nearby desk in Mr. Bunch's classroom. They were double cousins—their fathers were brothers and their mothers were sisters—and grew up as brothers. They were both seventeen—adventuresome, fun-loving tenth-graders. Sambo, Chesley and Leila Shaw's youngest child, showed an independent streak also evident in his headstrong and rebellious older brother, Rayford. Unlike Rayford, who had had a confrontation with his father and dropped out of school, Sambo managed to steer clear of Chesley Shaw's wrath, although Sambo told some whoppers to do so.

Once, when Sambo stayed overnight at Arthur's house, Sambo decided he would be the first person to ride a young, unbroken stallion the family kept in a corral on the farm. He managed to straddle the wild horse for a few moments before it bucked him head over heels through the air. Instead of breaking the horse, Sambo fell so hard he broke one of his legs. Knowing his father would be angry at him for trying to ride the horse without permission, Sambo invented an elaborate tale about how he had tripped on a tree root when running down a hill to jump into a swimming hole.

On another occasion, Sambo tagged along with Rayford and several of his older cousins when the boys went to a beer joint outside Henderson.

His mother and father thought he was going to a picture show. When the boys were getting ready to leave the honky-tonk, somebody dared Sambo to slip out with a small table lamp as a souvenir of his first visit to a bar. He made it to the parking lot before the bartender caught up with him and cracked him on the head with the butt of a pistol. Sambo received a gash on his scalp but counted himself lucky the bartender hadn't called the sheriff. The boy didn't have to think long to come up with a story. Chesley Shaw often remarked that downtown Henderson's brick streets became dangerously slippery when wet. Sambo told his father he slipped on a wet patch of street, fell, and struck his head on a license plate bolted to the back of a parked car. Chesley Shaw bought the story, though by then he had to be thinking Sambo was hopelessly accident prone.

After Katie Mae Watson sent a warning to Bunch's classroom that the students must immediately cease their noise, a frantic hush fell across the room, Arthur Shaw recalled.

Nobody was going to risk getting called out and spanked—then forced to stay after school and write "I will not talk without permission" five hundred times on a blackboard—with only a few minutes to go before the bell would free them for a three-day weekend.

The Reverend Robert L. Jackson drove toward New London High School. He heard the sudden thumping of a tire going flat and pulled off to the side of the road. He had a spare tire and jack in the trunk, so he wouldn't be stranded; the blowout meant, however, Jackson probably wouldn't make it to the school before classes let out. It was already three o'clock, and it would take at least a half hour to change the flat. Jackson had a small typing project he'd hoped one of the typing students would do for him, but now he'd have to find another way to complete the project. He stepped onto the road and walked back to the trunk.

While Jackson knelt to jack up his car, a woman he knew, Euda Alice Walker, drove past in the direction of the high school. She was probably heading to the PTA meeting, Jackson figured.[2] They exchanged a quick wave.

# 12

# Last Dance

Dozens of women, some dressed in Sunday finery and others in the plain clothes of housewives taking a break from afternoon chores, walked in pairs and small groups from the parking lot in front of New London High School toward the main entrance of the school. The double doors acted like a dam, blocking their flow, backing many of the mothers onto the schoolyard on both sides of the front walk. Word passed quickly among the women that a sign posted at the front door was directing them to the gymnasium behind the high school. The PTA meeting was being held in there instead of the school's auditorium, the regular meeting place, the sign informed.

The group, more than fifty mothers in all, set off for the gym, some of them going on into the high school and down a hall toward a rear entrance and others walking around the building on the outside, through a sun-warmed afternoon as pleasant as any March day they could remember.

While the women formed a line to enter the gym, streams of grade school children dressed in dance costumes marched single file to the command of teachers who had them halt and stand quietly until the mothers filed inside and found seats on the wooden bleachers.

One of the mothers filmed snippets of the crowd with a home movie camera.[1] Cameras sold for use by amateur filmmakers in the 1930s were nearly as costly as new cars, but one or two of the more affluent families in nearly every community owned one and brought it along on vacations and to events precious enough to be preserved on expensive film.

In the barn-shaped, wooden gymnasium, the women waited for their children to dance the Dances of the World.

The small movie camera whirred as a chain of second graders dressed as feathered Native Americans whooped and bounced, arm in arm, across the floor. Older boys in Spaniards' sleek, black garb and banded, flat-brimmed hats danced the flamenco with young ladies, gilded in mantilla veils of delicate lace and long dresses that swayed to the rhythm of castanets.

Minuet music, haunting and mellow, coaxed another round of dancers across the polished hardwood floor of the gymnasium. The girls wore white blouses, the boys white shirts.

The finale, the Mexican Hat Dance, brought boys bobbing beneath sombreros and girls whirling in white blouses and green and orange skirts. They floated like wind-strewn wildflowers. The grainy film captured the reflected light of dancers moving as children should—deliberate and rapturous.

It ended. The mothers applauded wildly. Some celebrated their private, winsome moment with a deep sigh.

The children bowed, filed out the door, and walked toward waiting school buses or clustered here and there near the high school to play games with their classmates until their mothers' gathering broke.

The dance show had ended on schedule at 3:15. The clocks now showed approximately 3:17 p.m.

# Part II. **Terror**

# 13
## 3:17 p.m.

Shop teacher Lemmie Butler, seated in his classroom on the lower level of the rear of the building, finished fiddling with the temperamental electric sander. He walked toward the power switch—a short metal blade, hinged on a wall-mounted plate, with two contacts open to the air spilling through the basement crawlspace door beside it.

John Dial, a fifteen-year-old freshman, bent his palms around the sides of a board and lifted it toward the band saw's blade. He turned his head to the right and for a frozen moment caught Mr. Butler's eye.[1]

Butler turned and lifted the switch. Metal neared charged metal. A blue filament of plasma arced. The air caught fire.

A violent heat, the concussive single beat of a monstrous heart, conjured chaos from oxygen. The shop became a blast furnace, white hot. Scorched and twisted inside a burning shock wave, Lemmie Butler died first. The blast flicked Dial and his classmates backward into the sharp concrete cloud of a disintegrating wall.

Flames raced back through the four-foot door into the crawlspace. The atmosphere fed madly on itself in a frenzy of deflagration. Every molecule of 62,500 cubic feet of air screamed and rent itself away from every other. A concrete basement wall, 250 feet long, cracked from the ground and tilted on its heels. Soil below and sturdy foundations around would yield no more, caging the relentless pressure, leaving one way out. The dragon spread its wings.

At its base the school trembled. The motion intensified to a menacing rumble until, mere seconds later, the entire structure shuddered violently. The explosion burst skyward with the force of seventy pounds of trinitro-toluene (TNT) detonated beneath each square foot of basement ceiling.

In the English class above the shop, teacher Lizzie Ellen Thompson felt the tremor sweep through the building as the floor, walls, and ceiling rattled and shook.

"Jesus help us," she said.[2]

The maelstrom swallowed her.

The first floor shattered like porcelain as a blazing torrent erupted through the poured concrete slab on which the long building stood. Cement, timber, and brick splintered. Rolling balls of gas, burning blood orange, howled upward in a dense, searing, forty-ton hurricane. The first floor, blown to shrapnel, rushed toward the ceiling. Windowpanes shattered in sprays of glass. Desks and chairs hurled apart. Drinking fountains snapped loose from plumbing fixtures. Classroom walls disconnected and were pulverized into clouds of chalky gray powder. Throughout the chaotic scene were children and teachers, faces, fingers, nerves, and bone. All was being torn to pieces.

Helen Beard, walking through the hall with her sister at her side, suddenly was propelled upward, higher and higher, until she seemed to float alone and terrified in the sky. Twisting downward as her consciousness began to flee, she saw toylike cars and tiny men. The men were running. Nothing made sense.[3]

The blast enveloped Marie Beard within a chamber of chaos, instantly knocking her unconscious.

Steel lockers shot through brick walls like cannonballs. A textbook soared up through the ceiling and pierced the roof, leaving part of the book protruding through the top. A phonograph flew out of the music room and burst against a wall. A pair of scissors, riding the blast wave, stabbed deeply into the plaster of another wall. Thick timbers snapped like pencils. Iron girders, doubled over and twisted, fell, slicing in two the people between them.[4]

Students in Miss Louise Arnold's room braced as the second-story floor buckled beneath them, tearing free from its walls. Children felt their stomachs reach for their throats as the room dropped and banged down against the ground floor. The children, scattered and dumbfounded, gazed at one another with faces powder white from plaster dust. Miss Arnold and four students lay dead.[5]

The sound of the explosion reached the rear of the north wing, where twenty-two students were taking a test on *Treasure Island* in Grace Mc-David's English class. The building began crackling.[6]

Miss McDavid screamed for the children to hurry to the front of the room. They rushed toward her and huddled around her as the roof crashed down behind them and a gritty, choking cloud of gray dust swirled into the room.

Shrapnel in Miss Lizzie Thompson's English class spun through the air, slashed open Corine Gary's scalp, and crashed into the girl's shoulder. A mass of tumbling bricks and mortar collapsed on Miss Thompson, crushing her.

In a study hall next to the library, Juanita Gibson was in the middle of drawing a circle on a sheet of paper when her pencil made a sharp jut—away from the circle's curve.[7]

Books in the library spilled off the shelves. Joe King, reading a news article about Amelia Earhart and daydreaming about a sports event scheduled for the next day, was thrown from his chair as a deep, rolling rumble shook the floor. The walls split and the explosion's fierce pressure forced a mass of thick dust through the gap, filling the library in seconds.[8]

At calamity's fringe, some perceived the explosion as eerily muffled. Joe Watson, a running back on the football team, was in study hall reading *Gone with the Wind* when "all of a sudden, it came." A wall fell toward him.

Clinton Barton felt a powerful vibration just before the glass partition between the library and study hall shattered. L. V. Barber and Olen Poole, both in study hall, saw an ugly cloud pouring into the room. The building was shaking apart.

Clarence Slater, one of Lizzie Ellen Thompson's students, saw the walls burst out and the ceiling rip upward. He flung himself beneath his desk as debris fell and shifted all around him, pinning him down.

At the end of the building opposite the shop, the detonation tore through a classroom where Mrs. Lena Hunt's math lesson was nearly done.

A moment later, the teacher and twenty-five students were gone, engulfed by whirling rubble and collapsing beams.

"Crawl under your desks!" screamed Mrs. Homer Gary, a teacher in charge of the study hall, as the building shook and the room darkened with dust.[9]

Unbridled, force and fire passed through the scrambled mess, licked away the corners of the roof and leapt, roaring, into the open air. A sheet of flame flickered red against the blue March sky.

A two-ton concrete slab, tossed into the sky, hurtled toward the car that grade-school student Bobby Joe Phillips had been ordered by his mother to go sit in a few minutes earlier. The long rectangle slammed into the driver's side with the force of a highway-speed collision, tearing through the door and side wall. Shards of metal and glass filled the interior.

Seventh-grader Lillian Anderson was nearing the building, just about to go inside to get a drink of water, when a broken brick crashed through her skull.

Fifth-grader Bill Griggs was outside, emptying a wastebasket from his classroom, when the area of the building he'd just left disintegrated, instantly killing nearly all those in his classroom.[10]

Superintendent Shaw, standing on the front walk, began to turn. A deep, muffled sound came first, and then the blast wave, which threw him to the ground. Debris, small and sharp, sliced one cheek, then the other. On his back, the superintendent saw the red-tiled roof of his school rise into the air. D. C. Saxon, the janitor lying next to Shaw, tried to stand and flee this unthinkable, irrational spectacle, but the rushing debris cloud toppled and pummeled him from behind.[11] Farther away, a man stood frozen, watching the school bulge outward and snap apart. The entire structure lifted and dropped in on itself. Debris shot upward, tearing through the slower-moving floors and roof. The high school's side door exploded off its hinges and shot toward Junior High Principal Felton Waggoner, as he was approaching it from the outside steps. It missed, but another missile grazed his head, stunning him. He fell on his back and saw pieces of the building arcing across the sky above, trailing tendrils of reddish brown dust. Exterior walls collapsed outward, toppling down into the schoolyard. The disintegrating roof, still rising high above, cracked into massive sheets and began to fall. The pieces smashed into the school's ruined center, sending a second wave of dust and wreckage spiraling against the sky. Smoke and steam and dust swirled from beneath what eaves of the roof remained.

"Oh my God!" cried the mother of Helen and Marie Beard, who was sitting in her car in a parking lot in front of the high school. She'd been watching for her girls to come out the front door; instead she saw the building mushroom into the sky and pancake down. A force spun the car around in the opposite direction. Bricks smashed through the rear windshield and bombarded the right fender.[12]

The blast wave pushed a wall of fine sand, broken cement, and pulverized glass. It sheared walls even with the ground and scoured paint from window frames and door casings. It stripped flesh from bones, leaving some as bare and bleached as if they had been drying in the sun for weeks. It roared through the thick brick exterior of the school, carrying tiny, broken bodies into the air. Its freedom found, the blast began to fade into the atmosphere, relinquishing to gravity the children it had stolen. Twisted forms dropped onto the lawn, the road, and the giant pile of rubble. A bread truck passing on the road in front of the school, about seventy yards from the building, screeched to a halt as the driver tried to avoid hitting the small boy who had fallen from the sky. The driver jumped out and found the boy sprawled on the pavement, bleeding and unconscious. He loaded the child into his bread truck and sped away to find help.

Elementary school children, lining up to board their buses, screamed in panic. A teacher herded as many as she could into a nearby ditch as the rolling gray cloud erupted toward them. Debris—concrete, wooden, and human—rained on the vehicles.

Molly Sealy, ten, felt something jar the bus she was sitting in in front of the grade school. A teacher on the bus stepped outside, and Molly and other students followed her. They saw smoke and debris rising into the sky.

"Get these children back on the bus!" another teacher shouted. The group fled back into the bus trailer.

"The children were wild with hysteria," Louise Taylor, principal of the elementary school, said. "Some tried to run toward the school. Some fled toward our building. Others tried to crowd onto buses."[13] She knew what lay beneath the collapsing wreckage across the way, but could do nothing to help them. She turned to her children and ordered them into the buses.

"Drive away!" Taylor yelled at each driver. She came to Lonnie Barber's bus. "Get them away from here!"

A mix of shock, confusion, and fear crowded Barber's instincts. Four of his children were inside or near the building that had just exploded. Barber wanted to spring from the bus and plunge into the disaster, to tear apart the pile of stone between him and his children. He realized, too, that the parents of the children on his bus would soon feel the same way, once they heard what had happened. Duty and love battled fiercely for primacy. Clenching the steering wheel, Lonnie Barber drove away and took the children home.

The cavernous wood-frame gymnasium behind the school, where the parent-teacher association was meeting, quivered from the explosion's tectonic thump. A rafter shook loose and clattered onto the bleachers. Heads swiveled around, and eyes snapped wide as hunted doe. Red dust billowed through the joints in one of the doors, and seeing it, Lorine Zylks Bright took a halting step back.

Drawn by the sound of windows shattering near the gym's roof, Mildred Evans looked up and saw treetops outside lash about like willows in a gale. Teacher J. H. Bunch and senior high student Catherine Hughes had just reached the gym. Bunch pivoted toward the nightmarish scene. Nearly everyone in Catherine's business class had already died.

"It was just like a West Texas sandstorm—black, heavy fog. The heavy brick dust covered the grounds. Bricks and glass fell around us. We couldn't see for three or four minutes. It was black as night," he said.[14]

The dust cloud rushed toward Carroll Evans, his neat white home, and his young son playing outside. Evans scrambled out of the house, racing the debris arcing through the air toward his boy. He reached his son and, bending over, shielded the child's head in his chest. The cloud enveloped them, and they began coughing, gasping. Picking up his child, Evans ran. They were suffocating. Bricks, heard more than seen, hurtled through the air. Evans nearly tripped down the ditch between the school and his house, and scrambled madly up the other side, his son wailing. Mildred Evans dashed out of the gym. She saw her husband race toward their child and vanish into the cloud. She ran to their house and arrived with the opaque dust. Putting one hand on the door lest she lose her way, she screamed for

Carroll and Duane. Her voice, shrill and terrified, carried Carroll's name through the murk. He followed the sound, clasped her arm, and together they stumbled inside their home.

A throng of mothers rushed the other way, pushing out of the gym and into the choking powder. They scrambled, blind, toward the wreckage hiding their children. Lorine Bright began a frantic search for her daughter, Georgia Lorine, who went by the nickname Darween. After finishing her dance at the start of the PTA meeting, Darween had asked to go out and play in front of the high school with a friend. Her mother had consented.

"With returning awareness, I realized that something had to be done," Lorine Bright recalled in her memoir of that day. "I thought, 'I must lift every bit of that rubble to find my child crushed beneath.' I felt the urge to claw at it with my hands."

As Bright stumbled around the corner of the building, she saw a girl standing behind a second-story window. The girl looked terrified, mouth agape in a scream, her eyes drawn to Lorine Bright's eyes. The girl's eyes spoke: *Save me.* Bright could do nothing for her, and she saw no sign of Darween between boulders and boards scattered across the lawn where her daughter had gone to play. Lorine Bright briefly snapped and started walking in circles, bent at the waist, clucking nonsense at first, and then praying over and over: *God, don't let my child die!*[15]

A short distance away, hidden behind wreckage, Darween Bright's face was turned toward the sky, frozen. She felt certain she saw her mother shoot out of the gym like a rocket soaring into the heavens.

Mrs. Phillips, Bobby Joe's mother, ran to the parking lot, blood pounding in her ears, to find her seven-year-old son. She emerged from the choking cloud of dust and saw the remains of the car to which she'd sent her boy. Falling to her knees, she screamed. The car was crushed nearly flat. She was unaware that Bobby Joe was huddled out of sight, frightened, clinging to the children whose games he'd joined after disobeying his mother's order to stay in the car.

Eleven girls in the home economics cottage directly behind the high school rushed outside into the dust storm. A great crashing noise, a cascade of broken glass and metal, had followed the roar they had heard. Outside, a student lay on the ground with her leg shorn off at the knee. The girls picked her up and carried her away, looking for help. Cletis Wells, a senior, broke away from the group and began searching for her sister, Doris Lucille. She quickly found her, slumped on the ground. Cletis's small hands wrapped around her sister's wrists as dust billowed around them and bricks fell to the grass. Her eyes welled with tears. She could find no pulse. Cletis stood and ran, her cries for help joining a rising chorus of screams.[16]

Inside the tangled wreckage, hundreds of children awoke in a nightmare. A thick, gritty dust cloud obscured all but the closest chunks of rubble around and on top of the living and the dead. Consciousness brought with it pain and the knowledge only that something monstrous had come. Bill Thompson wondered if the school had been bombed from above. The roof had collapsed on his class, breaking in such a way that it pinned Thompson's face and arms against the desk he'd swapped with Ethel Dorsey. Many of his classmates were crushed. Under another rubble pile, Walter Freeman struggled to breathe in the thick air. He did not know it, but his back was broken. He bled and felt the weight of another person's body pressed against his. Somebody nearby moaned, and then fell silent.

Eighth-grader Erwin McMilton, thirteen, had jumped to his feet when the building began to vibrate, and he plunged under the teacher's desk. Now the dust stung his eyes and clogged his throat. Panicked, he picked his way over sharp concrete and brick, and heaved himself from a window to the ground outside. At the other end of the ruined building, Corine Gary's head stung from the grit-filled gash in her scalp. Warm blood streamed down her face. She clawed for her friends, Chloe Ann Carr and Irene Emma Hall, who had been sitting on either side of her. She tried to pull them free, but they would not move. A hand gripped hers. "They're dead," the person said, helping Corine stagger to her feet and leading her off into the dust-filled cave of broken hallways.[17] Juanita Gibson, at another end of the school, ran with her study hall classmates through the same suffocating cloud. Jostling blindly through a corridor, she tripped and felt the bracelet her mother had given her begin to come loose. Juanita paused, pressed against a wall, the gritty air rushing in and out of her lungs in gasps. With shaking hands, she fastened the bracelet and then followed others to a bank of windows. They saw a drain pipe attached to the wall outside but could not reach it. Through their feet they could feel the shifting vibration of parts of the building still collapsing. Juanita climbed through the window, hesitated, then leapt. She caught the pipe, scratching her hands on the rough brick exterior and zipped to the ground.

The windows, ringed in shards of glass, beckoned all who could see them. They were hinged at the bottom and opened outward in a half-V. Most had already been blown open. Children in the second-floor library peered out. The drop to the ground looked to be twenty feet at most. L. V. Barber squeezed through the opening first and shoved off, pushing himself far enough away from the building to clear the same open windows on the ground floor. He landed hard on his feet, jarred but unscathed. Barber looked up and saw Evelyn Rainwater ready herself on shaky knees and leap. She did not push hard enough and fell too close to the building, plunging through a window below. Others landed badly on soft grass or hard, angled debris, snapping their legs and arms. Olen Poole had started to jump but, seeing this, decided to try another escape. He and the students remaining in the library formed a human chain and shuffled along a dust-filled, sagging corridor. Shaved brick and glass, suspended in the air, stuck to their eyes and coated the insides of their mouths. They felt their way toward a stairwell, but the stairs were gone. They pushed on to the next stairwell. It was mangled and clogged, but passable. They picked their way down and escaped through a gaping hole in the wall.

On the lip of a destroyed wall of what had been the second story, a group of children huddled together. Donald Mathis and others from his class were stranded. The structure—a classroom a few moments ago—teetered on the verge of collapse. Donald found a piece of pipe running down from the wall, apparently still securely attached to it. He told the other students they could use the pipe as a slide and helped them swing from the wall to get a grip on it. One by one, his classmates clung to the pipe and slid haltingly, a few feet at a time, until they passed out of sight into the wreckage below.

Joe Watson climbed up through a maze of debris and pulled himself out onto a portion of roof. The roof had fallen across the collapsed wreckage, a pile nearly half as tall as the school had been. The boy looked back into the hole from which he had freed himself and saw eyes staring up at him, some darting and frightened, others glazed and unblinking. He climbed back toward them and began helping classmates out of the wreckage.[18]

Rubble blocked the twenty-two students in Grace McDavid's English class from the windows. She asked Calvin Corrie, William Fredericks, and another boy "to go find a way out." "We found a place about four feet wide in an adjoining locker room," Corrie said.[19] The boys returned to the classroom and led the others out through the tight, jagged opening. On the other side, the windows were unobstructed. "We let ourselves out of the window on the second floor." The slope of the school grounds meant that here, the drop was only about ten feet, but the thought of falling to rubble-strewn lawn terrified some of them. One at a time, they slid out. With their hands on the jagged window sill, they lowered themselves as far as their arms would allow and let go.

The dust cloud began to clear above Clarence Slater. Still pinned beneath the ruins of his first-floor English classroom, he looked up and was stricken with fear. Clarence was staring into the sky. He lay still, trying to calm his pounding heart. Somebody screamed, "Fire!" Adrenaline clambered into his blood stream, commanding heart, lungs, and muscle fibers to twitch and surge. The chemical roared. Clarence tore himself free and scampered away.[20] Small, disjointed crowds, remnants of classes bumped into one another, catching hands and stumbling through a haze of plaster powder. Joe King ran with them toward the only light they could see. They made their way out of the wrecked building even as parts of it continued to fall. Joe Watson, his mouth thick with brick dust, joined a group that climbed out onto the roof. Here, the air sang with screams, some crisp from the lawn below, others muffled and weak. The children found a stairwell that was wobbly but still standing.

Outside was a new horror.

King looked up and saw "the body of our neighbor's little girl . . . hanging up in the wires next to the telephone pole," he recalled. "I recognized her by the coat she was wearing."

"There were heaps of dead bodies lying all around. It was awful. You couldn't look anywhere without seeing a pile of dead boys and girls," Joe Watson said. Though badly bruised, Watson would not leave. He began pulling bricks from the pile, digging into the wreckage toward the cries still ringing in his ears.

"Everybody was saying, 'What happened? What happened?'" King said. "You could hear people hollering and crying."

Just then, Della Westbrook arrived, panting, at the chaotic scene. She had walked across campus to a lunch stand just before the explosion. "I started running across the grounds to where children were dying," said Westbrook, the high school's librarian. "Many already were dead. The screams and cries were horrible."

Louise Taylor watched the last school bus shut its doors and drive off. She turned and rushed toward the ruined building. She saw the crowd from the gymnasium reach the rubble, "screaming, frantic mothers clawing with bare bleeding hands" at the wreckage.

The explosion spent itself, the debris settled, and the enormity of the tragedy began to mark its witnesses. A town had lost its future.

With blood streaming down his face, Superintendent Shaw gazed in horror and disbelief at the ruin of a generation. Sambo, his youngest son, was right in the middle of it. Hundreds have perished, Shaw realized at once. Screams and moans surrounded him. From somewhere inside the miasma a woman cried out, "Good God, all our children are dead!"[21] Shaw threw his hands to his face. His glasses had vanished.

Nearly every pane of glass in every building had shattered or cracked. Trees stood bare, their thickest branches ripped away. Combat veterans of the final years of World War I looked, disbelieving, at a landscape they'd seen before.

Ralph Estep rushed in his ambulance to New London with a load of emergency supplies, including glucose and caffeine. This man who had seen people cut to pieces beneath train wheels and faces blasted away by buckshot looked upon the carnage at the school and began to weep. He helped those he could and collected those he could not.

"I gathered two tubs full of hands, arms, legs, and feet for which we could find no bodies," Estep said. "I helped to gather nearly a bushel basket full of shoes—tiny shoes that kiddies wear—in which we found no feet. They were just shoes, laced and tied and which had been blown completely from the victims' bodies. I watched a doctor administering morphine to a little slip of a girl. Still conscious, she was suffering the agony of the damned."[22]

Estep watched another man rush to the doctor. His chest heaving, the man said they'd found the remains of the doctor's son.

Other fathers and mothers needed no intermediary. Estep remembered watching a red-eyed man digging for his son amid the rubble. The man found an arm protruding from a heap of bricks and boards. As he tugged to pull the body loose from the pile, the man's face turned white with recognition.

J. B. Dial, a decorated veteran of the Great War, rushed into the wreckage to find his sons. Dust still sifted down through the dead air. Panic-stricken, with a surge of adrenalin, Dial grabbed a slab of concrete and heaved it upward. A little girl wiggled out from a narrow space behind it.[23]

"That's my child!" a woman shouted with hysterical joy.

The first wave of responders—oil men, shopkeepers, truck drivers, preachers, barbers, a professional violinist—washed onto the wreckage. Nearly all had someone to find, but to look at this great disjointed mass was to lose hope. L. A. "Tiger" Mathis, Donald's older brother, did not even know where to begin. He joined a group of men who formed a line and started pulling debris from the huge pile and passing it, hand to hand, away.

A blizzard of paper from loose-leaf binders lay scattered throughout the wreckage and across the campus. Hundreds of textbooks had been tossed helter-skelter. On a small blood-smeared pamphlet, mashed into the debris, was written, "Tips on First Aid."[24]

Felton Waggoner's eyes swept the detritus and locked on the monstrosity at its heart. He muttered a prayer at the wreckage, even as its worst came into focus. Waggoner walked numbly forward into a field of small bodies, crushed and torn and missing pieces, and it was too much even to cry. John Nelson, the son of math teacher Johnnie Marie Nelson, walked into view, and in his face Waggoner saw what he was feeling. Nelson asked Waggoner if he'd seen his mother. Waggoner would not find out she was dead until the next day, so he told Nelson he had not. Nelson thanked him and turned around, and Waggoner saw the hair had been burned from the back of his head. The boy walked away, looking for what he'd lost.[25]

# 14

# Thunder on a Clear Day

A boy sat on the front steps of an unpainted wooden house. Five-year-old Ben Meador's thoughts were lost in the vast blue expanse of the afternoon. The sunshine and warm breeze were enough to make him content for the moment. Birds flitted over a patch of woods in the distance. The day smelled like flower petals and earthworms.

Ben's father was at work in the oil field. William Floyd Meador Sr., forty-one, was a roustabout gang pusher. The oil patch title described a roughneck who goaded laborers, the roustabouts, to keep busy on the task at hand. Ben's mother Mattie, thirty-seven, was in the kitchen.

Ben's brother, William Floyd Meador Jr., thirteen, and his sister, Myrtle Fay Meador, seventeen, were at school. He hoped that they would come home soon, so he and Junior could play.

A small red wagon, Ben's Christmas present, stood near the driveway where the family's 1936 DeSoto sparkled in places sunlight touched glass and chrome. The car was the latest model and still smelled new inside, thanks to work in the oil fields staying on an even keel the past couple of years.

Junior Meador had delighted Ben that morning by pulling him around the house in the wagon a few times before the older brother had to catch the school bus.

Ben was daydreaming when a sound wave crested the treetops. The steps where he was sitting, the front porch and house, everything under him, shuddered. He heard a long rumble and then a ferocious boom that even as it vibrated through space was ripping into the fabric of the Meador family.

"I saw big chunks of stuff go up in the air and then I saw what looked like smoke or dust that billowed up," Ben recalled.

Mattie Meador flew out the door and grabbed her boy.

"Look," Ben said, pointing.

His mother gasped, "My God, that's the school."

She clutched Ben, yanked him up and flung him into the front seat of the DeSoto. They rushed off toward the strange cloud on the horizon, puffing upward, to the southeast not too far down the road.

Reverend Jackson tightened the last lug nut on his spare tire and began lowering the car down from the jack. All of a sudden, the ground shook, an earsplitting boom rocked across the sky, and trees along the road bowed backward in a wild gust of wind. Jackson's white fedora flipped into the air and sailed across the road.[1] The explosion came from the school campus, or just beside it, the preacher realized immediately. A broad cloud of smoke and dust rose over the tree line, not a half mile away. Jackson jumped into his car, cranked it, and gunned the engine. He raced toward the school.

Otis Jones, a hired man who lived and worked in Overton, was in the middle of digging another post hole for the new fence. He had earlier taken off his light jacket, but the afternoon was so warm he was sweating heavily as he took a cedar post and stood it upright in the hole. Judging from the base of the post, the hole needed to be a little deeper. He was about three miles from the school.

A rolling rumble and sharp thunderclap cracked right at his ears. Otis took an unsteady step forward, then backward. At first he thought lightning had struck something right at his back because the thunderbolt was so loud. He looked up and all around. There wasn't even a wisp of a cloud in sight.

Several miles down the road, Mrs. Ezzie Poole was bent over her washtub scrubbing clothes for her husband and children. She raised her head and stared at the sky. What on earth?

Three of her children were at school. The clap of thunder came from that direction. She instinctively started to take count of her brood. Classes were nearly over, so the three might be on the way home. Her youngest two, not school age yet, were visiting a nearby house where an elderly woman sometimes tended to them.

The old woman watching the children had felt something jar the house. Her hearing was not good, but she still had her wits about her. She tottered into another room where she found Mrs. Poole's little ones, standing still and looking surprised in a way children sometimes look when they've been up to mischief.

"Now you kids know better than to be jumping off the furniture," the old woman scolded.

The kids looked at each other quizzically. They hadn't jumped from anything.

Glasses on a shelf above the milkshake machine in Thomas Smoot's café rattled, and a force surged against the windows, making the panes waver in their frames. The café was on one corner of a crossroads in Old London, only a couple of miles from the school where Thomas's daughters, Helen and Anna, were in classes. Helen, seventeen, was the older, and Anna, fifteen, the leaner. Little jibes about her weight didn't seem to bother Helen. She was plump but hardly unattractive. She carried the extra weight well, used it to her advantage with quick wit, absorbed it into her personality, and seemed lovelier because of it. Her smile was a beam of sunshine, and if eyes could be said to twinkle, Helen's did.

A legion of friends at school made her president of the senior class. She reported for the *London Times* and worked on the staff of the school's yearbook, the *Londona*. Occasionally a blurb in the *Times* poked fun at Helen's size. A quip in a recent edition said, "Helen Smoot used to touch the floor without bending her knees but now she can bend the floor without touching her knees."[2] As likely as not, it was Helen herself who planted the remarks. Classmates elected her Senior Girl with the Best Personality. She was mentioned in the *Henderson Daily News* in a London School Notes column, appraising the Perfect Senior Girl:

She should be as popular as Ruby Lee Hooten,
Have the clothes of Geneva Blackwell,
Be as studious as Evelyn Hudkins,
Be the size of Yvonne McGary,
Have the eyes of Geneva Dorsey,
Have the complexion of Eva Ruth Jordon,
Have the eyelashes of Helen Stroud,
Have the graceful walk of Bernice Norris,
Be as neat as Geneva Gary,
Have the personality of Helen Smoot,
Be as pretty as Florence Lee.[3]

Beneath Helen Smoot's outgoing charm lay a sensitivity and creative vision that few of her classmates noticed. At heart, she was a poet. The delicacy of flowers, the nuance of butterflies, the purpose of raindrops, and the snowflake's transient offering captured her imagination. These were the gilt, glitter, and gold interwoven into this child's tapestry of the universe. Sunrise was God's transcendent painting. Sunset, a mysterious negative—the fiery omega.

Anna Smoot didn't have her sister's cute face, but like Helen, she possessed intelligence and a leader's gregariousness. Her peers made Anna the class president as well. Being a pair of presidents from the same family— and both girls—drew them close. They shared secrets, cracked jokes, and giggled. Sometimes they talked about romantic scenes in recent movies, such as *Rose-Marie*, starring Jeanette MacDonald and Nelson Eddy as young lovers, or new books, such as that panorama of ruin and love and the Old South at war, *Gone with the Wind*.

Thomas Smoot and several of his customers strolled to the front windows of the café and peered outside. Somebody suggested they might have felt an early tremor of an earthquake. *No*, Smoot realized. *That came from around the school.*

Smoot, who had worked near oil fields for much of his life, guessed the explosion was a steam boiler on one of the drilling sites dotting the school's campus. Smoot's four sons worked in the fields as roughnecks, but his immediate worries were for Helen and Anna.

"I'm closing up," Smoot told the customers. "Let's go see what happened."

Marshall Cox and his customers at the country grocery store felt the building sway and heard jars and cans vibrating on the store shelves. Within minutes, a car screeched to a stop on the gravel parking lot outside Cox's store and the driver shouted to people standing out front. One man walked back inside, looking bewildered. "May be an explosion at London School," he said.

Marshall Cox told his customers he was closing up so he could go check on Bobbie Kate and Perry Lee. His face had lost all color.

Several miles in an opposite direction, beside the Sabine River outside of Kilgore, young Paul Howard was helping his father chop a load of wood. As the explosion swept over their heads, the trees on the riverbank seemed to sway. Mr. Howard was a veteran old-field hand who had moved to the Black Giant out of the Smackover field in Arkansas.

"That was a boiler going up," he told Paul. "And I mean a big one."

Paul's twin brother, Silas Howard, was in the cafeteria of the Kilgore High School, where he had a part-time job helping clean up at the end of the school day. Silas was mopping the floor, and he had just poured sudsy water out over the center section, when the building shook for a moment. He felt the movement pass right beneath his feet. Looking back at the floor, he saw a fresh crack running the entire length of the cafeteria. The soapy water from his mop bucket was seeping slowly into the fissure.

Across town inside a two-story Kilgore office building, insurance salesman J. B. Downs was writing at his desk when the earthquake-like tremor made the walls and floor tremble for a few seconds. The windowpanes pinged like crystal glasses being tapped with a fork.

In a neighborhood on the other side of Kilgore, Mrs. Bud Sanders was standing with her hand on the front door knob, about to enter her mother-in-law's house, when the home's front windows rattled. She heard a distant rumble to the south, followed by a boom. An eerie sensation tingled against her skin. "Looking back, I can't help but wonder if the trumpet of the Lord might not produce these same feelings of apprehension and wonderment," she said.[4]

Mary Jones was stopped at a red light atop a hill, not far from New London, when she saw a spectacle that defied belief. The New London High School rose into the air, split into many pieces and crashed to the ground. She saw tiny dots—children actually, but tiny because of the distance—start shooting from the rubble like ants pouring from an anthill kicked by somebody's boot heel.[5]

All across the countryside, farmers pulled up on their mules and said, "Whoa." One of them, Sam Wooley, more than ten miles from the New London school, thought he heard a crack of thunder, although the afternoon was too pleasant for a storm. In nearly the same instant, Sam felt the fresh-turned earth at his feet seem to tremble, vibrating into the wooden plow handles. The impatient mule stamped at the ground.

Other farmers, those closer to the explosion, stood still behind their mules and watched the near horizon, where just then a plume of rust-colored smoke, splotched with white puffs and gray streamers, began to rise.

Roughnecks in the surrounding oil fields stopped what they were doing and looked around trying to determine what had just happened. Of all the people in the vicinity, they knew best what that sound meant—explosions were the roughnecks' worst occupational hazard.

One by one at first, then by the score, and within moments by the hundreds, men such as Joe Davidson and Floyd Meador set down their tools, scaled to the bottom of their derricks, shut off welding machines and blowtorches, and proceeded at a trot in the direction of the hellacious blast. When one of the men yelled back to the others, "It's the school!" and that word passed from man to man, the pace of the procession accelerated to a gallop and soon became a wild dash of thousands of men with hearts pounding in their throats.

A. H. Huggins, a telegraph operator in the Western Union office at Overton, about four miles west of New London, looked up from his machine and saw a man in tattered clothes with blood smeared on his face, arms, and hands. The man, New London's band director C. R. Sory, murmured, "There's been a terrible explosion. Hundreds killed. It's unbelievable, but true."[6]

Huggins later described Sory as "half-crazed," and for the moment he doubted what the man was saying. Then he glanced out to the street. People wandered past, their clothes shredded, faces ashen with dust, arms and legs blood-spattered. An ambulance passed in one direction, siren wailing, and a fire truck rushed by, alarms clanging.

The operator gathered enough information for a quick dispatch to Western Union regional headquarters in Houston and tapped it out in Morse code:

THERE HAS BEEN AN EXPLOSION AT THE NEW LONDON SCHOOL HERE, REPORTED SEVERAL HUNDRED KILLED AND INJURED, FLASH THE NEWS TO OUR OFFICES IN THE VICINITY ASKING THAT THEY SEND DOCTORS, NURSES AND AMBULANCES AT ONCE.[7]

# 15
# Newshounds

In the cities of East Texas, the only hot news so far that day appeared to be the weather. Forecasters expected unseasonably warm temperatures that afternoon and possible showers or a thunderstorm in the evening.

Associated Press (AP) reporter Felix R. McKnight arrived early for his shift at the AP's office in Dallas, where he was slated to spend the entire day at a desk doing mostly rewrite work. In a nearby office building, United Press (UP) reporter Walter Cronkite, on loan to the Dallas office, assessed his workload that day as no more interesting than the rewriting he typically performed on a slow news day at his regular office in Kansas City. McKnight and Cronkite were both in their twenties and itching for stories with more oomph than routine reports on oil-field activities and running tallies of traffic fatalities.

Another wire service reporter in Tennessee, in fact, found little more exciting to write about than a farmer who showed up at a bank wanting to deposit a hundred dollars, all in pennies.[1] The gist of the short feature concerned the grumpy bank teller who had to count the coins one penny at a time.

In the nation's capital, the ongoing power struggle between President Franklin D. Roosevelt and the U.S. Supreme Court had reached a lull. The Roosevelts stumped for the president's education agenda, Franklin in Georgia and Eleanor in Oklahoma.

It was a slow day for news even in New York. A flurry of interest developed when a distraught woman leaped in front of a subway train.[2] But for the Big Apple, a showy suicide was hardly more extraordinary than the bank teller counting pennies in Tennessee. A short piece about the woman would be buried deep inside the next day's editions.

One glimmer on the news front: Female aviator Amelia Earhart took off on one of her daring flights. Elsewhere in the world, Arabs rioted against British colonialism and Jewish immigration into Palestine. Ernest Hemingway filed dispatches on the Spanish Civil War. The pope prepared to deliver a radio broadcast deploring the evils of Communism.

In New York City, United Press's most-prized columnist, Henry Mc-Lemore, a flamboyant globetrotter recently returned from covering devastating floods along the Mississippi River, prepared to don his sportswriter hat and report on a professional boxing match set to take place the next day at Madison Square Garden.[3] Destiny had other plans. By midnight, he would be in a cramped makeshift newsroom in remote East Texas, fifteen hundred miles from his desk in New York, covering the most riveting story of his storied career.

Back in Austin, Texas, reporters hunted for fresh angles on the birth of Governor James V. Allred's third son, Sam Houston Allred. The catchy tidbits were filed in early briefs: Sam Houston Allred was born on March 17 in Sam Houston's bed in the Sam Houston Room of the Texas governor's mansion. First Lady Eleanor Roosevelt planned to drop in on Governor Allred and his wife, Joe Betsy, to take a peak at baby Sam. Bits of hard news emulsified into pabulum.

Labor organizers in the oil field around New London had been fanning rumors of a potential strike in 1937 that would shut down production in a pocket of the nation where the economy was growing strong again. Most people felt it was idle talk. Roughnecks were such rugged individualists that it was difficult to believe they would ever walk off the job, especially when so many other men with hungry families were drooling for employment in the oil fields.

Even so, the AP in Dallas sent Felix McKnight to East Texas to check out the rumors. McKnight spent several days in late February and early March 1937 talking with oil-field workers and their families as well as the owners and managers of the oil companies and gasoline refineries driving the boom.

The young South Texas native was impressed with the beauty of East Texas, the rolling little hills with thick pine forests, hardwood river bottoms, the growing towns, Henderson so tidy and neat and spiked with church steeples, Kilgore earning its rowdy reputation nightly, the neighboring villages of Old London and New London with the farm community social order mixing with oil-field culture.

McKnight took names and developed a rapport with enough local contacts, in the towns, oil fields, and company headquarters, to be able to keep an eye on the situation in East Texas if anything developed.

Sarah McClendon considered herself a crusading journalist early in her career. It was true on several levels. As a woman ambitious to carve a lasting place for herself in a profession dominated and controlled by men, she developed a brash, outspoken, and tenacious approach to even basic newspaper reporting, an approach she would one day take to White House press conferences.

Soon after graduating from the University of Missouri's School of Journalism in 1931, McClendon snagged a job reporting for a pair of newspapers in her hometown of Tyler, Texas, a small city at the edge of the East Texas oil boom. At the time she was hired, the co-owned *Tyler Courier-Times* and *Tyler Morning Telegraph* were launching a campaign with the Chamber of Commerce to push support for a modern new hospital in the city. The oil boom spurred so much growth across the region—accompanied by frequent job-related injuries and increased traffic accidents—that Tyler's cramped hospital facility, with fewer than twenty beds, became woefully inadequate.

"My job was to find out what it would take to build the hospital, to find out who opposed the project, to find out how to get around that opposition," McClendon recalled in a memoir.[4] "I saw myself as a fearless, crusading reporter. The pay was ten dollars a week."

McClendon's chief responsibility, though, was to cover "society news" for the newspapers' "women" sections. It galled her.

By March 18, 1937, the modern hospital was one day away from becoming a reality. A grand opening ceremony for Mother Frances Hospital was scheduled for Friday, March 19. McClendon had devoted much time during recent weeks to working on a special section about the glistening new facility, which the Tyler newspapers had published the previous Sunday.

Other than the anticipated hospital opening, it was a sluggish news day in Tyler. McClendon spent the morning on routine projects for the *Courier-Times*, the afternoon newspaper. Typically, if she could grab an additional byline by covering hard news for the *Morning Telegraph*, she'd work on through the afternoon and evening. This day, the twenty-six-year-old reporter felt caught up enough to schedule a midafternoon appointment at a beauty parlor.

When McClendon emerged from the beauty parlor and set out down the sidewalk toward her office, something about the afternoon struck her as odd. The pace of shoppers, businessmen, lawyers, and others on the sidewalks and street corners seemed to have slowed down a notch from the normal midday bustle. Many had even stopped in their tracks. "When I returned to the office, it was clear that something was terribly wrong," she recalled. "Everyone was just standing there, stunned."[5]

# 16

# Holy Sisters

Dr. C. C. McDonald took his seat at the head table during an afternoon meeting of the Tyler Rotary Club. McDonald, president of the Smith County Medical Society, was there to speak about the Mother Frances Hospital opening the next day after a formal dedication ceremony. Among the most prominent doctors in the region, he'd led the drive to build the gleaming facility. He'd supplied local reporters, including Sarah McClendon, much of the background the Tyler newspapers had used for a special hospital section published the previous Sunday.

Russell Rhodes, the former manager of Tyler's Chamber of Commerce, introduced McDonald. "Certainly he deserves, more than anyone, the credit for the hospital which we are about to dedicate," Rhodes said. "The doctors gave him authority to go ahead as their representative or we would not have a hospital today."[1]

An artful and entertaining speaker, McDonald typically opened with an anecdote. The physician kept a selection in his repertoire, drawn from personal experience and stories he'd heard working closely with other doctors in Tyler. He spoke frankly and with a sense of self-deprecation, tossing in splashes of local color and an occasional bawdy wrinkle. McDonald referred to the time of his birth in 1906 as a "pioneer" era in Texas medical practices.

"Mother hung a white cloth in the window when it was time for father to go for the doctor," he said in a memoir of his medical career. The doctor who brought McDonald into the world "was a well-educated physician who had been reputed as being a 'good doctor if you could catch him sober.'"[2]

McDonald obtained a permit from the sheriff's office and started carrying a .38-caliber Colt handgun in an arm holster during the early years of the oil boom. This was after sometimes rowdy oil-field roughnecks started showing up in his office bloodied and ill-tempered from accidents at work or brawls in a tavern. He never had to use the pistol, but its presence was "comforting" when it came time to ask some of the rougher roughnecks for cash on the spot in payment for his services.

Among friends, McDonald might use a favorite story about a urologist named Livingston: "Dr. Livingston had a unique way of handling patients successfully. This is illustrated by the traveling salesman who came into his office for examination of his prostate. After completing, he told the patient the bill was $2.00.

"The salesman, scowling indignantly, sputtered, 'That much for just thirty seconds of work?'

"Livingston handed the man a rubber glove, and offered: 'Put it on, and stick your finger up my a— and we will call it even.'

"This settled the matter," McDonald deadpanned.

When it came to Tyler's new hospital—the first modern medical facility in East Texas—there was no joking around. C. C. McDonald could take much personal credit for the project's success, although bragging was not his style. Besides, everybody in the room knew how much toil and sweat McDonald put into it and applauded his leadership. The nineteen doctors who joined McDonald in the effort had taken to calling him "Chief."

Opposition to the idea from those who suspected taxpayers would be saddled with enormous debt was unrelenting—despite wide awareness that a hospital was needed.

McDonald recalled once working at a local hospital that experienced recurring power outages during an ice storm. He improvised by using a car headlamp and storage battery to light the operating room during an appendectomy. The makeshift system failed by the time the surgeon was ready to close his incision. In the emergency, an assistant shined a flashlight on the patient's belly. It was not until the next day that an X-ray revealed a clamping device had been sewn up inside her abdominal cavity. The surgeon had to reopen the woman to remove the tool.

Opponents of the new hospital were not bad people, McDonald said. The "gentlemen were honest, sincere businessmen who had grown up under very conservative circumstances in a small agrarian community of limited resources. They had been trained to a lifestyle that required 'Squeezing the dollar until the eagle defecates.'"

Some of the opponents worried what would become of the local economy when the oil boom inevitably played out. A few demeaned the plan to build a new hospital as a scheme by the doctors to enrich themselves. That was hogwash, McDonald knew. These docs in Tyler didn't have much to gain personally from supporting the push for a hospital, but twenty of them, including McDonald, had put up their own money to get the ball rolling so the city could apply for a grant from Roosevelt's Public Works Administration.

In the end, supporters were able to have Mother Frances Hospital built and equipped at no cost to the taxpayers after brokering a deal with the Sisters of the Holy Family of Nazareth to invest in the facility and manage hospital operations.

McDonald assured everybody at the Rotary luncheon that the hospital was fully ready to open for business following tomorrow's ribbon-cutting ceremony. More than a dozen Sisters of the Holy Family—hospital-trained nurses—were on the job already. The twenty doctors who backed the plan were set to become part of the staff.

McDonald was scheduled to be a guest of honor that evening at a formal banquet celebrating the launch of the facility.

All morning and afternoon Mother Mary Ambrose kept the nuns in her charge jumping from one project to the next. Bishop Joseph P. Lynch, head of the Roman Catholic Diocese of Dallas, was scheduled to arrive in Tyler by early evening. Mother Mary Regina, the provincial superior of the Sisters of the Holy Family of Nazareth, had arrived already. Her order had signed a contract with the city to operate the hospital. It was a coup for the Catholics, outnumbered by Protestants in this region ten-to-one. Tyler had just one Catholic church and no parish school. A Baptist group—the largest Protestant sect in East Texas—made a pitch for the contract, and the city's decision raised concern about a possible backlash from anti-Catholic factions. The Sisters of the Holy Family won the contract because of the order's experience at operating hospitals, an outstanding reputation, and the offer of a sweeter deal for the city than others put on the table.

Twelve sisters, all practical nurses, formed the staff. But this afternoon, as no patients would be admitted until after the dedication tomorrow, the nuns busied themselves with housekeeping chores and last-minute touches to make Mother Frances Hospital shine. It was said that even the heads of screws were gleaming when the sisters finished polishing the hospital that day.[3] Mother Ambrose was a taskmaster of the old school, a strict spiritual leader who equated orderliness and cleanliness with godliness.

The hospital was named for the order's founder, Frances Siedliska, born in 1842 in Poland to wealthy, landowning parents. She received a noblewoman's education, including voice, music, poetry, and other arts instruction, from tutors in her home. Her parents placed minor significance on religious practices, but Frances developed into a devout, practicing Catholic in her teens. She felt drawn to the life of a nun and a need to spurn affluence and contemplate matters of the spirit. Her father objected to the very idea of his beautiful and cultured daughter becoming cloistered in a dungeon-like convent. Frances had something different in mind. In 1875 she started the Sisters of the Holy Family of Nazareth, based in Rome with convents in Paris and London. Ten years later, she and eleven sisters arrived in the United States at the request of a priest in Chicago to serve a community of poor immigrants from Poland. When Mother Frances Siedliska died in Rome on November 21, 1902, she had led the order for nearly three decades and nurtured it well. By 1937 Sisters of the Holy Family were maintaining more than a hundred schools, eight hospitals, and two orphanages in the United States alone.

The doctor's group at the newest hospital, a five-story beacon of progress in a growing city, invited all of Tyler and East Texas to drop in and take a look. Three hundred out-of-town doctors received personal invitations to inspect the hospital and attend a Friday luncheon in the larger of the hospital's two dining rooms. An adjacent kitchen provided a fully equipped food service unit, complete with a conveyor belt and elevator lift to transport food trays to the various floors, where nurses could distribute them to patients' rooms while the food was still warm.[4]

The Tyler municipal band was to play a fifteen-minute concert to kick off the grand opening at 4:00 p.m. on Friday. Guests from West Texas to Washington, D.C., were en route for the event.

"On the eve before the opening all was ready: beds covered with colorful spreads, furniture arranged," according to archival documents referenced in a Sisters of the Holy Family newsletter. "Interior decorators chosen by the hospital committee were busy preparing assortments of flowers for the wards and the rooms; the atmosphere was very pleasant. Nobody there was idle; each came with the sole purpose of helping to make the dedication a success.

"All that was in the hospital was very modern, perfectly planned, and furnished beautifully. There were large operating rooms, offices, and a library—all with the finest equipment."[5]

The sisters thoroughly scoured the kitchen area, even though it had never been used. They washed hundreds of dishes, glasses, and eating utensils as the items were removed from manufacturers' packing crates. It's not known whether the meticulous nuns used the kitchen's chief novelty, an electric dishwasher, or washed them, as they were accustomed, by hand. They did use the hospital's automatic laundry to wash scores of new linens and towels for all the beds and patients' rooms.

The hospital contained an isolation ward for patients with contagious diseases; a unit for broken bones and skeletal deformities; a radiation department for treating cancer; an X-ray room and diagnostic lab; an eye, ear, nose, and throat facility with special equipment for removing obstructions from breathing and food passages; a nursery with a glass partition so fathers, grandparents, and friends could look in on newborns without contaminating the sterile atmosphere around the babies; and a pharmacy.

A room on the main floor was converted into "a small but beautiful chapel." The custom-made altar wasn't yet installed, but a small organ was in place.

"Since some of the Sisters had a designated ward on the first floor as their living quarters, that room became a temporary 'warehouse' for whatever could not be arranged in place at that time," the newsletter said.

"Imagine, if you will, stacks of sheets in one corner; in another, a huge pile of blankets; in another section, pillows; in still another, towels galore. In addition, there were under each bed suitcases, shoes, bedroom slippers. . . . Any thing that seemed superfluous on the higher floors was deposited in the 'common' room.

"The upper floors shone with order and cleanliness. The patients' rooms were like well-furnished parlors. The third floor maternity section was none worse, and the children's bassinets were fit for children of a king. All was in such readiness so that if any person questioned what still had to be done, the only suitable reply would be: 'Straighten out the sisters' quarters.'"[6]

Their living quarters would not be open to the public anyway, so the sisters postponed that job for the first thing Friday morning, when they expected, finally, to have a little time to themselves to meditate, pray, and tidy up their rooms.

Mother Mary Regina was busy with innumerable tasks she'd assigned herself around four o'clock Thursday afternoon, when a sister approached her and said the Mother Superior needed to take an emergency phone call. When Regina put the phone receiver to her ear and listened for a moment, her face changed from the pleasant expression she always tried to wear to a look of grave alarm.

"Yes, we'll send help immediately," she said, with urgency in her voice. "And we will open the hospital this afternoon."

# 17

# Radio Man

Ted Hudson awoke on that Thursday with a feeling that his dream was about to come true. This was his first day at the helm of a new radio station in Henderson, Texas. It was the town's first station, the fruit of Hudson's planning and promotion of the idea for years.[1]

Hudson, a native of Shreveport, Louisiana, had moved to Henderson in 1931, soon after the oil boom began. The region offered fertile ground for entrepreneurs. Hudson saw no reason why Henderson shouldn't be able to sustain a radio operation tailored to the community and supported by East Texas advertising dollars. It seemed incredible to him that a town of more than ten thousand residents in a county with a population of seventy thousand didn't already have a radio station by 1937.

Nothing surpassed radio as a diversion from the hard times of the Depression. Americans bought approximately four million radios between 1930 and 1932. By the end of the decade, an estimated 28 million homes had at least one, and nearly 90 percent of the population spent more than four hours a day listening to everything from news and weather to music and forerunners of the situation comedies and melodramas that would become equally popular on TV in another couple of decades.[2]

"Before they can go happily to bed on Sunday nights, millions of people wait up to hear Walter Winchell chatter about the news," said a story in the first issue of *Life* magazine, published November 23, 1936. The story detailed how Gypsy Rose Lee, the famous stripper, was a recent guest on

Rudy Vallee's hour-long variety show. Vallee earned more than $100,000 to host the show—$1.6 million in 2010 dollars.[3]

Jack Benny attracted the biggest following, with an estimated 18 million weekly listeners. Political columnist Dorothy Thompson commented on the serious news of the day on NBC's *America's Town Meeting of the Air*. Less adventurous listeners tuned in to CBS radio's *Just Plain Bill*, the "barber of Hartville," a vehicle for "the real-life story of people just like people we all know." For those who couldn't quite handle the stimulation of Bill's rollicking adventures in normality, Oxydol offered Ma Perkins, "America's mother of the air. Brought to you by Procter and Gamble, makers of Oxydol."[4]

Maxwell House Coffee sponsored *The George Burns and Gracie Allen Show*, and Wheatena, a hot breakfast cereal, sponsored another favorite, "All hands on deck, here's *Popeye*. . . . Wheatena is his diet, he asks you to try it, with Popeye the Sailor Man!"[5]

Music made up more than half of radio programming and was mixed with adventure serials such as *The Lone Ranger*, variety shows, soap operas, and a few educational programs such as *Invitation to Learning* and *Science on the March*.

By 1937 radio had become the nation's nervous system, transmitting signals coast to coast.

Soon after moving to Henderson, Ted Hudson immersed himself in civic and business activities and began talking up the radio idea with anyone who would listen. His father, a railroad train engineer, imparted to Ted a yearning for adventure. Ted, now thirty-two, discovered in himself a born entrepreneur's relentless drive, optimism, and instincts. He'd already secured the money to open a radio, washing machine, and appliance store in Henderson, but radio remained his true love. As a little boy tinkering with a ham radio in the attic, Ted had picked up snippets of the Russian Revolution—an excited mob shouting revolutionary slogans in a foreign tongue. With his flabbergasted parents standing behind him that night, he learned the power of radio—its immediacy and its ability to carry one solitary voice around the globe. Ted resolved to be the announcer on a coast-to-coast newscast.

The new radio station occupied the top floor of the Randolph Hotel, in downtown Henderson, where Hudson rented an unused penthouse to house the station's studio and control room. He'd made practice runs on the system for two weeks. The station hit the airwaves at 7:00 a.m., broadcasting network programming interspersed with Hudson's announcements of news and events.[6] Hudson had some experience calling high school football and baseball games, but this was his debut as a regular radio announcer. He apparently had the talent to pull it off. "His keen sense of humor and his knowledge of the games he announced made him one of the best sports commentators this section has ever known," according to an article in the *Henderson Daily News*.[7]

Hudson piggybacked his Henderson broadcast on the signal of KOCA in Kilgore, about twenty miles north. After the 7:30 *Eyeopener Program* furnished by a network, Hudson had a few minutes at 7:55 to make local announcements. The late afternoon edition of the *Henderson Daily News* from the day before, Wednesday, March 17, offered him a template and included the New London PTA meeting, scheduled for 3:00 p.m. in the high school auditorium. All parents, the announcement said, were urged to attend.

Hudson must have felt a surge of confidence after surviving his first live segment on the air without a glitch. At 8:00 a.m., his station went to a thirty-minute Pentecostal Church program. At 8:30 a.m., a variety show started. The rookie radio man had some time to contemplate his next news and announcements segment at 8:55 a.m.[8] So far, so good.

If Hudson had any jitters about going on the air, they quickly dispersed. Besides, who was listening? The station was brand-spanking new; Hudson doubted more than a few hundred people, among them his closest friends and neighbors, knew to tune their radio dials to listen to him this morning. He was talking to family. His seven-year-old daughter, Mary Lou, had promised to tune in for a few minutes before she left for school. Hudson gave Mary Lou the honorary title of "engineer" at the new station, and she immediately set about trying to correct her father's grammar.

The 3:00 p.m. network show *Rhythm Time* had concluded, and the next show, *King Richard's Orchestra*, which started at 3:30 p.m., was well under way. Hudson was nearly through the afternoon of his first full day as a professional radio announcer when he noticed commotion outside his studio in a hallway of the Randolph Hotel. He heard snippets of a conversation, voices loud enough to sound excited, alarmed, or distressed. After sticking his head outside the studio, he overheard several people discussing an explosion that supposedly happened at New London High School, ten miles northwest of Henderson.

Hudson immediately called a friend and arranged to borrow an airplane. A few minutes later, he was flying over the disaster site. It looked far worse than anything Hudson had imagined. Debris was scattered in a wide, twisting swath, and hundreds of people were scrambling about the ruins. As far as he could tell from the air, the school was just gone—smashed into a heap of rubble that resembled scenes of bombed towns in news photos from Europe. He turned the airplane back to the south.

After landing at the Henderson airstrip, Hudson wasted no time getting to his panel truck, loading it with radio transmission gear, and heading toward the stricken community.

# 18

# Into the Ruins

Bill Thompson's heart slowed as he sank into a state of shock. The previous instant, a flicker in time, lodged in his brain as a flash of some moment in his future: déjà vu waiting to occur, again and again.

It was strange—whirling through space as though his desk had become a wild carnival ride. The boy twirled over and over in a realm between life and death until compacted inside a tangled mass of debris, he was sucked back down by the forces of gravity at war with the physics of exploding gas.

Bill saw nothing. Only one of his arms was free to move up and down. The rest of his body felt locked as if in a mousetrap. He pinched himself. This was no dream.

Blood trickled down his face and neck. It was sticky and warm. A ringing in his ears gradually gave way to other sounds, a distant commotion. Voices. He was not alone.

E. D. Powell was working in his garden about a quarter of a mile from the school. He heard a loud boom and felt the ground shake. Powell, an oil-field worker, figured a storage tank had blown up. A moment later he saw a great cloud of dust or smoke billowing skyward from the direction of the school.

Arriving at the scene, he saw bodies of children, some blown onto the campus and some hanging from shattered windows. He began digging in the debris, pulling bodies from it and keeping an eye out for his own children. He first found Edna, twelve, and then Eloise, fourteen.

"My heart was gone," Powell said later.[1] "They were our babies."

Ralph Carr stood on the porch of a building near the school and watched in disbelief as the structure rose into the air, hung suspended for a split second, and crashed back to earth with a roar. He dashed toward the wreckage, praying that his sixteen-year-old daughter, Chloe Ann, was somewhere safe from harm. He was one of the first people to enter the ruins, climbing over mounds of debris and working his way through the wreckage until he became hopelessly blocked from going any farther.[2]

He could see through the debris into part of a classroom where students were sitting at their desks, covered in gray dust—dead. Chloe Ann was among them. Carr could get no closer to his child. He wept.

H. G. White had just gotten back to his seat after talking with math teacher Lena Hunt when the boy felt an object slap against his head, a quick hard blow that momentarily stunned him. Something broad and heavy pressed into his back, pinning him to his desk.

A woman screamed from somewhere above the dark cocoon of broken wall and ceiling plaster that encapsulated him. Dust in his nose and throat made breathing difficult. He was hurt and bleeding, and the woman's scream seemed to be moving somewhere out of sight.

He heard a crash and then a shaft of light shot down into the hole where H. G. was pinned. Suddenly the screaming woman was down there with him. She stopped screaming when she saw the boy.

Miss Ann Wright, a first-year teacher, had been in a nearby classroom that was demolished. Several of her students had been killed instantly in the explosion, which had trapped Bill Thompson beneath the rubble. Wright had stumbled across the ruins, screaming hysterically, until she crashed through a sheet of plaster atop what had been Lena Hunt's classroom. Mrs. Hunt was dead, buried somewhere in the debris.

Miss Wright broke away some of the plaster wall that pinned H. G. to his desk, and she threw out broken pieces as fast as she could. Within a minute or so, she had tossed out enough for H. G. to wriggle his body as Wright tugged him from beneath his armpits. The rubble gave him up, dislodged him into the arms of the teacher. H. G. and Miss Wright climbed up out of the hole. He felt an amazing sense of freedom and litheness, in spite of a pounding headache. Blood matted his hair, and grayish powder covered his body and those around him. Everyone looked like ghosts.

H. G. glanced back into the hole where he had been trapped and saw another boy, a classmate, who appeared to be dead. Blood had gushed out of the boy's mouth and nose.

H. G. walked toward an outside water fountain that two women were using to splash water on students. One held the fountain's valve open while the other caught water in her cupped hands and poured it over the children's wounds and dust-covered faces. H. G. bled from a hole in his head over his left eye. The woman washed his face, then looked up and asked him to move aside. A high school student staggered around the north side of the gym toward the women at the fountain. As they began washing his face, he collapsed and did not move again. Pieces of notebook paper had scattered across the campus, and people were using them to cover the faces of the dead. One of the women picked up a sheet and placed it over the young man's motionless features.

Third-grader Jimmie Jordan had disappeared from her sister's side. Elsie staggered through the mess looking for her, but the dust and debris prevented her from seeing far ahead. People fleeing the building jostled her, everybody lost and confused, going one direction then the next. Children all around her cried, and every now and then, somebody screamed.

Elsie saw Jimmie's hands sticking out of a pile of rubbish beside some windows. She climbed over the heap and began tearing it apart. She slipped and fell against a cracked window, and it shattered. A sharp dagger of glass sliced Elsie's face, cutting her eyebrow and eyelid in half. With blood blinding one eye, she kept digging, throwing out pieces of plasterboard and shards of tile. When she finally pulled Jimmie free, Elsie saw a dime-size hole above her eye. Blood poured out of it. Elsie tried to find a pulse and couldn't, but thought she might not have done it right. She stopped the bleeding by holding her hand on Jimmie's wound.

Elsie carried Jimmie in her arms until she reached a place in the ruins where she could get out. A woman saw them and noticed the bad cut over Elsie's eye. "Let me take the child. You're hurt yourself. We need to get you both to a doctor."

Elsie didn't want to let go of Jimmie. The woman gave her no choice.

"We're taking her to get help," the woman said. They put Jimmie on the open bed of a truck filled with other children, most of whom looked dead. Elsie climbed on too and wrapped her arms around her unconscious sister.

Helen Beard awoke on the ground between cars in the parking lot. Cement dust completely covered her body. Blood was streaming from the back of her head. One of the first people she saw amid a crowd of people was her mother. Helen pushed through the crowd until she was able to throw her arms around Mrs. Beard's waist. "Mother," Helen said, before becoming too woozy to speak.

The right fender on the Beards' car was crushed into the wheel, so Mrs. Beard asked a friend to take her and Helen to a hospital.

Mr. Beard and his son, Alton, who survived the explosion unscathed, stayed behind to search for Marie.[3]

Felton Waggoner waded into the scrambled wreckage and began separating children from the ruins. He picked up the living and the dead, carried them out, and laid them atop a gentle slope, on the grass beside a sidewalk.

Time and again, he struggled into the demolished building and emerged holding a child in his arms. Waggoner was a tall man—six feet, five inches—and looked like a giant to the younger students. Many recalled seeing him striding back and forth, carrying a precious bundle each time, thrusting a measure of discipline into the chaos and hysteria surrounding them all.

Bobby Clayton, pinned in a narrow gap beneath a row of steel lockers, saw Mr. Waggoner maneuvering through a cross section of collapsed walls and over a ragged hump of shattered joists and fallen beams. Bobby's father worked in the oil field for a natural gas company, and the boy had begun attending New London just three weeks before, having transferred there from a little country school in Arkansas. Bobby called out to the junior high principal, but his voice was so choked with dust his words barely formed on his lips. Waggoner couldn't hear the faint plea for help. The tall man moved off in another direction.

Bobby, ten, settled back and tried in vain to relax. The sturdy lockers had stood against a wall at the back of the room, just behind Bobby's desk.

When the room blew apart, the lockers fell over against him and knocked him to the floor under the desk. A gash in his scalp bled. He hurt all over. As far as he could tell, the others in Mrs. J. D. Nelson's classroom were buried under a heap of rubble, dying or dead.

Teachers Carroll and Mildred Evans held each other with their bodies clinched around their toddler, Duane, their terrified hug lasting until the air cleared enough to see the high school—what had been the high school—in a scrambled heap of bricks, boards, tile, pipes, wires, twisted steel beams, and jagged concrete boulders.

Carroll gave Mildred and Duane a gentle push back inside their home, and he headed straight into the ruins. Evans tried to find the science room where he taught his last class and where his colleague, Willie Tate, was teaching a large group of students about the moon's orbit and phases. The mound of rubble that had replaced that part of the building proved impassable. Evans picked his way down to the basement level and into what was left of the industrial arts shop where his friend and next-door neighbor Lemmie Butler taught.

When he saw the scorched body of a man splayed across a desk, Evans knew it had to be Lemmie. He patted around the corpse until he felt Butler's pocket watch. Evans stuck it in his own pocket to take to Butler's wife.

F. M. Herron jumped into his car and joined a caravan of vehicles that headed from Overton toward the school. When he arrived at the edge of the disaster, he assumed the worst. Herron hardly uttered a sound before he struggled into the debris pile and began carrying out the bodies of children. He had no idea of the whereabouts of his own—Juanita, fourteen; Inez, twelve; and F. M. Junior, ten. These bodies were so torn he didn't know how any parent would recognize a son or daughter.[4]

Herron lifted a dead girl and carried her to the line of bodies on an embankment. Women were laying sheets of notebook paper over their faces. Herron gently placed the girl among the dead and turned to go back into the ruins. But before he took two steps, he stopped, and then spun around to look at the girl again. She still had on one shoe, which Herron recognized.

*Juanita.*

L. V. Barber realized he could do nothing for the girl who jumped from the second-story window of the study hall library. She'd sliced an artery in her leg going through the glass of the first-floor window. A small group of students huddled around Evelyn Rainwater, a girl known for her beautiful gray eyes, as blood drained from her into the schoolyard dirt.

L. V. jogged around the corner of the only wing that still stood and looked out at the wreckage of the rest. He couldn't imagine anybody had survived the collapse but set out anyway, searching for his brothers—Burton, sixteen, and Arden, twelve—and his fourteen-year-old sister, Pearl. He found Burton, milling among a crowd of survivors, within about fifteen minutes. Someone had showered him off, exposing extensive burns. Burton had been in the shop, where the explosion originated. The blast had blown apart the column he had been standing behind, tearing his face, shoulder, and leg.

Nobody L. V. talked to said they had seen either Pearl or Arden. He went to a part of the school where he suspected Pearl might have been in class and saw rows of bodies mangled and twisted beyond recognition. He turned his search to Arden, the family's baby, a fifth-grader whose classroom sat in the middle of the explosion's most destructive swath. It would take a miracle, L. V. Barber admitted to himself.

Walter Freeman, twelve, was sitting at his desk in the back of Lena Hunt's math class, in the opposite corner from H. G. White's desk, when the explosion brought the school down around them. Walter woke up on the floor under a desk, feeling numb through part of his body, stinging and hurting in other places. He saw some light seeping in from the direction of a stairwell in the hall that led up to the outside. With excruciating effort, Walter pulled himself forward into the hallway. It seemed like he was inside a bad dream. He remembered seeing Mrs. Hunt at her desk, with the blackboard behind her, when something crashed down on the teacher. He also remembered seeing a quick flash almost at the same moment, as he careened from his desk into a vortex of debris. Now he couldn't stand up, but he managed to crawl another few inches using his shoulders, chest, and one arm. A stick protruded from his other arm. Walter tried to pull it out but it wouldn't budge, and that's when he realized it was bone.

His back was broken, several ribs were cracked, the sight in one eye was blurred, and a piece of steel was embedded in his head; he had a concussion. Walter didn't then know the extent of his injuries or how perilously close to death he was. He just focused on the shaft of light ahead of him and pulled himself toward it. He heard someone near the stairwell say, "There's one. Let's get him out."

Two women hurried down the steps and saw the boy with a blood-smeared face and his overalls nearly ripped off his body. His eyes were open, blinking away drops of blood. They carried him out into the sunshine.

Walter saw the big oak tree behind the school with some of its branches stripped off as if a storm had hit it, and the mangled body of a child hanging from one that remained. He passed out.

George L. Hardy of Arp heard the explosion, and soon afterward, he saw emergency vehicles streaming east in front of his house. "The London school!" somebody shouted from a car. Hardy grabbed his hat and coat, jumped into his car, and started for the school. By the time he reached the outskirts of New London, he was sweating profusely. Hardy, sixty-three, loosened his collar and took off his coat. After he'd gotten as close to the school as possible, he parked the car in the weeds on the side of the road. Then he set out in a trot. He was too old and out of shape to make a full run.

When Hardy saw chalky white men coming out of the collapsed building carrying dead children drenched in blood, he clutched his chest and collapsed next to a fallen piece of wall. George Hardy died later that evening, felled, a doctor said, by a heart attack induced by shock.[5]

Preston Crim had been sitting near the windows in Ann Wright's fifth-grade English class, next to Claude Joseph "Joe Bo" Kerce, a couple of rows over from Bill Thompson.

Preston, eleven, held a green-striped fountain pen and copied down a homework assignment Miss Wright had put on the blackboard. Kids were talking in soft voices because the teacher said they could visit quietly in the last few minutes before the bell. Bill Thompson, Preston noticed, was making eyes at Billie Sue Hall. Joe Bo, also eleven, was gazing out the window. He was the class cutup and got paddled often, but everybody, including the teachers, liked him and couldn't hold back the laughs when Joe Bo's comedic charm hit high gear. His nickname was a droll coupling of his middle name—Joe for Joseph—and the name of a faithful companion, his little dog Bo. Joe Bo seemed a natural fit.

Preston Crim had no indication anything was wrong until a strange force slapped against him. "All of a sudden it felt like there was a strong wind—something blowing against you real hard—and everything was going around and around and you couldn't stand against it," he recalled. "It was just turmoil, and then, almost as soon as it happened, it was over. And then it was just complete destruction. You couldn't see anything."

A piercing scream sliced through heavy dust. It was Ann Wright, yelling her lungs out. Joe Bo Kerce took command and pushed the teacher toward an opening where the windows had been and through it. Preston followed them.

"When we got outside you couldn't see your hand in front of you because of the dust," Crim said. "We started running and the first thing you do is run into some parked car out there and bounce back, torn up. We made our way to the front of the building where the buses always waited."

The only certainty at that moment was something crazy had happened, turning school out earlier than expected. "That's all us young kids could think about. We didn't realize how serious it was," he said. "We got up there and saw the school—just leveled out."

Joe Bo glanced at Preston and saw blood running down his shoulder and a coating of plaster dust stuck to his green corduroy outfit. Preston looked at Joe Bo, whose scalp and neck bled in spots from bits of concrete blasted everywhere by the explosion.

"Well, Preston," Joe Bo said, "this ought to get us out a couple of weeks."

When the dust cloud parted, the boys discovered a terror far worse than the scenes of any horror movie they'd ever watched. This was not fiction flickering on a movie screen; it was as real as the taste of blood in your own mouth.

Students were leaping from second-story windows of a wing of the school that remained upright. Some made hard landings and didn't get right up, but rolled and moaned. A girl named Evelyn Rainwater was hurt badly. Students clustered around her were talking about how it happened.

A boy said he had yelled, "Don't jump! Don't jump! We'll come get you down."

She jumped anyway but didn't push far enough away from the building to miss the outturned window on the first floor. One of Evelyn's legs crashed through the glass, impaling her body on the steel window frame. Blood gushed down her leg. A boy put his arms under Evelyn's arms, pulled her off the window frame, and carefully laid the unconscious girl on the grass.

Her dress below the waist quickly became soaked with blood.

"Somebody please come help this girl!" the boy yelled. "She's bleeding to death!"

Preston Crim saw a man emerge from the ruins carrying a schoolboy. "Evidently he was one of the first on the scene and he found his son the first thing," Crim said. "I could see [the son's] feet dangling—turned different directions like his legs were crushed. His abdomen was opened up and his intestines were hanging and he was still alive, begging his daddy to kill him. His daddy was just walking like a zombie in a trance."

Joe Bo Kerce took off for home, running across the school grounds and down the side of a road. His heels were steadily kicking up little spouts of dust as he faded from sight.

Ledell Dorsey sat in a daze in the corner of what remained of her classroom, now reduced to a small portion of a two-story section of the building standing like a precarious pedestal amid the ruins. So much dust covered her she blended with the floor and walls, becoming almost invisible, like a silver moth enmeshed into the gray powder. She was conscious but in a twilight—frightened and alone.

One of her classmates, Helen Rainwater, had jumped out through a window in the room, but Ledell was afraid the second-floor window was too high off the ground for a safe jump. She waited, hoping someone would come to help her down soon.

A man stumbling across the rubble saw a small human foot sticking out of the debris, wiggling. He fell to his hands and knees and started shoveling away broken pieces of a wall, using his bare hands. A child's legs, midsection, and shoulders became visible, and a moment later, a young girl looked up at him with clear, frightened eyes. It was Billie Sue Hall, the fifth grader Bill Thompson had wanted to flirt with before the bell rang. The school explosion had cut short their romantic interlude.

Billie Sue was not hurt badly, although she was scared speechless and in a confused daze. She glanced around, looking for her teacher. She had seen Miss Wright an instant before the room blew apart. The teacher had clutched a student with her arms and dived under a table, pulling the girl underneath it with her.[6]

When ten-year-old Molly Sealy hurried off the school bus, she saw her mother standing at the side of the road with four other mothers who were neighbors. The neighborhood was not far from the school, separated only by a deep ravine and patch of woods. The women had come running from their homes to the bus stop soon after they heard the explosion.

Catherine Sealy grabbed Molly and gave her a tight hug. The other mothers watched as the door closed and the bus pulled away. No other children had gotten off.

Clarence Moore left work and hurried to the high school as soon as he heard about the explosion. He hoped to find that his sister-in-law, Marie Patterson, had gotten out of the building without harm.

Clarence went straight to the part of the building where Marie worked in Superintendent Shaw's office, and his heart sank when he saw the destruction. His brother-in-law, Pat Patterson, was already there, searching in the ruins.[7]

"Any word about Marie?" Moore asked Patterson.

"No," Patterson said.

Moore asked if his wife, Billie—Pat and Marie's sister—had been told yet.

Billie was in the office with Marie, Pat Patterson said. "We'd come by to give Marie a ride home, and now I'm afraid we have lost them both."

Olen Poole thought a radiator near the study hall had popped a seam. The fifteen-year-old heard no massive explosion. "It sounded like—you take a big sack of nails and dump them out—then hot gas and dust came boiling in," he recalled.

The boy felt his way through the cloud until he found an open window. It seemed as though he was all by himself, although he knew other students must be all around him. He was scared.

"So I dropped out of one of them windows and it wasn't about four or five feet to the ground, because the building was kind of built into that hill," he said. On the opposite side, it would have been a much steeper drop.

Near the school, he saw a teacher's parked car with a big hole shot through it. "I knew then it was worse than a radiator blowing up. So I went around and there's a concrete wall coming out the back of this building and there was a body laying on this wall. I didn't recognize him. His head was in bad shape. I knew he was dead.

"I come right around . . . and I got to where I could see the building was just a pile of brick," Olen said.

Only part of the easternmost wings—the ends of the prongs on the E-shape of the building—were standing amid the ruins. The middle prong, which had been the auditorium, had collapsed, with the end toward the stage sticking up out of debris.

Olen located his three younger brothers, who attended the elementary school, waiting on a curb about to board a school bus. He made certain they were okay and then took off running down the road toward his home.

"People would stop me and ask me what the explosion was and I'd tell them, 'The school!' They didn't believe me."

When he raced into the house, Olen caught his mother off guard. She knew nothing about an explosion. "When I told her, of course, she went to crying. I told her all my brothers were all right."

Olen couldn't stop thinking about the dead boy against the wall. The sight of it, so shocking at first, now caused an unaccustomed anguish in his heart. He thought and thought, but he couldn't decide who the boy might have been. There was just no telling, because he was so beat up. Olen was almost sure it wasn't his best friend, Charles Hasbrook, although the boy had been about Charles's size.

Oil-field worker Homer White, thirty-seven, was at the wreckage soon after the explosion, helping remove debris and bodies and searching for his son, also named Homer, whom everybody called by his initials, H. G. The boy's dad and his wife, Edna, had quickly located another son, Max Wade, who was okay.

A small girl who knew the Whites told them she saw H. G. soon after the explosion and his head was bleeding, but she didn't know where he was now. Homer and Edna White felt their hearts sink.

Edna White, a thirty-year-old homemaker, scurried about, looking all over the place for her boy. Her neck and shoulders ached with spasms of grief, which she compressed by catching her breath, clenching her teeth, and balling her fists. Each time her eyes pooled with tears, she wiped her face on the sleeve of her dress.

Many of the bodies she saw were crushed beyond recognition.

"What was he wearing?" Homer White asked Edna.

"Khaki pants, a plaid shirt, and little high-top boots," she said.

Homer made another round to reexamine bodies that already were laid out on a grassy place near the ruins. Halfway through, he spotted a body about the size of H. G.—dressed in khaki pants, a plaid shirt, and high-top boots—with blood-spattered sheets of notebook paper over the upper portion. He lifted the paper and nearly doubled over in horror. The child's head was gone.

He started to go look for his wife and break the news, but then had a second thought. A few weeks earlier, he had taken the boy's boots to a shoe shop for repairs. The shoemaker replaced the worn-out leather across the sole of each boot with a strip of new leather. White went back to the body, gently picked up one small foot, and examined the boot. The bottom was crusted with dirt. Taking out his pocketknife, the burly oil-field worker scraped the boot bottom clean enough to see that this boot had never been half-soled. With a reprieve from the anguish that had surged into his chest, Homer White resumed his search.

Out in the country, a school bus stopped on a lonely stretch of road, and a first grader stepped down out of the bus trailer. *"Go straight home,"* a grown-up told the child.

The bus disappeared around a bend in the road, leaving six-year-old Billie Anderson standing alone, more frightened than ever before in her life. She knew only that something terrifying had happened to the high school, and her sisters Allene and Lillian didn't meet her as usual to ride the bus home with her.

Billie stood at the edge of a big field with oil wells scattered here and there. She could see her house, small and dark, far off in the distance, all the way on the other side of the field. Her mother had told her to never cross the field alone. She was supposed to cross it only with her older sisters, but now she had no choice.

Trembling, Billie took a few steps into ankle-high grass and found the path, a narrow strip worn smooth; for years many feet had beaten down the grass and wildflowers until it was just a ribbon of red dirt. She walked as fast as she could, imagining that wolves might come out of the woods before she could reach the house. Clouds had drifted across the sky and made it seem later than it was—dimming the landscape and setting off a chorus of crickets chirping.

Billie was almost in tears by the time she reached the front steps of the Andersons' small house. A woman was sitting on the porch, but she wasn't Billie's mother. Billie recognized the woman as a maid who worked for a family living near the Andersons. The woman stood up immediately and took Billie by the hand.

"Come with me, child," the woman said. "Your mother and father are out looking for your sisters, so you're going to stay with us until they get back."

Bud Price, manager of the Overton Chamber of Commerce, raced to New London as quickly as possible. He followed a line of police cars, fire trucks, and ambulances with lights flashing and sirens blaring. He had expected his sister, Mattie Queen, to leave school early and meet him at her apartment in Overton. He had dropped by the apartment, but Queen apparently hadn't been able to leave as early as she had expected.

At the school, Price first checked the parking lot for Queen's car. When the school exploded, it cast slabs of concrete, desks, rows of steel lockers, wooden beams, and chunks of smaller debris across the thirty to forty cars parked in front of the high school. Price hurried through the lot, glancing into each car. He felt sure he'd recognize it easily, but now many of the vehicles looked very similar.

After they had met for breakfast that morning, Queen had walked to her car, stopped and strolled over to see Bud before he left. "She told me to be sure to come by her house that afternoon because she had something important to tell me and was going to leave school early to meet me," Bud Price recalled.[8] "I walked over to her car, which was new. I noticed a pair of wooden shoes in the car. Queen often took items to show students. I watched as she drove off and wondered why at the corner she turned back to her apartment rather than to the school. I found out later she had gone back to the apartment to tell her roommate to be sure and be there that afternoon because she had important news to tell. She kissed her good-bye and left."

Bud couldn't find Queen's car anywhere in the parking lot, so he figured the music teacher must have left early after all, and they had missed each other coming and going.

He walked over to where rescue workers were pulling the wreckage apart to look for the survivors and the dead. They obviously needed all the men they could get, so Bud rolled up his shirt sleeves and went to work. It was a ghastly task.

"At this time there were no stretchers to carry the bodies on. We used the metal window frames," Price said. "I was working with a man I didn't know. I heard him mutter, 'This is worse than the Battle of Marne [a bloody World War I battle in France, during which thousands were killed and wounded].'"

A father approached Price and asked if they had been able to find his daughter.

"We have," Price said.

"Did she die innocently?"

"Yes."

Later, Price confessed, "I hope God will forgive me that lie because in fact she was trapped in metal and concrete and died while we were cutting her out with a torch."[9]

A truck raced down the oil lease road boiling up a cloud of dust behind it.

The crew working at the site had finished loading tools onto its truck and was ready to call it a day. The men looked up and saw the boss's truck speeding toward them. The truck stopped fast, and the manager called out the window, "The London school exploded! Men, they can use all the help they can get."

Oil-field worker Marvin Dees and the four men on his crew now understood where the loud boom they had heard originated. The crew truck had first-aid supplies aboard, and most of the men had at least a smattering of emergency medical training. The foreman said, "Let's go and see what we can do."

"We jumped in our truck and went on up," Dees said. "Traffic was beginning to congregate, and they weren't letting people through unless they could help. They could see that we had a truck with a winch on it and we also had first-aid equipment, so they flagged us right onto the perimeter of the disaster area.

"Oh, my gosh. It was just a big pile of rubble where there used to be a school. We couldn't believe our eyes. Parts of the building—some of them were the jagged pieces of concrete in the walls—were standing a little bit. Rubble was just scattered everywhere. There were big chunks here and there. It was an awful scene."

The men jumped off their truck and started running helter-skelter to help wherever they could, Dees remembered. "There were a lot of bodies scattered around, and you could see blood here and there and parts of flesh here and there. There were a lot of shoes scattered around. I guess they were just blown out of their shoes."

The first task was to load the wounded onto vehicles so they could be rushed to clinics and hospitals, Dees said. They separated the living from the dead and laid bodies at a clearing near the rubble. "We covered them as best we could, with clothing or paper or whatever. In other words, when they were covered, we knew they were dead."

The rescue work was disorganized in the early phase. Men rushed about and lent a hand wherever it was needed—carrying a body, lifting a hunk of concrete, holding pressure on the wounds of children to keep them from bleeding to death.

Cries for help rang out from students and teachers trapped in the massive debris. At first, there seemed no way to reach some of them, Dees said.

"It just so happened that a truckload of baskets from a basket factory was passing by, and the driver stopped to help," he said. "Somebody came up with the idea: Let's just form a basket brigade and remove a lot of that debris that will fit in a bushel basket, like bricks and mortar, tile, whatever would fit. Somebody said, 'Let's form two lines from about the center of the site out to the perimeter.' We formed two lines facing each other. They were loading the baskets up around the center, and they would pass the basket to two men, and they would pass it on to two men and so on out to the perimeter, and they would dump the basket. And then we would pass the empty baskets back up to the center.

"That's how we got organized, so to speak. We got settled down to this basket brigade, and we moved a lot of debris."

Superintendent Shaw wandered across the ruins trying as best he could to help somewhere. Dirt and blood smeared his face and neck. He had found his glasses, although the frame was warped and a crack shot across one of the lenses.

"There are children under here," he said to each person he met. "There are children under here."

His sense of responsibility as the person in charge of a demolished schoolhouse, the responsibility for hundreds of dead children, began to crush him. An overpowering hopelessness crept into his mind.

He sensed almost immediately that this disaster resulted from his decision, with the school board's approval, to tinker around with the heating system and save some money. How blind, how pointless that seemed now. The first angry question the inquisitors would ask him, Shaw felt certain, was why the richest country school in the nation needed to save a few dollars on heating fuel.

The small man with round spectacles wandered as far into the ruins as he dared without getting in the way or making the situation worse by getting himself trapped in the unstable underpinnings. Roaming the debris, he eventually thought of a situation in which he and the school board would have been less culpable for what had happened. It was not unheard of across rich Texas oil fields for natural gas pockets to bubble up into caves or excavated holes beneath structures and cause explosions when some idle spark touched the gas. Something like that had happened recently in Texas or Oklahoma, Shaw recalled. It seemed at least feasible that it could have happened here.

Torn books with pages bulging from the bindings were scattered far and wide. Textbooks, library books, composition tablets, encyclopedias, anthologies of literature, arithmetic exercise pamphlets, geography books with maps—all the wisdom of the world pitched across a chaotic gulch. Lost somewhere in the heap, near where the superintendent's office was demolished, had to be Shaw's personal copy of the 1935 London yearbook—the school's first annual—a handsomely bound tribute to the accomplishments of the students, teachers, and the superintendent himself. The first *Londona* was dedicated to Shaw: "To one who has a clearer vision of our modern student life and its activities; one who is ever in sympathy with school interest; one who upholds the highest ideals before his pupils; and to one whom we love and admire." The dedication summing up Chesley Shaw's legacy was buried in the ruins.

The superintendent made his way as near as he could to where Sambo's classroom would have been. Peaks and valleys of rubble stretched toward a partially standing wing of the school that seemed remote and surreal, unconnected to anything, with the football field in the distant background. Sambo is gone, his heart told him.

# 19

# Newsflash

The two major newswire services in Dallas, the Associated Press and United Press, each were preparing for a shift from the regular dayside crew to the night operation. The change took place every day between 3:00 p.m. and 4:00 p.m. Soon after 3:00—depending on the level of traffic on the newswire—the electrical nerve centers in the main offices were closed down, and all activities for the rest of the day, until about midnight, were shifted to smaller auxiliary offices.

The UP and AP were fierce competitors. Each had hundreds of newspaper and radio clients counting on them to deliver any breaking news story faster than their competitors' wire service—without sacrificing accuracy. Newspapers and radio news editors posted stories on tight deadlines, usually giving themselves an hour or more to edit a report, enough time to double-check the facts and fine-tune each element of the story. In the wire services, the motto was "a deadline every minute." Rarely was there a spare moment even to grab a dictionary. This was the trench warfare of the news business. The wire services had offices in every major city in the United States; they were often located in downtown buildings not too far apart. Such was the case with the AP and UP bureaus in Dallas.

Veteran reporter Felix R. McKnight was about to close the AP day office after a long afternoon working at the rewrite desk. McKnight looked the part of a city reporter. His hair was combed neatly with a sharp, straight part on one side, and his tie was knotted up high against the collar of his white dress shirt. His sideburns were short. He wore a light sports coat.

Most of the copy he put out that day was dull sounding in spite of his best efforts to enliven it. A couple of old newsroom slogans helped him on days like this. The first was "You can't make a silk purse out of a sow's ear." The other was even more potent: "It is what it is." No amount of embellishment could polish flimsy facts; great facts made a clean, lean story shine like a lamp in the dark.

One of the phones rang. McKnight grabbed the receiver, "AP, McKnight."

The connection was bad. The man on the other end got out a couple of words through gulps of air. "Terrible, terrible explosion. Hundreds dead."

"Slow down. Say again."

The man paused and identified himself as a stringer from East Texas. McKnight knew the name. The stringer was crying as he tried to get his words out. "The school blew up," he muttered.

"What school? Where are you calling from?"

"London school—the oil field. The children—"

"Did you say children dead?" McKnight blurted.

The next line was too garbled for McKnight to understand. He knew the man; he was a reliable stringer. "Are you sure there are people killed?" McKnight asked.

"Yes. Many children are dead. Please send us help. Doctors. Ambulances. I've got to go now."

"No, don't hang up," McKnight urged. He managed to jot down the phone number before the man hung up.

McKnight jumped from a table where he sat to a swivel chair in front of a teletype machine. He typed out a quick, short advisory: "An explosion at or near a school in the East Texas oil field has caused multiple injuries and possible fatalities, according to a usually reliable source."[1] He sent the advisory with a bell signal so that editors would know this was no ordinary story and more was coming.

The AP bureau chief, Fred Dye, had overheard bits and pieces of the exchange, and he already had a Texas map spread on a table near where McKnight was working. "There's no London in the oil field," Dye said.

"I believe it's called New London. I saw the school when I was in East Texas the other day."

"There's no London or New London on this map," Dye said.

Another phone rang and McKnight snatched the receiver off its cradle and cuffed it against his ear.

"Yeah. Yeah. Yeah." He was scribbling notes as he listened. "You're sure about all this? Okay. We need a number to call you back. Okay. And call us back when you have more."

McKnight slammed the receiver down. "That was an executive at Humble Oil. He confirmed it's a school and says hundreds possibly are dead."

"Get something on the wire," Dye said. "Then get down to the explosion—and take Bill Rives with you."

Twenty-six-year-old McKnight swiveled back to the teletype machine and started furiously pounding the keys. The first code he punched into the teletype tape was the multiple bell alarm for a newsflash. It was approximately 3:45 p.m. It would take more than two hours to drive to New London—not counting unexpected delays, McKnight knew from experience. Adrenaline surged to his fingertips.

Commotion also filled the UP office, located in another downtown high-rise.

Walter Cronkite, twenty, was on the desk filling in for a regular staffer who was on vacation. Normally Cronkite was based in the Kansas City bureau, but he had been called in to the Dallas office a couple of days earlier. He was getting ready to leave the office at the end of his shift when an advisory from the UP bureau in Houston rang bells in a teletype receiver.

A major story is developing in East Texas, the advisory said. "Hold the afternoon wires open."

"The word came down the wire to Houston that they were going to need a lot of medical help up in New London, that there had been a serious explosion," Cronkite recalled in an interview with KHOU-TV in Houston.[2] "I don't think the first report said a school. We were holding the afternoon wire open for the late newspapers when word started developing that it was a school and it looked like there might be hundreds dead. It was hard for us to believe that it was that serious, but Bill Baldwin, the bureau manager of the UP in Dallas, and I hopped in a car and started right away for New London."

Editors at the *Tyler Morning Telegraph* and the *Courier-Times* quickly decided to send Sarah McClendon as the lead reporter to cover the disaster. She knew the region as well as anyone and knew the quickest routes to take over back roads to get to the school. Her editor assigned a photographer to drive, as McClendon herself didn't yet drive, and told them to rush to the site of the explosion and immediately phone back with some facts about the true extent of damage and death. If the story was as bad as it sounded, they would put out an extra edition late that afternoon and send more staff to the scene, the editor said.

News of the disaster spread rapidly from New London to all the surrounding communities and into Henderson by telephone and word of mouth. Neighbors raced next door to tell neighbors, motorists waved frantically and shouted what they knew to other motorists and to clusters of people gathering on street corners and along the roadsides.

Rookie radioman Ted Hudson, driving a panel truck, joined a stream of traffic that included cars driven by Alvin Thompson and numerous other parents rushing to the school grounds to look for their children. Hudson's own daughter attended school in Henderson and was safe at home. He wasn't driving to New London as a radio newsman—he didn't think of himself as any kind of reporter—but just because it seemed the right thing to do, as he would say later.[3] He was going to offer to help in any capacity that might be needed.

A procession of vehicles was leaving New London with lights flashing and horns honking. Injured children, some with blood smeared on their necks and faces, were visible in some of the cars. Children were also sprawled across the beds of pickup trucks. The cars and trucks were obviously heading toward the Henderson Hospital. The traffic at times became clogged in either direction. Somewhere in the procession, typing teacher Hazel Shaw was driving toward the school with Myrtle Meador, one of her students, in the passenger seat. Shaw and Meador had been at Henderson High School waiting for a typing and shorthand contest in which Myrtle was a finalist. When people at the high school noticed ambulances and emergency vehicles pulling into the nearby Henderson Hospital, Myrtle ran over to see what was going on. She came back, pale in the face, and told Miss Shaw what had happened. Now they were rushing back so Hazel Shaw could check on her father, the superintendent, and her brother Sambo and other relatives and many friends; Myrtle Meador was worried sick about what might have happened to her brother, Junior, and also knew that her parents would be searching for her as well as Junior.

Although Hazel Shaw had no way of knowing it, an old friend of hers from her childhood in Minden, Texas, Avis Adams Griffin, was at that moment with her husband in one of the vehicles in the same flow of traffic toward New London. Avis, now a Henderson resident, was expecting New London teacher Mazel Hanna, one of her best friends, to spend the weekend as a guest in her home. Mazel, Avis, and Hazel were classmates at the Minden School when Chesley Shaw was headmaster there. Hearing about the explosion, Avis decided to hurry to New London to make sure Mazel Hanna and the Shaw family were all okay. Dr. C. C. McDonald was driving himself and a nurse to the site of the catastrophe to offer medical assistance. Harold Emerson, a traveling violin teacher from Dallas, was teaching lessons in Henderson when he heard about the explosion; he jumped in his car and headed toward the disaster to help in any capacity he might. Two cars filled with ten nuns who were staff nurses at the new Mother Frances Hospital moved along in the traffic, which hit a fast pace at times and then invariably crept to a halt amid a cacophony of blaring horns, sirens, and voices shouting between vehicles.

This was a big mess, Ted Hudson and others in the jam concluded.

Soon after reaching the disaster site, Hudson decided to rig a makeshift broadcast station. Somebody needed to send a plea for emergency medical supplies, doctors, and nurses. He started searching for a live telephone wire among the lines that had been blown away from the building.

With any luck, he had enough equipment in his truck to patch together a mobile transmission center. Hudson rushed to finish the task before dark.

Henry McLemore had zoomed to the top of his profession with such alacrity that it seemed appropriate he loved to write about racing horses, speeding cars, and spectacular runners. At just thirty, the United Press reporter was known the world over for his syndicated sports column—often brightened with comic asides about his own or other people's foibles—and brilliant reporting from championship boxing events, grudge-match football games, and World Series showdowns. He was also surprisingly adept at covering sensational stories, hard news such as the devastating flooding in eleven states along the Ohio and Mississippi river basins in January 1937.

McLemore was a dapper man with a puckish grin, a Georgia gentleman who had assimilated into New York City without losing his own brand of style and charm. Whether he liked to travel or not, travel was his motif as a writer. If the Kentucky Derby were taking place, McLemore was there. He staked out the hotels and bars in Indianapolis for days leading up to the Indy 500. This week his column might be datelined London, England; next, Nassau, Bahamas. His apartment was in New York, but his home was in airplanes, ocean liners, passenger trains, and automobiles. He once drove his car from New York to Columbus, Ohio, to cover a football game between Notre Dame and Ohio State. He returned by train, totally forgetting the car.[4]

McLemore reported on cockfights and mob wars, high-stakes gambling, political conventions, the international tensions beneath the surface of the 1936 Olympics in Berlin, Germany. When German guards blocked him from entering an Olympic dressing room, McLemore pulled from his vest pocket an old speakeasy card with gold lettering and waved it in the guards' faces. Bedazzled, they let him pass.[5] In a column from Czechoslovakia, McLemore compared a taxi ride through Prague to taking a few laps around the Indy Speedway with racer Ernie Triplett.[6] Writing from St. Augustine, McLemore explained he was in Florida looking for the fountain of youth. He hoped to bring home a glass of its fabled water for Babe Ruth to drink.[7] The globetrotting scribe datelined one piece from somewhere in the Swiss Alps, admitting his ineptitude as a mountain climber. "When Mount Everest finally is scaled and a flag planted in its eternal snow, I promise I won't be the man to do it," McLemore wrote.[8]

On the morn of a much-ballyhooed boxing match in June 1935, McLemore wrote, "James J. Braddock, just one year ago relief case No. 11732 on the rolls of the state of New Jersey, tonight fights Max Baer for the heavyweight championship of the world." McLemore predicted an easy victory for Baer, adding that if Braddock won he, McLemore, would spend six months doing penance in Rangoon, Burma.[9] McLemore's next column began with the dateline: RANGOON, Burma.

On March 18, 1937, McLemore was not off on one of his exotic treks but at his own desk in the New York office of United Press, mulling over a lightweight boxing match he was scheduled to cover on Friday at Madison Square Garden. The afternoon was dragging. If he was itching to leave the office and go exploring, the wire service boss walking toward him might have read his mind. "Swing by your apartment, get some travel duds—including extra shirts—and go straight to the airport," the boss told him.[10]

He was heading to a little hamlet in Texas called New London—posthaste.

Lib McKnight had parked her car near the curb on a busy street in downtown Dallas. She was there to pick up her husband when he finished work. When Felix McKnight appeared on the sidewalk, he was carrying an armload of stuff from his office and was followed closely by his fellow reporter and friend, William T. Rives. They were in a rush. As soon as he reached the curb, Felix said, "Lib, I've got to have the car." A big story was breaking, he explained hurriedly. The AP bureau chief would find her a ride home, he added.

She jumped out of the car. Her husband gave her a quick kiss, and then he and Rives dove into the car and screeched away into the afternoon traffic.

Before leaving the office, McKnight had called the Texas Highway Patrol to see whether any patrolmen were heading out to New London. His contact told him an officer was leaving in a few minutes. McKnight could trail the patrolman if he made it to a rendezvous point on the outskirts of Dallas in no more than, say, fifteen minutes, the contact said.

"We'll be there," McKnight assured the highway patrol dispatcher. "Tell him to look for us."

Walter Cronkite and UP bureau manager Bill Baldwin were driving out of Dallas in the same rush-hour traffic. They stopped briefly at a roadside bootlegger's venue to purchase supplies.[11] Although liquor was legal again across the nation after the repeal of Prohibition in 1933, much of Texas remained officially dry because of local option laws. Even so, booze was readily available, as always, at bootleggers, speakeasies, and some apothecaries that kept whiskey on hand for medicinal purposes, so to speak. And it wasn't uncommon in those days for editors and reporters to keep a pint or two handy—either for their own use or sometimes to share with news sources to help loosen their tongues.

Cronkite had yet to make a name for himself. He was just twenty years old, with little more than one year's experience as a reporter, en route to his first major story—a huge one that was about to test the skills of some of the best journalists in America. But in certain ways, Cronkite had been preparing for this assignment since he was a boy, when he first decided he wanted to be a newsman.

He was born in St. Joseph, Missouri, a Kansas City bedroom community, on November 4, 1916. His father, a dentist, moved the family to Houston, Texas, when Walter was ten. After graduating from Houston's San Jacinto High School, where he wrote for the school newspaper, Cronkite enrolled at the University of Texas in Austin. In 1935, after two years at college, he decided to drop out and pursue his career in the trenches of a real newsroom. He accepted a job with the *Houston Press,* taking on the typical rookie assignments—obituaries, luncheon speeches, church news, dribbles of police beat work gleaning information on burglaries, drunk driving arrests, and traffic accidents for the newspaper's police blotter and news briefs. The most critical lesson drilled into him by an old-school editor was the overriding importance of accuracy in everything he reported, Cronkite recalled. After a year, he left the *Houston Press* to become the one-man news and sports department of a Kansas City radio station. The job was short-lived. A few weeks after signing on with KCMO, Cronkite was fired because of a dispute with the station's program manager over Cronkite's unwillingness to air a phoned-in "news" item before checking out the facts himself. His newsman's instincts and training were right—the story didn't check out—but the program manager's clout nevertheless put Cronkite on the street looking for a job. He landed one with United Press at the wire service's national headquarters in Kansas City.

"Banks of teletype machines clattered twenty-four hours a day, an insatiable maw demanding sixty words of copy every minute," Cronkite recalled in his memoir, *A Reporter's Life*.[12] "Our competition across the street, the AP, was doing the same thing. Our job was to write better than they, and get our copy to the newspapers first. It was a blistering, relentless battle. It was said that somewhere in the United States or among our worldwide clients, there was a paper going to press every minute. It meant that we faced a deadline every minute."

The wire service was a great finishing school in the educational process of becoming a reporter, he concluded.

"We couldn't spend much time in contemplation," Cronkite wrote. "We wrote fast, and because our client newspapers always compared our stories with the opposition's, fact by fact, we had a powerful incentive to be right."

It also was a good place for a reporter in the right place at the right time, like Cronkite, to get a big break. Had he not been on a temporary assignment in Dallas, but at his regular desk in Kansas City, he wouldn't have been sent to a school explosion in East Texas. He and Baldwin were on their way to New London to plant the UP flag and establish a foothold. The wire service already was preparing to send in the big guns—Delos Smith from New York, one of the fastest and best writers among UP editors, to head the staff at New London; Washington, D.C.–based Tom Reynolds, one of the best hard-news reporters in the nation; and Henry McLemore, the renowned sports columnist and news feature writer.

Sarah McClendon would boast for decades that she "broke the story" about the New London school disaster, suggesting she was the first reporter to get the news out.[13] Her claim was a stretch. Reporters from the *Henderson Daily News* were close enough to have heard the massive explosion and felt the walls of their newsroom vibrate from the shock wave. Many of the first victims pulled from the rubble were transported straight to Henderson, which had the closest hospital. *Henderson Daily News* reporters were on site quickly enough to gather data for the first comprehensive special edition about the explosion, published late Thursday afternoon.

Even so, McClendon unquestionably was among the first at the site and her dispatches reached beyond local outlets, stunning the outside world with horrifying details of the catastrophe. She was there soon enough to be an eyewitness to horror, to hear mothers screaming, jumping from beams to boulders on tons of debris that lay atop their children. Tyler was only about twenty-five miles from New London, even closer along the back roads that locals such as McClendon often traveled. Unlike most of the reporters racing toward the disaster, she had a home in East Texas—it was a place where her roots were deep and she knew many people. She had an on-site reporter's knowledge of the oil boom and historical grasp of the region and its residents.

Her father, Sidney Smith McClendon, was a native of Monroe, Louisiana. He arrived in Tyler on a stagecoach and went into business selling books, stationery, and musical equipment, including Baldwin pianos. Her mother's family had lived in East Texas for generations and had included a number of prosperous bankers and lawyers. McClendon's maternal grandfather was a judge on the Texas Supreme Court. Sarah was the youngest of Sidney and Annie McClendon's nine children.

"It was like a vision from the end of the world," McClendon wrote of arriving at New London with photographer Kenneth Gunn at her side. "Most of the school had, literally, vanished, leaving a rubble-littered cradle to show where it had been."[14]

McClendon gathered enough information to dictate a preliminary story over the phone to her office in Tyler and then to the International News Service in Dallas. This was within about an hour after the explosion, according to McClendon's calculations.

"After telephoning out my story, I simply pitched in," she recalled.[15]

On the open road, McKnight jammed his gas pedal to the floor to keep up with the state highway patrolman, who was speeding as fast as a hundred miles per hour on some of the straightaways. Here and there, people popped outside onto their porches as the officer's sedan flashed by on U.S. Highway 80, screaming toward East Texas along with dozens of other sirens that seemed to be coming out of everywhere.

Bill Rives was bracing himself at times between the floorboard and front passenger seat of McKnight's car. With no seat belts to secure him, Rives was left to cling to the passenger door armrest with his right hand and press his left palm against the dashboard, lest one of the frequent stretches of ruts in the road toss him into McKnight's lap or against the windshield. The patrolman finally slowed as the automobiles approached the city limits of Terrell, the first town of any size east of Dallas. Seeing the main route had been cleared for emergency vehicles, the highway patrolman accelerated again and barreled through downtown intersections at speeds McKnight clocked on his speedometer at fifty miles per hour. Both reporters' heads thumped into the roof as the car bounded across dips in the streets.

McKnight and Rives, twenty-five, had so much in common they were like brothers. Native Texans, they hailed from white-collar, middle-class families and were nurtured as city boys. McKnight was born in Dallas and grew up in San Antonio. Rives was from nearby Victoria. A shared passion for sports and sportswriting had lured the young men into the news business. They became close friends in the early 1930s working as fellow reporters for the San Antonio *Light*. The bustling South Texas city gave the boys a quick education in hard news—the police beat, city government, and the courts.

Neither man had covered a catastrophe. The closest McKnight had come was the Gulf of Mexico, where he had been dispatched to meet a hurricane churning toward the coast. The skies stayed dark for several days, and the warm waters of the gulf were whipped into an angry frenzy of whitecaps, but the hurricane fizzled.

McKnight knew he was racing toward a big story. The challenge pumped adrenaline into his system like gasoline into a carburetor. His mind flitted past his car, and the patrolmen racing ahead of him. It reached for the scene, groping in the darkness of the unknown. He thought his experience provided him at least a basic understanding of what lay ahead. He was wrong.

With Bill Rives riding shotgun, McKnight's confidence swelled. The bureau chief at AP decided to send two reporters in case this was a real disaster. Even one child injured or killed in the hallowed safe haven of a school would be grist for an important story, the sort of viscera that gathers communities a little closer together and convinces a few more people to pay for the news. If the initial reports of catastrophic damage and dozens of casualties were true, McKnight would need the backup.

They worked well together. McKnight was fast and exceptionally well organized under pressure. He had a rare instinct for reading people quickly and cultivating their trust. Rives had a keen eye for nuances of a story. His training as a sportswriter had instilled him with poise for reporting fast-breaking news on tight deadlines. And it had given his prose, like McKnight's, a sparkle.

McKnight wished he'd received more time to prepare himself before rushing away from Dallas. He and Rives had about ten minutes to prep before leaving the office. McKnight would have liked more time to explain the situation to Lib, but after three years of marriage, she understood the job's demands. A stampede of other news writers, including United Press reporters—the AP's chief rival—was hurtling toward East Texas. Careers in this business rose or fell on timing.

Lib and their nine-month-old daughter, Joan, would be fine without him for a night or two, McKnight knew. He planned to call and check on them during his first break after filing the story from New London.

Rives repeatedly spun the tuning dial on the car's radio, but so far no special news reports about a school disaster had interrupted the ho-hum afternoon lineup of gospel singers, swing music, farm reports, and routine network programming.

"Mac, something nutty about this thing," Rives said.[16] "We might find twenty-five dead. But hundreds? It's impossible."

It seemed so. Still, McKnight felt better knowing Jackson Krueger, another former San Antonio *Light* colleague, was on the AP rewrite desk in Dallas that night. Jack rounded out the team. Regardless of what challenges McKnight and Rives might face in East Texas, a pro like Krueger would solidify the effort. He could take a slab of rough copy and carve it into tight prose.

Jack Krueger was another longtime friend. He and McKnight had been pals as children and remained close as young men. They even had some of the same blood. During McKnight's junior year at Texas A&M, a serious stomach ailment landed him in the hospital, and he had to endure an emergency ten-hour surgery. Krueger provided blood for a transfusion. After McKnight went to work for the Associated Press in 1933, he recruited his buddies from the San Antonio *Light*, Rives in 1935 and Krueger in 1936, to join him at the bureau in Dallas. Now their mutual trust, talent, experience, and news instincts were about to combine on one of the major stories of the twentieth century.

McKnight was an offspring of the new century. He was born August 2, 1910, to Nancy and Luther McKnight. The family moved to San Antonio when Felix was eight years old. His father was a salesman for the Diamond Match Co.

Felix graduated from Main Avenue High School, where he was sports editor at the student newspaper. In 1928 he went to work as a sportswriter for the San Antonio *Light*, saved enough money to start at Texas A&M, and continued working for the *Light* in the summers. While attending A&M, he earned $2.50 a game covering Southwest Conference sports for the *Light*, *Dallas Morning News*, *Houston Chronicle*, and *Fort Worth Star-Telegram*.

Texas A&M at the time offered almost nothing for an aspiring journalist, McKnight recalled in an interview for this book. "They'd never heard of a journalism school. The closest thing to it was a rural sociology course I took," McKnight said. "In that class they taught you how to gather swine and poultry reports together for the weekly newspaper."

The stomach surgery caused McKnight to miss several months of college in his junior year. With the Great Depression raging and money in short supply, he left A&M in 1931 to take a full-time reporting job with the San Antonio *Light*. And there his real schooling began.

The afternoon was nearly spent. Rives moved the radio dial from station to station but still picked up only music and entertainment. They were almost in Tyler, the city nearest to the school explosion.

McKnight calculated that he had driven 110 miles in 100 minutes. He veered off the main east-west highway and headed south on a back road toward Tyler. The bureau chief in Dallas, knowing the direct routes would be blocked by police and clogged with traffic, had called an editor at the Tyler *Courier-Times/Morning Telegraph,* an AP member newspaper, to arrange an escort who knew back roads into the New London area. McKnight and Rives met him at the paper.

From Tyler, they followed a *Courier-Times/Morning Telegraph* delivery truck over narrow, oil-topped roads toward the school. About ten miles outside New London, a car sped toward them; the driver was frantically waving traffic aside.

"I saw the back of the car," Rives recalled.[17] "It was piled with bodies." The reality that the first report of hundreds killed in an explosion was no exaggeration washed over him.

When they were about two miles from the school, a barricade across the road blocked further access to vehicles. McKnight and Rives set out running. It was twilight when they reached the top of a hill overlooking the New London campus.

"We looked and saw a million-dollar schoolhouse scattered over a block-long area," McKnight recalled. "We saw a thousand men crawling over the ruins, silent, sweating, clawing at brick with raw, bleeding hands. Oil company trucks formed a semi-circle in front of the ruins. Motors hoisted cranes in and out of the gnarled steelwork. Floodlights poured daylight shafts on the scene."[18]

The reporters raced down the hillside.

# 20

# A Blue Patch of Sky

Bill Thompson heard faint voices above him and the sound of work boots tromping through the mess. As the sounds grew closer, he called out, hoping his words would carry all the way to the surface. He had not been able to move for nearly an hour, and his body felt numb. His head had stopped bleeding. He still couldn't see anything.

Metal clanked somewhere, and a motor growled. The boy now heard men stomping all around just above him. A vague fear crossed his mind that the movement might cause the debris to collapse more tightly around him, cutting off his air, and then he saw a wedge of sunshine cut into the darkness. "Here I am," the boy said. "I'm down here."

A man on the surface called to other rescue workers, "Here's one alive! Get some help over here! Fast!"

The boy could see hands and arms as the men pulled away broken sheets of plaster and shattered boards. A triangle of blue sky appeared above him. The man looking down in the hole smiled at him. The roughneck's face glistened with sweat. Dirt was smudged across his cheeks. He had the mug of an amateur prizefighter who'd been on the losing end of too many bouts.

"How you holding up?" the man said.

"I think I'm okay."

So many hands grabbed him and lifted him up from the hole it seemed he was riding on air. The men set him down, and he immediately stood up and started to walk.

"Hey, whoa there," a man said. "You need to see a doctor."

The boy felt woozy but generally okay. The cut on his head was sore, and he ached from bruises. No limbs seemed broken. His eyesight was clear. "I need to go home," he told the man.

"No, you need to go to a hospital. You sit down right over there until I get back with some help."

When children in Japan participated in earthquake drills at school, they crouched beneath their desks. Tenth-grader Max Holleyman didn't remember where he learned that—whether it was in a civics class or something he might have seen on a newsreel at the movies—but it was the first thought that popped into his mind when he heard a roar and a rumble sweeping toward his classroom. He shot straight up at first, and then dove under his desk as the classroom darkened.

"It went black," he recalled. "Everything went black—pitch dark."

After a few minutes, Max could perceive enough light to follow it to a window. He climbed out and immediately went to search for his sister, Betty Kathryn, eleven, whose sixth-grade classroom was on the backside of the school, facing the gym. Max saw scores of women running out of the gym. He studied the wreckage to determine where Betty Kathryn might be. She was on the first floor, but all that area was smothered beneath other parts of the school, which had fallen on top of it, including the big red-tile roof, which was scattered in pieces. Finally, he saw a standing stairwell that led into the wreckage, and he climbed down the stairs. Dust was so thick he could hardly see, but he stopped short of stepping on a boy on the stairs because the child was shuddering and panting. Max bent down to get a better look. The boy was dying, and there was nothing Max could do for him. He headed farther down the stairs until he came to a massive ball of debris that blocked him from continuing. He saw a classroom door, off through the wreckage, where a child was crushed beneath a cascade from above. Max retreated back up the steps and out into the afternoon sunshine. A cluster of women stood wringing their hands at the entry to the stairwell.

"*Can you get in through there?*" one of the mothers asked.

"Don't go in there. It's bad. It's a bad thing," Max said. The debris was too large to remove by hand, he told them.

He hurried back toward the section of the building that was partly standing. Max passed the band director, C. R. Sory, who had backed his car onto the campus and was lifting a badly hurt girl into the backseat. The girl was Mrs. Sory's niece; she lived with her uncle and aunt so she could attend school at New London. Mr. Sory got blood on his arms and face when he loaded her into the car. She was too far gone to help. Max saw a large group of students standing below the hull of a two-story section, still intact, although it looked as if a giant with a huge saw had hacked off the wing from the body of the school. The second-floor hall opened into thin air.

"The second floor was a library and there was a student that had jumped from the second floor and gone through the glass [of the lower window] and almost cut her leg off. There were students very bravely getting that child off that window," Max said.

"Is anybody in here?" a voice said from within the broken hull of the building. "Is anybody alive in here?"

Ledell Dorsey struggled to her feet but stayed close to the corner of the classroom where she had remained, paralyzed with shock and fear, for nearly an hour after the building shook violently and broke apart all around her. The fifth grader suddenly saw a person appear, moving slowly through a cracked wall where a dusty shaft of sunlight pooled along an empty hallway. "I'm over here," Ledell said.

The tall teenager, a senior high student she'd seen before, came toward her.

"Come with me," he said. "I'll get you down from here."

She was afraid to move.

The boy took one of her hands. "Now come with me. You've got to follow me. This building could fall."

"I'm scared," she said.

"It's okay."

He tugged her hand, and Ledell followed him. The boy led her to a window that was not so high from the ground as the windows in her classroom had been, and the boy convinced her she wouldn't be hurt in the short jump. The teenager turned and walked away, back into the shadows, looking for others who might have survived.

People tried to warn Carroll Evans that a section of building where he was searching for survivors seemed to be teetering on the verge of collapse. *It's dangerous,* they told him. *Of course it's dangerous,* he wanted to shout back at them—*it's a disaster.* He struggled forward with the beam of his flashlight searching the crevices. He spotted a child, a girl pinned against a desk by a block of concrete. The girl was unconscious.

"Somebody bring me a jack!" Evans hollered.

A young man showed up quickly with the sort of industrial jack house movers used to lift buildings off their foundations. Boxhead and the boy situated the jack so that the base rested on a concrete slab and the lift arm wedged against the desk under which the student was trapped. Evans pumped the jack handle back and forth until pressure from the lift began to crack seams in the wooden desk. With a few more pumps, the desk burst apart, shifting under the weight of the concrete above. The sudden movement set the girl free but sliced off part of her arm. Evans tore a piece of fabric from his shirt tail and fashioned a tourniquet.

"I carried her out there to the gym and her mother came out there and took her out of my arms," Evans recalled. "Then I went back around there and I looked around and the whole building was down."[1]

The girl he rescued died from her injuries.

Evans found another opening and plunged back into the wreckage. He first came across a boy pinned beneath a slab of concrete. The slab was too massive to move with jacks, so nothing more could be done for the boy until a crane could be used to hoist it. That would be too late, Evans knew. The teacher put a piece of board beneath the boy's head, to elevate it slightly. "Rest quietly until help comes," Evans said.[2]

F. M. Herron learned that his son, F. M. Junior, had gotten out of the building without a nick. The ten-year-old took off running for home and didn't stop until he was hugging his mother on the front porch.

Juanita was dead, and Herron was determined not to lose hope of finding his daughter Inez among the students who had survived. Even so, he went back around and looked over bodies that had been carried out since he last surveyed the dead. Men and women in pickup trucks and cars were hauling them away to morgues soon after they were identified as being deceased. Inez, his oldest daughter, was not among the bodies left behind.

Herron hadn't found out anything about Inez in the nearly three hours since the explosion. He asked about her every time he saw a surviving student or a teacher or anybody who might have information. Finally, he received a hint—hearsay, really—that Inez was injured and transported to one of the hospitals or clinics somewhere in East Texas, or perhaps to Shreveport. Yes, a second person said, a girl who might have been Inez was taken away in an ambulance headed for Shreveport because the closest medical facilities were beginning to fill up.

Herron left the ruins, swung by his house to pick up his wife and son, and they headed east toward Louisiana.[3]

His wife looked pale. His son remained silent. Herron ran one of his hands through his mussed gray hair, smoothing it as best he could, and caught a glimpse of himself in the car mirror. His face was the color of schoolroom chalk. He pushed down on the accelerator, hoping to make Shreveport before dark.

Rescue worker Marvin Dees had worn his gloves bare handling material passed from man to man in the basket brigade. Some men in the line had no gloves, and their hands were bleeding. Dees didn't realize it at the time, but he would discover later that the leather soles on his new work boots were being shredded by sharp objects underfoot.

After a while, a murmur passed down the lines that Salvation Army workers had set up stations where volunteers could get gloves, coffee, sandwiches, and cigarettes. The men took turns visiting the Salvation Army stations for a short break and a smoke. Some munched on sandwiches. Before returning to the basket brigade, they each received a new pair of gloves.

"Everything you touched was sharp," Dees recalled. "Sharp edges on the tile, broken brick, and concrete—all those jagged edges were pretty sharp."

A sickening feeling settled into the pits of their stomachs as they worked their way deeper into the ruins, he said. "You just kind of got nauseous, and as time went on, you got more nauseous. We knew that death was all around us—that had just happened. You were in an area that, an hour before, these people were living, and you knew that now some were dead and some were still trapped and you didn't know how many."

"Every once in a while, you'd hear somebody yell, 'Dragline. We need a dragline,'" Dees said. "There were some [victims] that were trapped underneath and that's when the draglines came in handy. And someone would pull a winch line over to a big piece of concrete or a steel beam or whatever and drag it out of the way, and then the basket brigade would get in there and get the small stuff."

Fifth-grader Walter Freeman woke briefly when something cold touched his forehead. A volunteer at a makeshift hospital in an Overton church tenderly brushed his face with a damp cloth. Walter opened his eyes and saw a black woman standing over him. Seeing that he was conscious, she beamed.

"You be still now, child," she said.

Walter didn't feel like moving anyway and could have moved very little even had he wanted to. It was soothing to feel the woman bathing his wounds with the cool rag. Other students, some of them groaning, lay on cots all around him. The woman asked him his name.

"Walter," he whispered.

She was writing on a note pad. "And your last name?"

"Freeman."

She asked for his parents' names, and Walter told her, although it took some effort. He didn't want to talk anymore. He felt awful, groggy and nauseous.

A doctor and several nurses moved among the children. Against one wall, the volunteers were lining up the bodies of children who died en route to the triage or at the medical station. The men were covering them with tablecloths, quilts, or sheets of paper they found in the church's closets and pantry.

Sisters Jimmie and Elsie Jordan were stretched out on side-by-side cots, both with their heads swathed in gauze. Elsie held her little sister's hand, comforted by her warmth, though Jimmie had not opened her eyes or said a word since Elsie found her in the debris. Elsie knew that Jimmie was badly hurt by something that had knocked a hole in her head, and that she might even die. But she wasn't going to let go of Jimmie's hand even for a minute because she was afraid the grown-ups might mistakenly think Jimmie was dead and put her against the wall.

Bobby Clayton lay on a nearby cot with his head bandaged. His mother had found him soon after the explosion and sat with him. A nurse came by and told Bobby she needed to give him a tetanus shot. He rolled his eyes toward a girl on the next cot over and said, "Give her the shot first. She's hurt worse than me and may need it sooner." Bobby's mother smiled down at her boy. She would repeat the story many times in the weeks to come. Later, Bobby disowned the hero mantel. With a sheepish smile, the ten-year-old admitted he directed the nurse's attention to the girl on the next cot as a ploy to keep the dreaded needle away from his own arm a few moments more.

At the disaster scene, Bud Price carried an armload of trash to dump at the debris collection pile a short distance from the ruins, and to get there he took a shortcut across the parking lot. On his way he spotted a car he hadn't seen in his initial survey of the parking lot.[4]

Debris and dust covered the car. Price put his face to a window and peered inside. A pair of wooden shoes sat on the backseat. He'd found Queen's car, and now his heart raced as he developed a plan to go look for his sister. He'd first check the nearest medical stations and hospitals, and then the funeral homes in Overton and Henderson. And then, if necessary, he'd spread the search, circling through the countryside to hit Kilgore, Longview, Nacogdoches, Jacksonville, Tyler, and other outlying communities. He didn't find her at the Baptist church in Overton. He drove a couple of blocks to the American Legion Hall, which was being used as a temporary morgue and information clearing house for the victims. When Price walked in, passing under a sign that read "Gentlemen Please Remove Your Hats"—for patrons of the skating rink inside the hall—he was instantly struck by the overpowering fumes of formaldehyde. He covered his nose with a handkerchief and resumed his search, going from body to body.

Suddenly, he noticed a pair of his friends standing over by a wall. Price waved and said hello. They lowered their heads and didn't speak, and he knew.

When he found her body, only a small cut marred her lovely face. But the back of her head had been flattened by a blow; one leg was nearly severed.

"I found out she had been in her room with eight pupils. Only one survived. That little girl's last memory before she blacked out was going forward to hug Queen," Price said.[5]

A pair of rescue workers later told of finding Queen, clinging to life, in the ruins. She was conscious and spoke to them, they said. When they picked up the piano teacher, one of her feet fell off. She reached and picked up the foot before they carried her out of the wreckage.[6]

The big news that Mattie Queen Price had planned to tell Bud that afternoon remained a mystery he puzzled about, from time to time, for the rest of his life.

Cars crowded along the street outside the American Legion Hall as parents pulled up, parked, went inside long enough to survey the bodies, and then left for another hospital or morgue. Floyd Meador's 1936 DeSoto was at the curb. Five-year-old Ben Meador was alone in the car, sitting in the back-seat, occasionally raising his head to peek outside.

Oil-field worker Floyd Meador and his wife, Mattie, were inside, scanning the bodies. They were looking for Myrtle Fay, seventeen, and William Floyd Meador Jr., thirteen. Myrtle was supposed to be away from the school that afternoon at a typing contest in Henderson, but when her parents were helping remove the dead and injured from the ruins, a classmate of Myrtle's told Mattie that Myrtle didn't make the trip to Henderson.

"She stayed back there in the typing lab," the girl said with tears in her eyes.

But Floyd and Mattie found no sign of either of their children in the American Legion Hall. They walked back to the DeSoto.

Just then, a flatbed truck loaded with more bodies pulled to a stop at the door of the hall. Rescue and recovery workers had covered them, as best possible, with linens and sheets of newspaper. The truck normally carried watermelons.

Floyd Meador walked to the truck and quickly spotted a body that was covered with a blanket except for the legs.

"I know those feet," he said. "That's my boy."

Wilson and Corine Jordan found their girls at a medical station in Overton. Elsie's face had a serious cut from her hairline to the top of an eye. The eleven-year-old child was conscious and alert but extremely upset about Jimmie's condition. The third grader had been unconscious since Elsie dug her from debris after the explosion. A doctor looked at the hole in Jimmie's head and told her parents there was nothing he could do for the child.

"A brain surgeon from Dallas is in Tyler," the doctor said. "Get her in an ambulance and over to Tyler as soon as you can."

Wilson Jordan, a thirty-two-year-old oil-field worker, left to locate an ambulance. Corine, twenty-seven, stayed with her daughters. The Jordans lived on the other side of a hill from the New London school campus. Corine had heard the explosion and quickly climbed to the top of the hill to see what had happened. When she saw the destruction below, she had fainted. Now that she had found her girls alive, she never wanted to let them out of her sight again. Wilson returned and said there was an ambulance outside with room for Jimmie. They could get Elsie on the next emergency vehicle bound for Tyler, he told Corine.

Wilson Jordan carried eight-year-old Jimmie out to the ambulance. She was totally limp and light in her father's arms. She was a tiny girl with dark brown hair, incalculably precious to the roughneck placing her in the ambulance and immeasurably loved by the stunned housewife holding back tears so as not to alarm their older daughter.

Similar emergency medical stations and temporary morgues were being set up all around New London—in churches, hotels, and grocery stores. Perry Lee Cox, the fifth grader who tried to cut school that morning, was taken to a doctor's office over a grocery store in Arp. The bread truck driver who saw Perry drop out of the sky onto the road in front of the school, had loaded the boy into his truck and rushed him to the only doctor's office in the vicinity he knew about. The doctor examined Perry and realized the boy was too hurt, inside and out, to have any chance of recovery. A brick had slammed into his head above his right eye, an arm and leg were broken, and his insides were scrambled, damaging all his organs; amazingly, his heart continued to beat. The doctor decided it was best not to move him; he just kept the unconscious boy as comfortable as possible while a search was made for his parents. The doctor found a small pocketknife in one of the boy's pockets; the knife's handle was painted with fingernail polish. "Get a description of his clothes and this pocketknife on the radio," the doctor told one of his helpers.[7]

The boy's father, Marshall Cox, was at the disaster site searching for Perry.

Alvin Thompson quickly found out that his daughter, Lanelle, a third grader, was safe and sound. She was in the grammar school rhythm band and had performed during the PTA dance program. Lanelle and some of her friends were walking back to their school, passing the high school, when it exploded. A concrete boulder and shower of bricks landed all around Lanelle, but the child escaped without a scratch. She was on a school bus headed for home. Now Alvin was hunting for Bill. He was walking the corpse line on the school grounds, carefully studying all those in trousers for any indication one of them might his boy. His heart sank a couple of times when he saw bodies about Bill's size and stature. He went back to one body three times before definitely ruling it out. Although he was deeply sickened by the sight of mangled children and the rancorous stench wafting through the ruins, Thompson made his way toward a line of men who were passing out debris from hand to hand.

Roughneck Joe Davidson was at the head of one of the lines, digging and sorting through rubble, finding other men's children but so far no sign of any of his own four. Nearby, a barber and beautician had teamed up to help with minor injuries, mainly sewing up cuts.

Fifth-grader H. G. White was taken by car to a rural doctor's office. Dr. J. T. McClain, a veteran of trench warfare during World War I, sorted out the four bloody children sprawled across the passenger seat. Most of the blood appeared to be from one badly injured boy. H. G. White looked to be the next most seriously hurt. McClain told H. G. to keep hand pressure on his head wound and wait on the front porch. The doctor lifted the bleeding boy out of the car and carried him inside to the office.

After a few minutes, McClain hurried out onto the porch and examined H. G.'s cut. The physician stitched the gash in his scalp and told him to go tell his parents that he was okay. H. G. leaped off the porch and started running for home. A woman he knew offered him a ride, so he jumped in to make the trip faster.

When they pulled up in front of the house, it looked deserted. "It was an old tin-roof, four-room house, just a square block. We had gas lights. Gas mantels in each room. It had a big porch on it but didn't have a bathroom," White recalled.

He knew his mom and dad must be at the school looking for him, so he asked to be taken back to that terrible place. The woman, a Mrs. Miller, drove fast.

"It was two miles to the school. We went up and down two or three hills, still on an old country oil road, and another half a mile, we met my mother and dad. They were coming home," White said. "When we met them, both cars stopped right in the middle of that road and my mother grabbed me and she was shouting, 'Praise the Lord!'

"A lot of people don't know what shouting is, but I told them it was kind of a hallelujah jubilee. My dad was standing there crying. He hugged me."

# 21
# Valley of Death at Sundown

Bus driver Lonnie Barber drove his rig to the bus barn, parked as best he could in a hurry, jumped out, and marched straight off toward the school wreckage a hundred yards or so across the way.

Running the route had taken longer than normal because he had a mix of students from different parts of the district and found himself doubling back from time to time, to drop one off here and another there. The grammar school children were mostly hushed, although some sniffled and cried. At nearly every stop, adults were waiting for their children to bound off the bus trailer and into their arms. Barber tried to make sure all the students were left in the charge of some adult. He didn't return to the campus until late afternoon.

He found his oldest child, L. V., the eighteen-year-old senior, working in the rescue mission. They stared intently at each other for a moment. Lonnie didn't have to ask.

"Burton is hurt, but he'll be okay," L. V. said. "I haven't found Pearl and Arden."

"Take the car, go straight home, and tell your mother what's going on," Lonnie said. "Then come on back here and help me look some more."

"Yes, sir," L. V. said.

L. V. watched his father join those digging through the rubble. On his way to the car, he learned from a friend that Pearl had been taken to a hospital in Tyler. She was not gravely injured. Now he could take his mother

Wildcatter Columbus "Dad" Joiner (left) shakes hands with partner Doc Lloyd (right) after their discovery well launches the East Texas oil boom in October 1930. *London Museum and Tea Room*

Main Street of New London, Texas, circa 1932. *London Museum and Tea Room*

Oil field company houses, mid-1930s, New London, Texas. *London Museum and Tea Room*

Mr. and Mrs. Earl Davidson, whose daughter Ardyth was killed, in front of their general store. *London Museum and Tea Room*

Main entrance to the London Junior-Senior High School. *London Museum and Tea Room*

Typical New London school bus. *London Museum and Tea Room*

The New London Wildcat marching band at practice on the football field (notice the lights and oil well in the background). *London Museum and Tea Room*

Bill Thompson, fifth grader, astride his pet calf, Tony. *Bill Thompson*

Popular New London music/ speech teacher, Mattie Queen Price. *London Museum and Tea Room*

Superintendent William Chesley Shaw. *London Museum and Tea Room*

Coach Carroll "Boxhead" Evans (far left, in dark pants and sweater) with his 1935–36 Wildcats football squad. *London Museum and Tea Room*

The New London Champion girls' softball team taken the morning of March 18, 1937. *London Museum and Tea Room*

The New London typing classroom. *London Museum and Tea Room*

Paul Greer, senior, uncle of Carolyn and Helen Jones. *Carolyn Jones Frei*

Carolyn Jones, nine years old, fifth grade. *Carolyn Jones Frei*

Helen Jones, thirteen years old, eighth grade. *Carolyn Jones Frei*

Industrial arts students at work with a belt sander in the basement-level shop. *London Museum and Tea Room*

A Texas highway patrolman examines a car demolished when the school exploded. *London Museum and Tea Room*

Rescue workers scrambling to find students and teachers in the ruins. *London Museum and Tea Room, photo restored by Anita L. Brown*

A boy crushed in the debris. Hydraulic lifts being used in an attempt to remove him. *London Museum and Tea Room*

The shock of
devastation.
*London Museum
and Tea Room*

Combing the ruins.
*London Museum
and Tea Room*

A wing of the
school collapsing.
*London Museum
and Tea Room*

A tangled mass. *London Museum and Tea Room*

Rescue workers with torches and jacks. *London Museum and Tea Room*

The rescue mission in the late afternoon. *London Museum and Tea Room*

Student James Kennedy in shock, disbelief evident on his face. *London Museum and Tea Room*

The peach-basket brigade hauling out bodies, body parts, and debris. *London Museum and Tea Room*

AP reporter Felix McKnight, twenty-seven years old, frantically getting the news out about the explosion. *Joan McKnight McIlyar (daughter), photo restored by JoAnn Gosnell*

Injured student being rushed to a medical station. *London Museum and Tea Room*

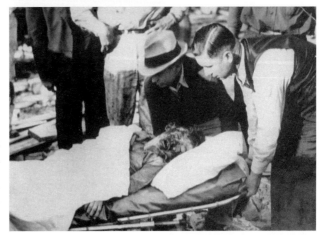

Bringing out the dead and injured. *London Museum and Tea Room*

Parents searching for their children by identifying pieces of clothing that were placed on top of mangled bodies. *London Museum and Tea Room*

A makeshift morgue. *London Museum and Tea Room*

One of hundreds of funerals. There were not enough hearses despite many being sent from all over the area. *London Museum and Tea Room*

Heartbreaking New London scene after the disaster. *London Museum and Tea Room*

One of the dozens of funerals at the Old London Baptist Church. *London Museum and Tea Room*

Gravediggers and coffin builders at work at Pleasant Hill Cemetery. *London Museum and Tea Room*

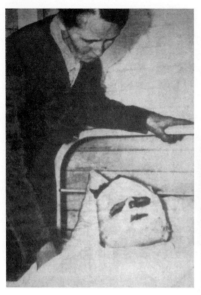

Emma Strickland watching over her son, Jack, who recovered from his injuries and became a Baptist minister. *London Museum and Tea Room*

Survivor Elbert Box, who lost a leg in the explosion, rowing with his wife, Louise. The pair met when she was his nurse at Mother Frances Hospital. *London Museum and Tea Room*

Ted Hudson, the novice radio announcer who rigged a connection from the site of the school explosion and did the live broadcast that was picked up on coast-to-coast radio. *Mary Lou (Hudson) Powell*

good news about all her children, save one. But he knew that would make it no less devastating for her to hear that Arden was still missing, and feared dead.

Carolyn Jones sat on the front steps of her house in the deserted neighborhood; her eyes were locked on the dirt road leading through trees, and she waited in silence. The afternoon light was fading to dusk. A puffy cloud drifting in from the south reflected a crimson sunset.

"I watched the car drive slowly up the lane. Mother and Ervin got out, carrying baby Ann [Carolyn's half sister]. Helen and Paul were not with them. I ran to meet them. They were mute, stunned. Only the baby gurgled in their arms," she remembered.

Carolyn's parents told her the clocks in the school had stopped at about 3:20 p.m., ten minutes before the school day was supposed to end. It wasn't necessary for anyone to comment on the bitter circumstances of the explosion happening just minutes before school was to be out. It would be one of those "what if?" questions that always go begging for an answer in the aftermath of a disaster. They fell silent. Carolyn could tell that her mother and stepfather had scant hope of finding Helen or Paul alive.

"Repair garages, roller rinks, gyms, church basements, dance and lodge halls—all vacant buildings were used as makeshift morgues. When the local hospitals were overcome with patients, ambulances carried the injured to more distance places," Carolyn recalled.

Every one of those morgues and hospitals had to be searched for Helen and Paul.

Ted Hudson now had the local radio station broadcasting from New London. His voice on the car radio "pled incessantly for volunteer doctors and nurses, ambulances and supplies," Carolyn said.

Hudson announced that the new Mother Frances Hospital in Tyler was opening a day earlier than scheduled to receive patients immediately.

"Lists of those who had been identified were read over and over on the radio," Carolyn recalled. "We recognized the names of our friends, the children of Ervin's coworkers, those who sat in class beside me, sang and prayed in the Baptist church."[1]

Bill Thompson decided he wouldn't wait for a stranger to whisk him away to a hospital. He needed to go home to let his folks know he survived. He realized his mother and father would be frantic by now. They didn't have a phone, so there was no way to find out quickly what they were doing or if they had heard that he had been saved.

Before he had a chance to set out for home, the men returned and put Bill into an ambulance. "You wait here, and we'll be right back," one said.

After they were out of sight, the boy climbed out of the ambulance and began walking away. The men caught him, put him back into the ambulance, and admonished him to stay put until they rounded up other injured children to send to the hospital with him.

"I don't know how many they were going to put in there. I guess stack them up," Thompson said.

He left again and made his way to a bus that a few students had already climbed aboard. After a moment, he thought better of that plan. On this day, a bus might take an extra hour or more to reach his house. He left the bus and found a car loaded with several of his friends. They agreed to take him home right away.

As soon as Bill reached his front door he felt a tremendous release of all the emotion he'd been holding inside since the explosion had pinned him in the dark. He felt a need to cry but didn't want his dad and mom to see him crying and think he'd been hurt worse than he had. Bill cleared his eyes with the cuff of his shirt. It didn't occur to him that his entire body was caked with plaster dust, his face was streaked with dried blood, and his hair was matted in a knot where the gash had clotted. He strode inside and greeted his mother in the kitchen. She didn't recognize him.

"It's Bill," he said. "The school blew up."

Bonnie Thompson was shocked. She had been busy with chores and hadn't heard about the explosion.

She snapped orders at Bill and his older brother Laverne, who was back home from a stint as a cavalryman in the army. Bill was told to sit down immediately, so she could take a look at his injuries and clean him up. Laverne needed to hurry out to the barn and reattach the family car's tires so he could take Bill to the hospital in Henderson. Ever since Alvin Thompson had received a dealer car to drive, the Thompson's automobile had been in the barn sitting up on jack stands, with its four wheels hanging from spikes on the wall. Laverne ran to the barn. Bill sank into a kitchen chair. Bonnie grabbed a damp rag and dabbed at the blood streaks on the boy's nose and cheeks.

At the schoolyard, Alvin Thompson surveyed bodies being loaded into a delivery truck. None resembled Bill. He decided to check the hospitals and morgues.

He hurried to his car, cranked it, and was about to drive away when a neighbor's child leaned on the driver's side window.

"They found Bill," the girl said. "He's at home."

Thompson gave an audible sigh of relief, thanked her, and then raced off toward his farm. Sitting with his back pushed hard into the seat cushion and his fists knotted on the steering wheel, he could see the rosy hues of sundown pooled in his rearview mirror. One glance into his own eyes grounded him, and tears flooded his cheeks.

Hazel Shaw and Myrtle Meador gave up trying to get any closer to the school than the outskirts of New London, where the traffic became hopelessly clogged and highway patrolmen were blocking further access by vehicle. Hazel parked on the side of the road, and she and Myrtle set out hiking the rest of the way, moving with a crowd of other people between cars and along the roadsides. It had taken them nearly an hour to travel about ten miles from Henderson to New London.

Myrtle saw her mother from a distance and hurried to catch up with her.

"Police had roped off the main part that had blown up, but there were pieces of body parts outside of that," Myrtle recalled. "The Tidewater Company had a cyclone fence on the south side of the school. They had stacked bodies there, two deep, wrapped in sheets. When I saw my mother it was quite a reunion."

After mother and daughter released each other from a long hug, Mattie Meador told Myrtle that her thirteen-year-old brother, Junior, was dead.

"It was such a violent explosion, bodies burst. His head had to be tied up like a sore thumb," Myrtle said.

They hurried away to find Myrtle's father. Floyd Meador was digging in the rubble at a place where the typing room had been, searching for his daughter's remains. He praised God for answering his prayer when he saw that she was alive.

"They leaned on the strength that God gave them. They were fine Christian people, and God helped them," Myrtle said. "It was three days before I could cry—that was such a shock to the human body to see something like that," she added.

Hazel Shaw soon learned hope was fading that her brother Sambo had survived the blast. She knew where his classroom was located—a part of the school crushed into a deep pile of debris. She also discovered that two of her cousins—Dorothy Oleta Shaw and Marvin Shaw—had perished.

Her father was alive, although deeply shaken. He was wandering through the ruins, almost incoherent, somewhere among more than two thousand volunteers in the rescue and recovery operation, she was told. Her mother, Leila, was holding up, although she had witnessed the explosion from her kitchen window, standing at the sink washing dishes, and felt ill with despair.

Hazel set out to find her father, knowing that he needed the strength and support of loved ones. Many people knew Chesley Shaw only from a distance, as a headmaster early in his career, principal of the Minden School, and superintendent at New London. He was set in his ways about some things—frustratingly headstrong. He was strict about rules of conduct he considered essential, not only as an educator but as a civilized human being. And sometimes he could be cantankerous. But he had a tender and sensitive side to his personality—an emotional vulnerability—that only those closest to the superintendent, such as his daughters, really understood.

He had inspired Hazel and Helen to follow his example and devote their lives to teaching children. It was a cause Chesley Shaw had remained faithful to all of his life, although his administrative duties as superintendent of a large school district had elevated him to a position outside of the classroom. He still loved nothing better than taking a field trip with students, especially the little ones in the grammar school.

Once he was finally making enough money to afford an extravagance, Chesley arranged his own version of a grand field trip, taking his two daughters on a cross-county odyssey to visit the Chicago World's Fair in the summer of 1933. Along the way, they stopped at historical landmarks, including Civil War battlefields; they drove hundreds of miles out of the way to reach the greatest battlefield in American history, Gettysburg. Chesley walked for hours with his daughters in tow across the Pennsylvania fields and hills where the armies of the North and South clashed in the first three days of July 1863, only a decade before Chesley was born, to determine the outcome of the war. His eyes brimmed with tears as he reminded Hazel and Helen of the blood spilled by those who gave their lives—more than seven thousand Yankees and Confederates, all Americans—to settle the grave issue of slavery and ultimately forge a stronger nation.

And then they headed back west toward Chicago, with Chesley driving the automobile at a pace so slow he was pulled over by a Pennsylvania state trooper. The officer didn't give Chesley a ticket but wounded his dignity with a lecture on the hazards of creeping along a modern highway no faster than a mule-drawn wagon. If he was going to drive like that, he needed to pull over and let faster traffic pass, the trooper scolded. Chesley was flabbergasted. The girls had to suppress giggles, watching their old-fashioned father being called a slowpoke to his face. Chesley drove a bit faster until he crossed the border into Ohio. He still seemed puffed up over the ordeal, but more than anything else, he was embarrassed, Hazel felt. He was a nineteenth-century man who had embraced the twentieth century with enthusiasm and considered himself a modern thinker, not a relic of the past.

Now, as she sought to find him in the maze of destruction, she felt grief from the loss of so many children and teachers, and at the same time she worried how all this would affect her father—emotionally and otherwise. Some people, no doubt, were going to find ways to blame him for the disaster, regardless of what was found to be its cause. The grandest achievement of Chesley's life lay in ruins. The crushed body of his youngest son lay buried somewhere beneath the rubble. So many children that he had adored had perished. She hoped, and earnestly prayed, that his family and friends could shield him from any greater loss.

When Felix McKnight and Bill Rives, panting and elbowing their way through a massive crowd of onlookers, arrived at the New London school campus, officials had set up a rope cordon to separate the mob from the rescue workers and establish a semblance of order.

"I'm Felix McKnight, Associated Press," McKnight told a highway patrolman on the other side of the line, handing the man his press badge. The officer glanced at it and passed McKnight and Rives through the rope barrier. Other highway patrol officers, men in American Legion uniforms and uniformed Boy Scouts were strung out along the rope to help keep order.

McKnight planned to survey the scene, find an official, ask a few key questions, and file a preliminary story within, say, about fifteen minutes. To do that, of course, he had to locate a telephone, and so far he'd had no luck. Everybody he asked about a phone just gazed at him and shrugged. "All the phones are out," one man said glumly. Another told him there were several working phones at the Humble Oil office about a mile away, but they were strictly reserved for emergency use only. McKnight had been at that office only a week before, when he was investigating labor unrest in the East Texas oil field, and he had made some contacts that might come in handy now, he figured.

"How could anyone survive this?" McKnight said, waving at the wreckage.

Rives told him that officials were estimating seven hundred students and teachers were in the school when it exploded, according to a highway patrolman.

"I recall the scene I'll never forget—and I've seen it a thousand times in nightmares," McKnight said later. "They were literally trying to clear that building by hand. They would dislodge bricks and rubble and cement and mortar and fill these peach baskets. They formed lines with about fifty men in each line and would pass the baskets down the line and start digging again."

The reporters headed for one of the basket brigade lines.

"We're from the Associated Press," McKnight told a roughneck who appeared to be in charge. "We're here to get this story out to the world."

"We don't give a damn," the roughneck said.

He ordered McKnight and Rives to join those in the rescue and recovery operation. McKnight initially was stunned and at a loss for words. He desperately needed to file a story without delay. But under the circumstances, he could not reason with these men, many of them parents of missing children, about the significance of a reporter's work. The story had to wait. McKnight wedged into a place on one of the lines and Rives found a spot in the facing line.

"And we passed those peach baskets from one man to the next," McKnight recalled.

The sun dipped below the horizon, glazing the debris field with a red afterglow.

Governor James Allred realized the chaos in East Texas could escalate, given the scope and horror of the disaster. He monitored the situation closely from soon after the explosion into the early evening. Hearing reports of monstrous traffic snarls as a crowd of thousands of people formed an almost impassable loop around the New London school campus, Allred decided to send National Guard troops to the disaster scene.

The order, directed to National Guard officers in Longview and Tyler, was to proceed with all available men in their companies and take charge of the entire situation. Allred appointed a team of military and state officials to establish a court of inquiry.

"They will decide on the procedure and act as officers of the National Guard. As such, they will have broad powers," Allred said.[2]

The governor declared martial law for a five-mile radius around New London. The first troops arrived within a couple of hours, riding in a convoy of military vehicles. With rifles slung across their shoulders, some of the guardsmen began herding the crowd back while others cordoned off the school campus with rope barriers.

When they drove into Tyler, Walter Cronkite and Bill Baldwin came to fully appreciate the wire service's decision to dispatch a team of top-flight reporters to help with the New London story. The staggering scope of the catastrophe became evident.

"Going through Tyler we saw lines of cars, ambulances and hearses and automobiles that clearly were carrying bodies in them, lined up trying to get to the two funeral homes in Tyler that were on the main highway," Cronkite recalled. "Then we knew we had a story on our hands."

The main road toward New London was barricaded by highway patrol cars. Officers were clearing only emergency vehicles through the road-block. Other routes into the oil-field region were clogged with enormous traffic jams. A car wreck with one fatality was backing up cars and trucks on one of the roads. To reach the disaster site as soon as possible, Cronkite and Baldwin had hitched a ride on a fire truck the city of Beaumont had dispatched to help in the rescue and recovery mission. The truck was equipped with a powerful searchlight.

"We got down to New London, and some distance from New London you could see the glow of the searchlights that were playing upon the rub-ble. . . . These great floodlights were lighting this scene of utter devasta-tion," Cronkite recalled. "By that time, it was dark. We saw this pile of debris that didn't even look like a building. It looked like a pile of debris that might have been bulldozed together into that little area and hundreds of men, looking like ants."[3]

When he arrived at the edge of the school campus, Cronkite's perspec-tive of the horror sharpened.

"In the rubble, men were digging with their hands, tears streaming down their filthy faces as they searched for their own children," he said.[4]

# 22
## Mother Frances

Walter Freeman couldn't help but wonder, time and again, if he was going in and out of a dream. He had been at school and was knocked down and hurt badly when the room collapsed. The nightmare next put him in the midst of other students, groaning and dying, and Walter tried to say something, ask some questions, but his voice was very weak. Then he awoke in an ambulance with a siren blaring, feeling it swerve to take a steep curve. Now, it seemed an angel was gazing down at him.

A black hood with a white collar curved around the beautiful oval of her face. She smiled at him. He wanted to say something but still felt deflated, too tired even to say hello. He heard the voices of men, his father in work clothes and a doctor in a white lab coat, standing in the doorway of the hospital room.

"Is he going to make it?" Mr. Freeman asked.

"If he makes it through tonight, I think so," the doctor said.

Although Walter didn't know what she was doing—or what she was, since he'd never seen a nun—he felt comforted by the sister as she swabbed his head injuries and gently probed his chest and arms. She was preparing the boy for surgery to repair the compound fracture in one arm and place a cast around his entire body, from head to toe, with slits for his eyes, nose, and mouth. His broken back and cracked ribs were not believed to be life threatening; doctors were most concerned about the concussion.

Walter Freeman soon drifted back to a semiconscious state, mixing the reality of his surroundings with dreamlike images, unaware that he was one of the first patients in the new Mother Frances Hospital in Tyler.

Walter's eleven-year-old sister, Jeanette, was with their mother, still looking all over the place for her other sister, Myrtle Marie, nine, who went by "Shug." Nobody had seen Shug since the explosion. They finally located her at a temporary morgue in Overton. Her head was wrapped in cotton and one of her legs was missing. Somebody had put a leg with the body but it didn't look to belong to Shug. "It took me a long time to get over that," Jeanette Freeman Martin said. "You never do really."[1]

Mother Mary Regina, provincial officer of the Sisters of the Holy Family, took it upon herself to open the hospital immediately upon learning of the school explosion.

She heard about it when a phone call came in late Thursday afternoon requesting medical assistance for disaster victims. She was visiting Mother Frances to participate in the formal blessing and grand opening ceremonies scheduled for Friday. All that could wait, she decided; these injured children were the highest priority for the new facility and its staff of sisters trained as nurses. Mother Mary Regina sent ten of the nuns straight to the disaster site, with instructions to return with patients coming to the hospital in ambulances and emergency vehicles, and then she started calling the offices of every doctor in Tyler and Smith County, urging them to report to the hospital as quickly as possible. A highly regarded brain surgeon was already en route from Dallas. Mother Regina instructed Mother Mary Ambrose, the superior charged with managing the hospital, to make a hundred beds ready to receive patients. When Bishop Joseph Lynch of the Diocese of Dallas arrived at the hospital a short while later, he praised Mother Regina's decisions and Mother Ambrose's quick work to organize a response to the catastrophe.

The formalities of opening the hospital, of course, were secondary to focusing all immediate attention on helping victims of the school explosion, Lynch said. He instructed the sisters to cancel the banquet and ribbon-cutting festivities planned for Friday. Doctors who already had arrived from out of town to participate in the activities would be needed instead to administer aid. The only official item left on Friday's schedule was a service for Lynch to ask God's blessings on the new facility.

"The hospital has already been dedicated by the blood of children," the bishop said.[2]

Reverend Robert Jackson was helping identify bodies at a funeral home in Overton when he heard a whimper from among those who were believed to be dead. He discovered the sound came from Marie Beard, who was critically injured but clinging to life. Jackson carried the little girl from the funeral home and put her in the backseat of his car. He took Marie to a makeshift hospital at the Rusk Hotel in Overton, where the only space available for another injured child was on the hotel's screened-in porch.[3]

One of her uncles found Marie at the hotel Thursday evening, and her parents arrived at her bedside about 11 p.m. Their daughter was still unconscious, but she was expected to survive.

Laverne Thompson had put his brother, Bill, in the backseat of the family car and driven him to the Henderson Hospital. When they arrived downtown, several blocks from the hospital, one of the dry-rotted tires blew with a loud pop. Laverne pulled over, jumped out, and hoisted Bill from the seat.

Bill said he was okay to walk, but Laverne wouldn't let him. He carried his brother across the street toward a taxi stand on the corner.

"He was in the explosion," Laverne told a driver. "Get us to the hospital."

Laverne stayed right at his side when attendants put Bill on a stretcher and carted him to a hospital room with a single bed. A few minutes later, they returned and set up a cot. Bill was moved from the bed to the cot, so the bed could be used for a boy with injuries that were much worse. Bill felt totally exhausted, as though he hadn't rested or slept for days. Laverne kept him awake, holding his hand and talking to him, until a doctor came to the room and checked out the boy's head injury. His scalp was cut and needed stitching, but he hadn't suffered a concussion.

Bill slept for a while, and when he opened his eyes again, his father and sisters were in the room. Alvin Thompson smiled at his son and patted his arm. When Bill awoke again, his mother was with him, inspecting his head where the doctor had stitched the cut and bathing his neck and arms with a damp sponge. A nurse came by and gave Bill a tetanus shot.

When he awoke later, it was night outside the hospital window. Bill recognized the boy in the room with him, Arliss Ray Middleton, a senior.

Arliss wasn't awake. He seemed to be having great trouble breathing. Mrs. Middleton and Arliss's sister were on one side of the bed. His father was on the other.

Bill could hear Mrs. Middleton praying, out loud, asking God for a miracle. Arliss's sister was crying. Mr. Middleton bowed his head and clenched his face in the fist of one hand. Arliss died later in the night.

Carolyn Jones waited in a car outside the American Legion Hall in Overton. Her mother and stepfather were inside, searching for Helen—Carolyn's sister—and Paul, their mother's youngest brother. It was nearly 9 p.m. when they found Paul Greer. "He lay on the floor in a line with the other children as though he had simply lain down for an afternoon nap," Carolyn said, recalling her mother's description of the boy who wanted to become a doctor. The hall's skating rink was being used as a temporary morgue.

"Finding Helen took longer," Carolyn wrote in a memoir of that day. "Ervin had been sleeping when she left for school in the morning, and could not picture the new spring dress she had worn. Mother, at the morgue, unable to speak, kept tracing with her fingernail on the car's upholstery the pattern of the pink and lavender print she had sewn.

"I finally fell asleep in the backseat, and when I woke, the grown-ups were talking in low voices outside the car. I heard the word 'mangled.' I understood that Helen had been found."

Ervin took Carolyn and her mother home, and then he went back to work the rest of the night at the disaster site.

"Mother and I lay on the double bed not touching, hearing the sirens of the ambulances, louder as they approached, and then fading into the distance as they raced toward Henderson or Tyler," Carolyn said. "Dogs barked and howled. I lay awake, thinking of the conversation outside the car, what they had seen inside the morgues. Finally I slept."[4]

When Felix McKnight was finally able to break out of the peach-basket brigade, he began a desperate search for an operable phone. He needed to phone in a story as soon as possible; he knew the bureau manager in Dallas and AP editors across the nation would be ready to pull their hair out if a story didn't come soon. He didn't have time even to sit down and scribble the story out in a notebook. Even so, much of it was written in his mind. He could easily dictate it, word for word, over the phone—if he only had a phone. During the search, McKnight continued to fill in gaps in the story.

"I scrambled over brick, steelwork, tattered clothing, shoes, schoolbooks, parts of bodies," McKnight recalled. "I started talking to people. None would say immediately what I wanted to hear."[5]

A Texas Ranger captain estimated 450 deaths. McKnight looked for a second source to confirm that number. A school official told him the death toll could be more than six hundred. The reporter stopped inside a makeshift hospital on the school grounds and talked to injured students about the explosion—gathering details and quotes to flesh out the story.

"It was time to get going. The nearest phone was a mile and a half away. I made it, clearing fences, gullies, weeds. In the oil field office sat the most determined woman I have ever known—a switchboard operator. Her phone lines were clogged. She would not listen to me."[6]

The woman said he might find a working phone in Overton, about four miles away. Frustrated, McKnight hurried back to the explosion scene, where he located Sarah McClendon, the Tyler-based reporter. McClendon told him she had a friend who worked at another oil-field office.

They dashed away to the other office, where the operator let McKnight sneak into an executive's office. He crouched in the dark, holding the phone cupped to his ear, as the operator put him through to the telephone company in Tyler. A woman answered.[7]

"I need to call Dallas," he told her.

"There will be a delay of three hours on your call," she said.

McKnight pleaded with her to no avail.

"Can I get through to Kansas City?"

"No."

He asked her to place a call to the AP office in Chicago.

"No."

"New York?"

"No."

"What about Seattle, Los Angeles, or San Francisco?"

"No."

McKnight came up with an ingenious plan he felt sure would get the operator's attention. He asked her to call the AP bureau in London, England. He could dictate the story to London and have them phone it back to New York.

"I guarantee you a thirty-minute call," McKnight pledged.

"I can't give you any station," the woman said.

He tried a backup plan.

"Give me the Western Union office in Tyler."

She put the call through, and a couple of rings later, a Western Union operator answered. Success at last, McKnight thought. He started dictating the story to a telegraph operator, with instructions to wire it to the AP office in Dallas. McKnight had dictated about seventy words when the phone connection snapped. The switchboard operator in the oil-field office had commandeered the line for an emergency call. McKnight stuck his pen in a shirt pocket and his notebook in a hip pocket; then he headed back into the night to find another way to file his story.

At least the AP had seventy words—three tightly composed paragraphs, packing a wallop. It was a start.

Medical services at Mother Frances Hospital shifted into high gear as dozens of explosion victims arrived in ambulance after ambulance. Crowds of curious pedestrians gathered on sidewalks near the hospital, straining to glimpse New London students being carted into the emergency entrance. Those close enough to see the children saw that many of them appeared unconscious and most were in bloodied clothes.

The people of Tyler had been eagerly awaiting the opening of the new hospital designed to serve the needs of the rapidly growing region. Tyler's metropolitan area had prospered from the oil boom and now had a population of more than fifty thousand. As the hospital neared completion over the past few weeks, people who worked downtown and many who visited Tyler to shop and go to restaurants had streamed by the construction site frequently to check the building's progress and gawk at the long-awaited medical center. At first, many people in the largely Protestant area were amused by the sight of Catholic sisters in long black tunics and headpieces shaped like hoods, with wide white collars and wearing silver crosses suspended from black cords against their chests and rosary beads hung from woolen belts. They wore plain black shoes. Their only adornments were simple silver rings worn on their left hands, signifying their vows of perpetual faithfulness to Jesus Christ.

The town had only one Catholic church and no parish schools. By now, though, the Baptists, Methodists, Presbyterians, and members of other denominations had become accustomed to seeing the sisters and often nodded or waved at them when they appeared on a downtown sidewalk or street corner. Not everybody was happy that a Catholic group received the contract to operate the hospital instead of a Baptist organization that also made a pitch, but most residents were so pleased about and proud of the modern new hospital—at no cost to the taxpayers—that most of the grumbling about who would manage it had ceased.

The first explosion victims arrived soon after the phone call asking for assistance. "Mother Regina was the first to open the door for them. Mother Ambrose directed locations to those conveying the victims," according to an article printed in the order's newsletter. "More wounded arrived, much blood streaming over them."

Mother Mary Regina and Mother Mary Ambrose had long experience working in hospitals, yet they were stunned by the sight of so many children with horrible, disfiguring injuries.

"Parents seeking their children were everywhere but found it a difficult task since all the children were so badly hurt. Two families wanted to claim the same girl since the features and the birthmarks were almost identical, and since the child was unconscious, one could not be certain whose girl it was," the article said. "It was questionable whether the little one would live since her skull was cracked and she underwent surgery twice. Another child was brought in without eyes. From the holes where the eyes were, parts of the brain were protruding. The latter lived only a few hours, never regaining consciousness."

Nuns returning from New London had viewed even more horrible scenes. Some of the victims were flattened as though their bodies were run through a press, they said.

Bishop Lynch went from room to room to say comforting words to children who were conscious. He counseled distraught parents to find solace through faith in God. Religious differences between Catholics and Protestants became insignificant at the time of crisis, as the entire community focused on supporting the victims.

"People, as if they fell out of clouds, gathered to offer their help," the article said. "It was amazing to see such selfless interest and sacrifice. Doctors as far as Pittsburgh [Pennsylvania] called to ask if help was needed; Red Cross volunteers came; some airplanes came to transport the victims.

"Nobody failed to recognize the sacrifices or self-giving of the people. They brought food, clothing, bedding, and even money for the parents of the victims. The telephone at Mother Frances Hospital rang endlessly with offers to supply medications and hospital instruments—free.

"Such was the evening before the blessing of the hospital. . . . Possibly no hospital was publicized as was this hospital named for our Foundress. All afternoon, evening, and night, and the following day, the happenings at Mother Frances Hospital were told and retold. The public stated that no formal opening was needed. God's Providence announced Mother Frances Hospital in a way not too pleasant, but a way in which people proved their love and concern for their neighbors just as Jesus taught them."[8]

Felix McKnight wasn't the only newsman looking for creative ways to file his stories. With telephone communications in and out of New London jammed by thousands of calls and many lines restricted to emergency uses, all reporters at the scene were stymied with similar problems.

Even local reporters, such as Sarah McClendon, had to improvise. Needing to return to Tyler in a hurry, McClendon climbed aboard an emergency vehicle loaded with injured children and heading for Mother Frances Hospital. This was shrewd. Not only did she get a fast, express ride back to her newsroom, where she could meet a deadline to get fresh material into an extra edition, she used the travel time to gather additional firsthand details from people in the truck and started composing a draft of the story.[9] Without good local contacts, it's doubtful she would have been allowed to ride with some of the victims. Many people at the scene were incensed by reporters asking questions and photographers snapping pictures at such a time, when children lay dead and dying all around. Some became hostile. One husky roughneck, irritated by flashbulbs popping all around him, wrenched a camera from a photographer and hurled it across the rubble. The photographer grabbed a spare from his backpack and started shooting scenes in a different direction.

McKnight trotted through the dark to his car, a couple of miles west of the disaster, and set out for Tyler across back roads he'd learned during his recent assignment to cover labor unrest in the oil field. He felt relatively sure he could use a phone line at the *Tyler Courier-Times*, an AP member newspaper. As a backup, he was planning, if necessary, to rent an airplane to fly his story to Dallas.

At about the same time, a chartered plane was zooming toward Tyler, cutting across Tennessee and then Arkansas, with a load of reporters and photographers from New York, including Henry McLemore and other United Press staffers assigned to the catastrophe.

Bill Rives scouted a huge crowd of onlookers just beyond where rescue workers were scouring the ruins, beneath glaring floodlights, for more dead and wounded. He spotted a group of teenagers clinging close together, some in tattered clothes, with several leaning their heads on their friends' shoulders. He took them for New London students who had survived the explosion, and his detective work paid off with a good sidebar—the typically short stories adjacent feature articles that explore individual elements within the major story.

Rives found an eighteen-year-old student named Martha Harris who was articulate and willing to tell her tale in extended detail. Instead of using her for one or two quotes, Rives took down her comments word for word so he could use them as a first-person account with her byline, written for the Associated Press.

"I was in the home economics building, about sixty yards from the school, when I heard a terrible roar," she told the reporter. "The earth shook and brick and glass came showering down. I looked out a window and saw my friends dying like flies. Kids were blown out through the top onto the roof. Some of them hung up there and others fell off two stories to the ground. I saw girls in my class jumping out of windows like they were deserting a burning ship."

Her sixteen-year-old brother, Milton Harris, jumped from a second-story window and received only a bruise on his knee. But all were not so lucky. Martha saw Evelyn Rainwater plunge into a first-floor window with such violence it nearly ripped the girl's leg off.

Martha Harris told Rives at least twenty-five of her friends were blown from the building, and their bodies were scattered near the home economics cottage. One part of the building caught fire and burned until men running with buckets of water put it out, she said. The men got the water from Alf Shaw's hamburger stand.

"The bodies of the kids were stacked up, after the explosion, just like you would stack up hot cakes," Harris said. "I'll never forget how I saw my friends' bodies torn. Some of them were blown to bits and never will be found."[10]

Walter Cronkite also found a student who agreed the reporter could use his comments for a similar first-person account. The byline said the story was by Charlie Clair (as told to the United Press). The boy said he was standing beside his desk in his eighth-grade classroom, reading from a book, when the explosion ripped through the school.

"Suddenly there was a dead silence then I heard a noise and was thrown up in the air. I saw other boys and girls thrown up in the air, too," he said. "Some of them were screaming. Some of the others were knocked down. I saw a lot of arms and legs being thrown around.

"Then I went unconscious. When I came to again, some man was standing over me, looking at me. . . . All around me were other children. Some of them were dead. Some of them were hurt. They were crying and screaming. People were running, nearly everybody hollering or screaming."

He realized he had been thrown some distance from the school, which now lay in ruins.

"It was awful. It made me sick and I lost consciousness again.

"When I came to again things were a little bit quieter but folks were still hollering. A lot of mothers and fathers were crying.

"I was lucky. I wasn't hurt much."[11]

Ted Hudson's makeshift radio studio was set up on the back of a flatbed truck. Using a flashlight to read a message he'd just been handed, Hudson said into the radio microphone, "We're trying to find the parents of a little boy at the doctor's office in Arp. The boy is seriously injured and he is unconscious. He's in khaki clothes. He had a little knife in his pocket that looked like it had been painted with fingernail polish."

Mr. and Mrs. Otis Wiley, friends of the Cox family, had been listening to the radio constantly since hearing of the explosion in hopes of learning the whereabouts of Perry Lee. When they heard Hudson's description of the boy in Arp, they looked at each other sharply. They set out to find Mr. and Mrs. Cox.[12]

Once he arrived at the newspaper offices in Tyler, Felix McKnight made arrangements for a local pilot to use his single-engine plane to ferry stories to Dallas, should that be necessary. Phone circuits in the Tyler area were just as overwhelmed as those around New London. McKnight plopped down at a typewriter and began pecking out a lead story for the Associated Press. A couple of minutes after he crafted a top for the story, the reporter's fingers began to dance wildly on the keyboard as though he were a pianist playing the molto allegro section of a concerto.

Sarah McClendon was at another desk in the newsroom. She had finished a front-page piece for the next extra edition—the newspaper's third since learning of the explosion, scheduled to hit the streets around midnight—and now she was working on a roundup story about Tyler residents providing medical assistance and doing other jobs at the disaster scene.

Jim Donahue, publisher of the *Tyler Courier-Times* and *Morning Telegraph*, tapped McKnight on the shoulder. "Here," said Donahue, who had been on the phone. "Here you are. Dallas."

McKnight was ecstatic. "For thirty minutes I pumped the story at rewrite man Dave Cheavens," he recalled. "It was 8:30 p.m. Two hours to shake out one of the biggest stories of the year."

The opening line of McKnight's first AP dispatch from the scene would become a classic epitaph for the disaster. "Today," he wrote, "a generation died."[13]

Ted Hudson described for radio listeners much of everything he witnessed in the late afternoon and early evening. That's all he could think of doing;

he had no script to go by and most of the time he was alone at the microphone. Occasionally, a short station break gave him a chance to catch his breath. The networks cut in with national headlines and sports briefs, and then released the signal back to Hudson's ongoing, eyewitness account of the New London school disaster. All regular network programming had been suspended since he had gone on the air shortly before sunset.

Hudson was still under the impression that his broadcast was being heard only in a small area of East Texas, including Henderson and Rusk County, where he had many friends and neighbors. He imagined he was speaking directly to his friends and that image bolstered his confidence. Had he known that by 9:00 p.m. most stations across the nation had picked up the broadcast and that millions of Americans were listening to every word he said and each heartbreaking scene he described, Hudson might have been dumbstruck with stage fright, he later acknowledged.[14]

Each time a person handed him a strip of paper with a message or additional plea for assistance, Hudson read it over the air. The place where he'd set up his makeshift mobile broadcast station was not well lighted, so he had a volunteer hold a flashlight for him when he needed to read something.

He received a note that said First Lady Eleanor Roosevelt, at an event in Denison, Texas, expressed sympathy for the victims. "Something must be done to guard against such calamities," she said.[15] The radio man read the note.

Hudson took another note from somebody, held it under the flashlight, and read, "All men willing to volunteer for grave digging, please report to Room 106 at the Rusk Hotel."

He then read a list of morgues and funeral homes in fourteen towns where the bodies of explosion victims had been taken. Parents whose children were missing could visit those places and attempt to identify their remains, Hudson said. A lot of the dead were at the American Legion Hall in Overton, he said, but bodies also had been taken to Henderson, Arp, Wright City, Longview, Tyler, Jacksonville, Joinerville, Nacogdoches, Gilmer, Kilgore, Turnertown, and Gladewater in East Texas and to Shreveport in Louisiana.

Hudson asked survivors of the explosion to take the microphone and identify themselves, so that loved ones who might be listening would know that they were okay.

Carroll "Boxhead" Evans, who had been planning to visit his parents in Belton, took Hudson's offer. "This is Carroll Evans. I was not in the school when it exploded and I'm not hurt," he said, somewhat awkwardly, into the radio mic. Evans was always at ease talking with people, even garrulous most of the time, but talking on the radio was an oddity; he swallowed and adjusted the tone of his voice. "My wife, Mildred, and our son, Duane, are safe and sound. I hope my mom and dad in Belton are listening."

Evans wouldn't find out until later, but his parents already had started toward New London in their car, fearing the worst. Their son's voice coming over the car radio was the sweetest sound they had ever heard.

Mr. and Mrs. Marshall Cox were driving toward Arp as Carroll Evans was talking on the radio. There was just one doctor in the tiny hamlet, so the office was not hard to find. Marshall Cox swerved into the doctor's driveway and skidded to a stop in the gravel. He and his wife ran from the car and up the wooden steps to the doctor's second-floor office. When the doctor saw them, he nodded gravely toward Perry Lee, who was on a hospital bed next to a back wall. When the parents looked to the doctor for some sign of hope, the doc just shook his head no.

Perry's face was gray. Mr. and Mrs. Cox sat with their boy, each holding a hand, until he died about 10 p.m.[16]

Wilson Jordan sat at Jimmie's side in the Bryant Clinic in Tyler. Corine Jordan sat at Elsie's side in the nearby Mother Frances Hospital. Elsie kept asking her mother whether Jimmie was still alive. Each time Corine said yes, Elsie made her promise she was telling the truth.

"She's at another hospital," Corine told Elsie.

"Why is she there, and I'm here?"

"The ambulance just brought you here."

Elsie's head was wrapped in a gauze bandage that was swathed at an angle across her face, covering her right eye. Glass had sliced her eyelid, which had to be stitched, but by a miracle it hadn't cut her eyeball. She grew silent. "Promise?" she said.

Her mother patted her hand. "Promise."

At Bryant Clinic, Wilson Jordan was greatly relieved when a man came into Jimmie's room and identified himself as Dr. Albert D'Errico, the brain surgeon from Dallas. D'Errico gingerly removed a bandage from Jimmie's head, bent close to her, and shined his headlamp down to illuminate the hole in her skull. He used tweezers to remove splinters of bone and bits of debris from her wound. After he had cleaned it out to his satisfaction, D'Errico closed the hole with stitches. He told Mr. Jordan it didn't appear the object that punctured her skull went so deep that it caused brain damage. He carefully bandaged her head, finally wrapping gauze at an angle across her face, covering her right eye.

"If she survives twenty-four hours, I think she'll get through it," the doctor said.

Lonnie Barber and his son, L. V., learned that two of the Barber children were at the Bryant Clinic in Tyler. Pearl and Burton had been admitted to the small hospital with injuries that weren't life threatening. All the clinic's beds were filled with victims of the explosion. But Arden Barber was not there or at the new Mother Frances Hospital or at the Henderson Hospital or any of the other hospitals Lonnie and L. V. had checked.

Finally, a friend of the family who had made a round of the morgues and funeral homes went to where Lonnie Barber and his son were working in a peach-basket line and pulled them aside. The man told them Arden was among the dead. Lonnie Barber thanked him and then went back to work pulling debris from the ruins. L. V. stayed at his father's side. Lonnie Barber didn't typically express his emotions, L. V. said years later in an interview. But the quiet, gentle farmer and longtime school bus driver was deeply hurt on the inside—grieving for Arden and all the other children he had come to know and love who perished that day, L. V. said.

"Arden was just a little ole slender, happy-go-lucky boy. He always made good grades," L. V. said. "He was twelve years old."

Dr. D'Errico left the Bryant Clinic and went straight to Mother Frances Hospital, where he joined Dr. C. C. McDonald and other local surgeons in the hospital's state-of-the-art operating room. Considering the number of seriously injured patients already admitted, with most needing some type of operation, the doctors were braced for a long night of almost nonstop procedures. Mother Mary Ambrose had admitted more than twenty children by mid-evening and before midnight the number would reach twenty-five—most with life-threatening injuries. At the hospital's front door, Mother Mary Regina welcomed parents, relatives, and friends who were searching for loved ones. If a child's name was on her list, she sent family members to the patient's room or to the waiting area outside the operating room.

The hospital had one unidentified girl, about eleven or twelve, who was unconscious. Mother Regina allowed friends and family who were looking for a girl about that age to go to the room and peek in to see if they recognized the child. So far, nobody had offered a clue as to who she might be.

Mother Regina's list of patients included Eddie Gauthreaux, the third grader who had returned to Mattie Queen Price's music room to get his jacket. Eddie's skull was partly crushed. A notation beside the child's name said, "No hope held for recovery." The list described Marilla Davidson's injuries as a broken leg, severe head bruises, and multiple lacerations. Twelve-year-old Connie Downs was listed in "very serious condition" with a broken right leg, broken right arm, and suspected internal injuries. Chester Couser, sixteen, was in critical condition because of a fractured skull. A crushed backbone made Maxine Maddry's hope of survival almost nil. Ida Ray Smith was listed as having bruises about her face and head. A boy named Elton Dees was in critical condition with a fractured skull and severe leg injury. The full extent of injuries suffered by Elbert Box was still being assessed, though a leg injury had been bad enough to put him on the critical list. One of Morris Luxemburg's legs was broken and seriously lacerated.[17]

Teachers and school administrators also streamed through the hospital to help sort out the whereabouts of as many students as possible. Junior High Principal Felton Waggoner went from room to room, speaking to each child who was awake enough to realize a visitor was in the room.

"I'm so happy you made it out and are okay," he said to one young girl. "How did you get out of the school?"

"Don't you remember, Mr. Waggoner?" she said. "You carried me out."

More students and teachers were killed and injured in the junior high portion of the building than anywhere else. Waggoner had carried so many out that he lost track of all their names.

"I'm just so happy we got you out," he told the child.

By the time Will Anderson reached Tyler in his old Whippet, the car's engine was sputtering and popping. He'd driven the Whippet for many miles around East Texas, stopping at hospitals and funeral homes in Henderson, Jacksonville, Kilgore, and Longview. He was searching for his daughters, Allene and Lillian. Anderson had accepted the possibility that they might both be dead, but he held hope in his heart that one or both of them could be alive. His wife, Lola, had given him two scraps of cloth to help in the search if worse came to worst. The cuttings were from the material Lola had used to make each of the girls' dresses they'd worn to school that day.

But there was reason for hope. Some of Lillian's classmates had told Mr. and Mrs. Anderson that she was outside playing softball when the school blew up. Even so, she was missing. At the last stop Will Anderson had made, a friend had told him somebody else thought a girl who looked like Allene was at the new hospital in Tyler. He jumped back into the Whippet and drove to Tyler as fast as the old car would go. About the time he arrived at the hospital, the Whippet's motor backfired one last time, shuddered, and slung a piston through the engine wall. He trekked toward Mother Frances on foot, beneath street lamps.

Allene wasn't at the hospital. Will Anderson found a ride to the Bryant Clinic. Neither of his daughters was among the patients at that small hospital.

Anderson hitchhiked back toward New London and got out in Overton. At a morgue in Overton, where clothing articles were placed atop sheets covering the dead, he found matches for both scraps of cloth he'd carried in his pocket all over East Texas.

# 23

# Midnight of the Soul

Felix McKnight picked his way over and across the sprawling ruins, looking for a fresh angle for his next dispatch. The AP reporter paused to take notes at a spot where a rescue worker clutched an acetylene torch near a massive steel beam protruding from slabs of broken concrete. The roughneck gripped the torch in a gnarled fist, skillfully gliding the sharp blue flame at the tip of the torch across the beam. His arms glistened with sweat. Grime was caked on his brow and cheeks. The flame popped and crackled as it contacted cold metal. The torch hissed at first, then made a low roar as the worker squeezed pure oxygen into the nozzle. The acetylene burned fiercely, slicing through the beam like a carving knife through a fat ham. The steel gradually sagged and broke into separate pieces, loosening another knot in the heavily packed debris field.

Soon afterward McKnight's impressions of the scene were rolling out in words and sentences on clattering teletype machines in newsrooms throughout the nation and the world: "Acetylene torches by the score were brought into play, and bit through the twisted steel of the girders which had supported the building and which were torn asunder in the terrific blast," McKnight wrote. "The building was of brick with a tile roof. The explosion mushroomed the roof, blew the brick walls outward and then the roof settled on those inside the building who had not been blown out by the force of the blast. So powerful was the explosion that employees of a Humble Oil Company plant two and a half miles away said it made the ground shake."[1]

[163]

It began to rain. United Press reporter Tom Reynolds wandered upon the weary boss of a gang of volunteers leaning against the shard of a school wall. Water trickled off the brim of his hat.

"How many more in there?" Reynolds asked.

"God only knows," the man said. "We won't know until we get down to the clay. I mean, there is a possibility of finding more bodies until we reach the clay dirt of the foundation."[2]

The Salvation Army took charge of rounding up food for a ragtag brigade of about six hundred grave diggers, volunteers who had rushed to the school to help save some of the children and who now would be burying most of those pulled from the wreckage.[3]

The country doctor who had attended to H. G. White's head cut, J. T. McClain, later had jumped into his roadster and sped the about three miles to the disaster site. He wanted to see if he could be of more immediate help at the scene. Meandering through the rain, which suddenly began to fall harder, he saw men pulling bodies and pieces of bodies from holes in the ground no deeper than foxholes. McClain helped where he could, splashing through the mud each time some excitement arose where men thought they had located a living child. It was the grimmest sight his eyes had taken in since the battlefields of Europe.

The first newspaper coverage hit the streets in an extra edition of the *Henderson Daily News* early Thursday evening. A bold headline proclaimed, "Hundreds Perish in School Blast." The *Tyler Courier-Times* also produced an extra edition on Thursday. "W.C. Shaw, superintendent of the New London school . . . telephoned here this afternoon that he believed between 300 and 400 school children died in an explosion at the school," the report said.

The biweekly *Kilgore News*, normally scheduled for Thursday publication anyway, was delivered to homes in East Texas late that afternoon with an even higher estimated death count. The newspaper's headlines captured a feeling of hysteria that seized the region as the day wore on: "Explosion Kills 500 Children, Wrecked Building, Burying Mutilated Bodies"; "New London School Tragedy One of Largest in History; Students Meet Death under Tons of Heavy Debris."

There were a few bright moments, like nuggets of gold or diamonds turning up in a washtub of muddy water. Under some of the heavy debris that was clawed away, two children, a boy and a girl, sat huddled together, clinging tightly to each other. With grime-smeared, frightened faces, they gazed up into the glare of floodlights. As the children were helped into an ambulance, many in the crowd raised their arms, hugged, and cheered.[4]

But the jubilation was not frequent. More often than not, noted AP reporter Bill Rives, the rescue teams recovered corpses. There seemed to be no end to the bodies being piled upon the schoolyard.

Rives recalled arriving near the disaster site by car just before dark. Reporters walking in saw the football field lights blazing in the distance, casting an odd twilight glow against the commotion in the distance. An undercurrent of disturbing sounds caused reporters to step up their pace. When Rives approached, the scene looked like a quarry with debris piled fifteen feet high in places.

"Blood smeared an upturned brick," Rives wrote later that night.[5] "With a shout, the workers gathered available shovels and lights and stretchers were called. An arm, a head appeared—terribly crushed. In a few minutes it was on the stretcher, carried to a waiting ambulance and speeded to the nearest temporary morgue.

"The scene was repeated over and over."

Several thousand oil-field workers, many of them wearing khaki clothes with dark stains after working a full day's shift in the fields, dug frantically through the ruins. Many of them, like Joe Wheeler Davidson, were searching for their own children.

"Under the hot glare of arc lamps, amid the thunder of trucks, the blaring of loud speakers, the even pacing of military sentries, the occasional shriek of an ambulance, hundreds of men dug. The known death toll stood momentarily at 500. It was expected to reach 600," reported the *Henderson Daily News* in an extra edition. Various news organizations reported what they believed to be factual information about the death count.

A film crew shooting a motion picture for a newsreel recorded buckets containing body parts at a makeshift morgue near the school, reported the *Tyler Courier-Telegram*. "A bucketful of ribs, leg and skull bones, looking as if they had been boiled for weeks and as clean of flesh as a whistle were being exhibited. . . . These bones were actually picked up in this manner from the debris . . . showing that the sand cut the flesh from the bone. A piece of skull bone was cut away as neatly as if a surgeon's knife had performed a trepanning operation."[6]

"Two sorrowful parents moved as if in a trance, bearing the clothes of a young boy. He died in their arms and his body was gently taken from them. But they were afraid in the confusion they might not see him again, so they wanted his death suit," Rives reported.[7]

The AP reporter met a woman searching for her child, who "frantically snatched at a hand with two rings on it found" a hundred yards from the building. "A cry, and she turns away." The "scene of desolation and despair . . . made my heart sink," Rives wrote.

L. A. Mathis had been in the peach-basket line for hours, long after he learned that his brother, Donald, escaped from the ruins without serious injury. L. A. was weary, his arms and back ached, and his head pounded with an awful headache. Each time he grabbed one of the baskets, it seemed heavier than the last basket he handled, but he drew upon all his strength, took hold of it, and passed it on to other hands. No sooner had he passed off one basket, another came swinging toward him, bulging with bricks and broken boards. The last time he took a short break to relieve himself, Mathis discovered he had forgotten his gloves somewhere, probably when he was getting a cup of coffee at the Salvation Army disaster station.

The men were passing a thick rafter through the lines, a long wooden beam so heavy that many hands were needed to hold and pass its weight. Mathis grabbed the beam when it reached him and his hand slipped, so he had to shift his feet quickly and catch the rafter with his other hand at another spot. As it passed in front of him, he saw that his hand had slipped because brain matter was smeared across the beam. His stomach seemed to turn inside out. He puked. A moment later, he collapsed. A couple of guys stopped to help him. "You okay?" one said. Mathis came to. He felt too ill to stand back up, but he let the other men pull him to his feet.

"I'm okay," he said. "I need some gloves."

Somebody handed Mathis a new pair of Salvation Army gloves. He stepped back into his spot in the peach-basket line and resumed his former pace of passing the debris along to the next man without breaking the rhythm. Mathis and others who worked in the peach-basket brigade would remember that night for the rest of their lives, recalling vivid details of the ordeal decades later.

"I can't remember every little detail, but I can remember some details," Marvin Dees said in an interview more than seventy years later. "The overall picture is with me forever—the chaos, the noise, a lot of engines running, and people yelling orders, conversation here and there, and a lot of screaming going on. Especially at first. Especially in the first few hours, there was a lot of weeping. You'd see a scene here and there that was heartbreaking."

Graften Ferguson, a young apprentice carpenter, had shown up at the disaster site that afternoon. He and his brother were fishing on the Angelina River when they heard the explosion. The people in charge at first put him to work building pine coffins. Now his duties had shifted to digging graves. He became one of hundreds of men working with shovels and picks at Pleasant Hill Cemetery, the closest graveyard with a lot of available space.

By late evening, thousands of volunteers were working in teams to remove the debris at a pace that seemed almost surreal. Witnesses who fixed a long gaze on the operation were amazed to see the rubble field literally shrinking, inch by inch, as they watched.

All the oil companies in the region had dispatched crews straight from the oil fields to the disaster site. Crews from other lines of work also hurried to join the rescue mission.

"We dug out rocks until our hands were bleeding. We had women out there digging, too. It wasn't just us men," recalled A. L. Green, who had worked all day clearing a right-of-way for a power line near Texarkana before he, his father, and his uncle heard about the explosion and rushed to New London. Up until then, Green had seen people hurt in car wrecks, but he'd never seen the results of a violent death.

Although rumors had spread that many children were trapped alive in the debris, Green, who was seventeen years old at the time, remembered finding only the dead. "You had a bunch of little ole kids laying out there.

You'd dig one out and couldn't find the other part of him. I toted out arms. I toted out heads," Green said. "I've been trying to get it off my mind all my life and I ain't got it off yet."

Scattered among the thousands of roughnecks were men from all walks of life, such as Harold Emerson, a violin teacher from Dallas. Emerson, thirty-eight, had children of his own about the same age as those he was helping remove from the ruins. Early in his career he'd worked as an undertaker's assistant to supplement his earnings as a musician, but nothing in life had prepared him emotionally for this kind of carnage. No matter, he tossed off his suit coat, loosened his tie, and joined the peach-basket brigade.

All afternoon and into the evening, Mrs. W. H. Phillips desperately waited for word about her three children—she hoped for news that they had all survived by some miracle. Two of them, Virgil, twelve, and Camilla, ten, were in classes at the time of the explosion. Four-year-old James begged to go meet Virgil at the end of his class. Mrs. Phillips stopped for a moment at a store near the school. James, who had permission to walk home with Virgil, darted into the building. All three children were missing.

Mrs. Phillips's husband had been in a Shreveport hospital recovering from injuries he suffered in a recent car wreck, but W. H. Phillips was able to leave the hospital and be with his wife when they heard the news, piecemeal, that all their children were dead.[8] When she heard, Mrs. Phillips collapsed and had to be taken to a hospital.

An element of the blast that confounded veterans of many explosions in the oil field was that "while the building was shattered from the ground up, leaving no trace of the concrete basement floor, there was no hole in the ground," the *Dallas Times-Herald* reported.

"Workers . . . worked with their feet on the sandy clay . . . literally swept clean of the original foundation. Walls two feet thick at the ground line were sheared off as though with giant scissors," the newspaper said.

American Red Cross headquarters in St. Louis dispatched regional director Albert Evans to take charge of relief work. Evans left immediately with a crew of Red Cross workers for New London.

"Already on the field and laboring prodigiously were scores of volunteer doctors and nurses from all parts of the Southwest," the *Dallas Times-Herald* reported. "Despite their efforts, gravely wounded children, many . . . suffering from concussions and torn limbs, lay for hours without medical aid."

"Bricks, steel and the bodies of scores of children shot skyward," the story said. "All landed in a twisted heap. Acetylene torches cut into the pretzel-like steel girders in all parts of the wrecked building."[9]

Bill Rives stopped to speak with a rescue worker taking a break near a table set up by the Salvation Army. The man was chewing on a sandwich and taking sips from a steaming cup of coffee. "This is some story, ain't it mister," the man said.

Rives nodded and gazed across the debris field. He ended his next dispatch with a description of what he witnessed: men carrying the corpse of a child toward the body pile. "Some story. Yes," he wrote.[10]

Jan Isbell Fortune, a *Henderson Daily News* reporter, described clusters of women at the scene who "stood and stared straight ahead, unseeingly." The women had been standing there for many hours. Their faces sagged with exhaustion and fear glimmered in their eyes. Their dresses were soaked, torn, and dirty.

Fortune saw a small boy in blue overalls and boots. "Jerry's in there," he said, rubbing his red eyes with the back of his hand. "That's his mama back there and she thought maybe he'd get out alive like Bobby Johnson did. But my dad—he's working over yonder on that oil truck—he says Jerry's nowhere any more except in little bits, maybe. We always played fire engine after school, Jerry and me, and his mom, she'd make us sugar cookies to eat, after we put out the fire.

"There's nobody to play with," the boy said. "It's going to be awful lonesome in London now."

Fortune moved on, spotting an open history textbook on the ground, with a notation: "Here—Friday."

"A half-eaten sandwich, soggy, in oiled paper, was pressed into the mud," Fortune observed. "A rain-soaked sheet of loose-leaf paper was scrawled with part of a lesson, 'Texas is bounded on the north—'"

The reporter built up courage to "venture a question to one slight, drenched figure who had been standing there an hour, unmoving." This was the woman the boy had pointed to as Jerry's mama.

"Her yellow curly hair was disheveled and she wore a house dress and an apron, as if she had been in the midst of some simple, homey task when the roar of the crumpling building first came to her ears that fateful afternoon," Fortune wrote. "She was a young woman—not 30—yet her posture and manner gave one the feeling of old age. When she did not show by a flicker of an eyelash or twitch of a feature that she heard my voice, I ventured to touch her hunched shoulder gently and repeat my query. And slowly, like a sleep walker, she turned toward me a face that was a mask, expressionless, but with the most terrible eyes. Those eyes weren't seeing me at all."[11]

Typesetters at the *Henderson Daily News* worked late into the evening preparing general descriptions of some of the yet unidentified dead children. The list was stark:

Boy 12–14, dark brown hair.
Girl, 15, pink and green print dress, red socks, brown hair.
Girl, 11, blonde, small diamond rings on left hand, has a red stone set in yellow gold on right hand.
Girl, 16, brown hair, purple crepe dress with pink slip.
Girl, 13, green socks, print dress has a green carriage design with a man and woman in carriage, has a red and green check too.
Girl, 15, brown hair, blue waist on dress, light and dark blue and white plaid skirt, blue socks, tan shoes.
Girl, 11, medium brown hair, green and pink plaid dress.
Girl, 14, dark brown hair, tan waist on blue slacks, blue collars and buttons, red sweater.
Girl, brown print, white polka dot waist, brown skirt.
Girl, 11, red hair, dress white waist, brown flower and brown stripes, light and dark tan socks.
Girl, 12, dark brown hair, blue print dress with yellow, blue, and red flowers.[12]

At the temporary morgue in Overton, a man stood gazing down at the body of a boy.

"This may be him," he said finally. "No, the feet don't look like him."[13]

In Tyler, a man stared at the body of a girl with many broken bones, the skin blue and cut all over. He fixed his eyes on the disfigured face. After a long while, he said, "I can tell by her teeth."

An attendant drew back the lips. The man bowed his head and squeezed his eyes shut, tears trickling down his cheeks.

"Yes. That's Mary."[14]

At one of the other temporary morgues, three bodies remained unidentified.

"There is not a mole or scar or mark," a nurse told a doctor. "There is only a ring on this finger."

"I think that will be enough," he said, telling her to put the clue out on a radio broadcast.[15]

Ted Hudson held tightly to the radio microphone and read through a stack of notices somebody had handed him: offers of help and condolences pouring in from all parts of the nation and telegraphs from people in foreign lands; locations of hospitals and clinics where injured children were taken; directions to places where undertakers were needed; and personal notes from worried parents. He read one from the neighbor of a family in New London whose children were missing. The father was out searching for them. The mother was waiting at home, just in case they showed up there. She was in great distress, the note said.

"Could someone please go to the house and sit with her for a while," Hudson said. He read directions to the house.

Henry McLemore and his United Press colleagues had landed at the Tyler airport and were en route to the disaster scene by car. The car's radio was tuned to Hudson's broadcast.

"Take me to that house," McLemore told the driver.[16]

Carroll "Boxhead" Evans knocked gently on the door of his next-door neighbor's home. A light was on inside Lemmie and Mary Butler's house, but nobody answered Evans's knock. He opened the door slightly and called out for Mary. She didn't answer. Evans stepped inside and looked around.

"Mary," he called again.

Neither Carroll Evans nor his wife, Mildred, had seen Mary Butler since the explosion. They didn't know whether Mary had learned yet about Lemmie being killed, although they felt somebody would have gotten word to her by now. Carroll ventured farther into the little house. Nobody was in the kitchen or the bedroom. Evans decided that Mary Butler must be at a friend's house or possibly at her church.

He took Lemmie Butler's watch from his pocket and placed it in the center of the small desk in the living room—Lemmie's desk.

Evans felt certain Mary would see it there as soon as she returned home. He hoped that in some way—even some small way—she would find comfort in it.[17]

Joe Davidson had helped remove many children, dead and alive, from the rubble, but he had heard nothing about three of his own: Helen, Anna Laura, and Joe Wheeler Jr. The son, whom they called by his middle name, had begun to take on his dad's rugged good looks. Of late, he'd grown taller and lost some of the baby fat that made him look pudgy in pictures that had been taken of him last summer. He'd never be slim but likely would grow to have his father's strong build. He'd already inherited his father's dark hair. Wheeler admired the man and wanted to follow his advice and go to the U.S. Naval Academy. Now in the ninth grade, he had become one of the most popular boys on the campus. His classmates elected him freshman vice president. Girls were noticing him. In a recent article about social life at New London High School, Wheeler was singled out as having the "best eyes" of any boy.[18] His younger sister, Marilla, might have poked fun at him about it, but the attention excited Wheeler.

Marilla had been taken away to a hospital in critical condition. Joe Davidson didn't know which hospital; he'd received only bits and pieces of information about her. So he dug. The roughneck's face was caked with grime and streaked with sweat and tears. His hands were cut and bleeding.

Reporters found out that Davidson might have lost all four of his children. One of his buddies had also passed along another tantalizing bit of information: the stocky roughneck with curly black hair, tinged with gray at his sideburns, was a decorated veteran of the world war. The reporters closed in, circling Davidson, and carefully choosing their questions, trying to be sensitive to the man's grief, yet knowing there was no other way to ask some questions but directly, in a respectful tone of voice.

Davidson stopped what he was doing. He felt relieved to talk about it for a moment.

"Were you in the war?" somebody asked.

"Yes," he said. "I was a Navy aviator, and I was shot down two times, but this is the worst I've ever seen."[19]

Davidson wiped his face on the sleeve of his khaki shirt and turned back to the job at hand. The reporters scrambled away across the ruins, hurrying to get Davidson's searing quote into their next cycle of withering reports.

Joe Davidson worked on until a friend tapped him gently on the shoulder. "You need to break off and go to the morgue. I think we've found the children," the neighbor told him.

Lightning flashed across the sky, and thunder rolled off in the night. The storms weathermen had predicted for two days were finally drifting toward New London. According to an ancient folk saying in the South, when it storms on the night of a death, a soul is entering heaven. A big storm on this night could only mean that God was preparing for a chorus of new angels, the old people said.

Graften Ferguson was digging graves when the storm hit. It began raining so hard that the shovel kept slipping from his hands. He was tired by this time and wanted to go home, but he kept digging in the slippery mud. The sides of the graves became so waterlogged they started caving in, dumping piles of mud back inside the holes. Graften and others started lining the graves with the wooden forms the carpenters had built earlier. The pine braces acted like a vault to keep mud from collapsing into the graves. The ground was so slippery the men were constantly falling down, and they were covered from head to toe in mud.

Men digging graves at Pleasant Hill Cemetery heard the scream of another siren around midnight and saw the flashing beacon of an ambulance floating across the darkness like the raw red eye of a storybook phantom, visible through a gap in the pine trees before it vanished.

Sam Bunting, eighteen, lay unconscious in the back of the ambulance. When workers dug him out of the debris, some thought at first he was just another victim for the body pile, but then somebody found a pulse in Sam's wrist. The only chance to save him, one man said, was putting him on a fast ambulance heading to the new Mother Frances Hospital in Tyler. "I doubt he will survive the trip," another man said.[20]

Shortly before rescue workers located Sam, they had found his sister Naoma under a different pile of rubble. She had a faint pulse but died before the ambulance had made it a hundred yards from the disaster site.[21]

"Mother Frances is this boy's only hope," a man said grimly.

The ambulance tore away as fast as the driver could go while weaving in and out of clogs of cars and maneuvering around National Guard barricades. A nurse kneeled in the back next to the gurney where Sam Bunting was as still as a wax figure. Now and again the nurse heard—or thought she heard—a low groan from deep in his throat. She held an oxygen breathing mask to his mouth and nose with one hand and used her other hand to clean blood and brick dust and mud from his wounds.

Once the ambulance reached the Tyler Highway and began the journey west, the driver pushed the accelerator to the floorboard. National Guard soldiers in army green gear and trucks were stationed all along the highway to keep it open for emergency and police vehicles only. The driver had lost count of how many trips he'd made between New London and various hospitals since late afternoon, but he knew he'd put many miles on the ambulance with runs that probably averaged eighty miles per hour on open roads.

As he was nearing the halfway point between New London and Tyler, the driver smelled smoke. An indicator gauge in the dash panel warned that the motor was exceedingly overheated. A few seconds later, flames shot out from beneath the hood and swept back over the windshield. By the time the driver brought the vehicle to a stop on the side of the road, the front end of the ambulance was engulfed in fire. He jumped out and helped the nurse pull Sam Bunting out of the vehicle as the flames flashed into the passenger compartment, burning the nurse's hands. Men at the side of the road who had seen the ambulance catch on fire were running back and forth from a ditch flowing with water from the earlier rains. Using buckets and cans, their hats and their hands, they finally showered enough water on the ambulance to douse the fire. But the vehicle obviously was out of service for now.

It is unknown what kind of vehicle was used to transport Bunting the rest of the way to Tyler. More than likely, a Texas Highway Patrol car pulled up to the site of the ambulance fire, and officers hoisted the injured boy onto the backseat and zoomed off toward Tyler even before the bucket brigade had extinguished the fire.

When the vehicle reached the emergency entrance at Mother Frances, Bunting was still unconscious, but his heart was beating. None of the flames leaping into the back of the ambulance had touched the boy. The nurse with burned hands and the ambulance driver helped convey Sam from the car to hospital attendants ready with a gurney to whisk him on to the hospital's emergency room.

Henry McLemore located the home of the two missing children. The mother was waiting by herself for some word. McLemore interviewed her while she waited. Sometimes they both fell silent and sat without speaking at all. McLemore originally was scheduled to cover a boxing match on this day, but the story he was on was immensely bigger than any sporting event. He had covered grief before, but never had he sat still in somebody's tiny parlor, his legs crossed, staring such grief in the face.[22]

Chesley Shaw and his son Charles, the oldest of the Shaw children, finally located Sambo's remains under a sheet at one of the makeshift morgues in Overton. They identified him by his wallet at 1:30 a.m. Chesley Shaw was trembling so much that several friends had to help hold him up as he left the morgue. Charles then drove his father home.

The moment they came through the door, Leila Shaw knew by the look on their faces that her husband and son were bringing to her the worst possible news—confirmation that her baby was gone. Hazel helped her mother to a couch in the parlor of the superintendent's cottage. Her father and Charles took seats nearby, and the family sat quietly for a while, occasionally sharing memories of happier times when Sambo was a little boy growing up in Minden. When they fell silent, the only sound in the room was the rhythmic tick-tock of the parlor clock.

Hazel worried about her father's health. His face was haggard and pale. A thin crack ran across one of the lenses in his spectacles, and he was bandaged where flying debris cut his forehead and cheek.

He'd survived losing another school once years ago, but that experience was nothing compared with this. His school in Minden had somehow caught fire one Friday evening and burned to the ground, but nobody was killed or even injured in the blaze. And nobody blamed Chesley Shaw, the headmaster. Hazel privately feared that some of the rougher residents of New London would wake tomorrow with blood in their eyes and seek misplaced revenge against her father.

Joe Davidson gazed down at the body of each child long enough to know for certain it was one of his. He kept a grip on his emotions, a response he had learned in battle, but this was the toughest hurt he'd ever known. After looking at his three children laid out at a funeral home in Overton, he turned away and faced a cluster of reporters who had flocked behind him, through the rain, from the ruins of the school to the undertaker's back room. His wife, Mary, was at home, inconsolable, locked within a living nightmare. Joe needed to get home and deal with whatever would come next, but first he would take a moment to talk out loud about this— somehow speak words. He was trained as a man of action, and act he must.

A reporter asked for the names and ages of the children he had just identified. Davidson sucked in a deep breath. "Anna Laura, eleven. Helen, thirteen. Joe Wheeler, fifteen. My daughter Marilla, fourteen, is in a Tyler hospital. She's in critical condition, I'm told."

Davidson sorted his thoughts. "I dreamed last night that Dewey Deer, my derrick man, fell out of the top of the derrick and was killed," he said. "I could see it just as plain as ever."[23]

The roughneck told the reporters he had tried to shrug the dream off as an overactive imagination at work on his subconscious mind, but now he didn't know what to think. When he started telling members of his crew about it, early that morning before the breakfast break, the men had warned him that it was an ill omen. He went ahead and told the dream anyway, Davidson said with a helpless shrug.

"I was a lieutenant in the U.S. Navy aviation service during the world war, but I never saw anything like this," Davidson said. "I was shot down in my plane twice, and I saw many a dog fight. I saw several of my buddies shot down as we were escaping from a German prison camp, but nothing like this."

Davidson said he received the Navy Cross and the Croix de Guerre, a highly esteemed French medal, for distinguished service in the war, yet he still wasn't prepared to face the deaths of his own children. He had hoped to send Wheeler to Annapolis after high school.

"Boy, it's tough," said Davidson, his voice husky with emotion. He felt he needed to say something more. A lump caught in his throat, and he turned away.

# 24
# Dawn, March 19

By dawn the rain clouds had cleared away from East Texas. The sun rose as if it were a normal Friday. Legions of birds, anticipating the spring, chirped and sang in trees and bushes all across the region. The countryside looked as fresh and clean as ever after being swept by the rainstorms.

Still the site of the disaster was a jumbled, muddy mess, although much of the debris had been removed during the long night. The mission was being called a rescue operation, but the workers had carted away only bodies for hours. Finally, they found an adult, a teacher, still breathing near the bottom of the heap. She died in an ambulance just minutes later.

*Tyler Courier-Times* reporter Jimmie Donahue was exhausted. Donahue had been assigned to spend the night traveling across the region between the makeshift morgues and funeral homes where the bodies were being taken. A misty rain fell most of the journey. The odyssey through hell began about 3 a.m. Friday, when Jimmie climbed the steps to the second floor of a grocery store in Arp, where clusters of parents were moving among the remains of nine unidentified children. At Crim Funeral Home in Henderson, Donahue watched a dozen volunteer embalmers at work on about fifty bodies. Workers were unloading forty coffins from a truck parked outside. The reporter drove to the blast site in a downpour of rain. Near dawn, as the rain was turning to drizzle, Jimmie saw a volunteer remove a head from the debris. It was the "cutest little girl," Donahue noted.[1]

Workers located a hand about twenty yards away, apparently the same child's, but found nothing more of her body. At Pearson Funeral Home in

Overton about forty embalmers were at work in rooms where the reporter counted at least a hundred dead. More bodies were in a garage behind the funeral home. Donahue counted fifty bodies at the American Legion Hall in Overton. Thirty-five in Kilgore, eleven in Jacksonville, and fourteen in Longview. At the funeral home in Longview, a handsome man wearing a shamrock on his jacket was pleading with everyone he met to help him locate his daughter. She had blond hair, he said. Her red-headed twin sister was already identified as dead in Overton.

Stumbling through the wreckage, one reporter spotted a steel radiator with "its ribs smashed and twisted as though it had been pounded with a two-ton pile driver." The mass of debris hinted at the ferociousness of the explosion. "A textbook, blown straight up, went completely through one of the remaining ceilings, through the wood base of the roof and stopped only when half of it was protruding through the roof. In one classroom, a pair of scissors such as children use in kindergarten to cut paper dolls was blown with such force that the blades went into the wall two inches."[2]

*Houston Post* reporter Pat McNealy Barnes saw a woman standing in the rain staring at the wreckage. She was holding a scuffed brown oxford shoe.

"Is that your child's shoe?" Barnes said.

"Maxine," she said. "They haven't found Maxine yet."

"What's your name?"

The woman didn't answer. She just kept staring at the wreckage.[3]

Ted Hudson's eyes were bloodshot and gritty after the sleepless night and his voice at times grew hoarse, but he kept talking into the microphone with only rare pauses. The networks patched into his broadcast were taking fewer station breaks than usual. They were staying glued to Hudson's description of the rescue operation.

Frequently, he read announcements, such as this one from Capt. Walter Elliott, head of the Tyler office of the Texas Highway Patrol, urging sightseers to stay away from the stricken area: "The road past the London school building, and all roads entering it will be blocked Friday by Texas highway patrolmen. All persons are requested not to attempt to enter the premises of the explosion unless they have business of a very urgent nature. Otherwise, they will not be permitted to go through."

Millions of people were listening. One man in a little Texas town, after listening to disaster coverage nonstop for hours, apparently went berserk. The sheriff's office was notified that the man was holding a gun on his family, blabbering about the school explosion, and threatening to shoot his wife and children and then turn the gun on himself. A sheriff's deputy killed him, "in self-defense," a news story said, with a single shot.[4]

Doctors at Mother Frances Hospital upgraded Marilla Davidson's condition, saying she was no longer at risk of dying from her injuries.

Sam Bunting was now expected to live, although his skull was fractured in three places and his spine was crushed. It was decided that the boy would not be told about his sister Naoma's death until his condition improved.

Dr. D'Errico, the brain surgeon from Dallas, was credited with saving the lives of several children.

Maxine Maddry took a turn for the worse, making her condition grave. She would be lucky to survive a day, one doctor said.

Walter Freeman made it through the night, and his condition stabilized. Walter's father and mother, in hushed voices, discussed whether to tell him that one of his sisters was dead. They decided it was best to wait; he'd been through enough for now.

Surgeons worked feverously setting and resetting Elbert Box's fractured leg. A serious infection had set in while Elbert was tangled in the debris. A doctor said the leg would have to be amputated if the infection continued to rage.

The little girl whose face was badly damaged was still unconscious. Two families waiting at the hospital now thought the child belonged to them.

Eddie Herman Gauthreaux's mother sat on one side of her comatose boy, and his father, E. J. Gauthreaux, sat on the other. Esterlene Gauthreaux went to the school soon after the explosion. She finally found Eddie among other injured children in the basement of the Overton Baptist Church. A car salesman drove them to Mother Frances Hospital in Tyler, but the brain surgeon could do nothing to help save the gravely injured nine-year-old. His mother now could only hold his hand, hoping her touch somehow brought him comfort. The ride from Overton to Tyler kept flashing through her thoughts. All the way out of Overton people were standing near the road, offering them blankets.[5]

Elsie Jordan's mother came to her side and took her hand. "Jimmie is awake," her mother said. Elsie sat up in bed. A bandage covered most of her head, but much of her face was visible. The bandage angled down across her damaged eye. "Is she okay? Is she really, really okay?"

"We think so. She thought you were dead and wants us to bring you over to her hospital so she can touch you and know that you are alive."

"Can I go?" Elsie asked excitedly.

"The nurses are arranging to have you taken to the clinic, for just a few minutes. But you must be still as possible and no cutting up."

Elsie smiled for the first time since the explosion.

A few minutes later, hospital attendants put Elsie on a rolling bed, took her out to an ambulance, and drove her the short distance to Bryant Clinic. They let her sit in a wheelchair on the ride in and down the hall to Jimmie's room.

Jimmie was lying flat on the bed, staring at the ceiling. A swath of bandage swept down over her eye.

"Guess who?" Elsie said.

Jimmie looked at her. "Elsie, is that you?"

"It's me."

Before anybody had a chance to stop her, Jimmie bounded out of the bed and tottered on bare feet across the room. Elsie stood up. The sisters in hospital gowns with almost identical bandages covering their heads embraced in the middle of the room, hugged, and patted each other's backs.

"I just knew you were dead," Jimmie said.

"It's me—no ghost."

Tears trickled down their faces.

"I love you, Jimmie," Elsie said.

"I love you too, Elsie," Jimmie said.

The storm clouds had swept on to other regions, and in the woods around the campus a few morning birds sang in the dripping trees. As the sun rose, casting vague light across the scene of wreckage and chaos from the night before, a mother and father sat on the ground next to the body of their son. They were silent and motionless. A reporter walking by them left them alone.

Nearby, a pair of oil-field workers held gently onto the arms of a mother, soaked and bedraggled from the downpour. The men were trying to convince her to go home, away from the desolate scene.

"I can't go away," she said. "I can't! My baby may be alive in there and calling for me."[6]

After a while, the men, both holding her, gradually and gently escorted the woman across an area where the ankle-deep mud was crisscrossed with the tracks of trucks and oil-field equipment.

# 25

# Hard News

Associated Press Dallas manager Fred Dye chided Rives and McKnight during a long-distance call: "The body count from various news sources sounded like wild estimates; instead of reporting estimates, start counting bodies!" McKnight and Rives knew Dye wouldn't listen to excuses or, for that matter, legitimate reasons for the count being so fuzzy. When the reporters started explaining bodies and parts of bodies had been taken to makeshift morgues for many miles around, Dye broke in with an order to go to the place with the most bodies and count them, one by one. The boss told them to divide up and visit as many morgues as possible, using stringers and other trustworthy volunteers to help with the count. The crucial facts in this story are bodies under sheets, Dye said.

McKnight and Rives set out first for the American Legion Hall in Overton. Long lines of parents were waiting to enter the building to search for children missing since the explosion. The men in charge were letting them inside just a few at a time, to keep from being overwhelmed by a mass of grieving family members turning the place upside down.

McKnight bypassed the lines, found a side door, and ducked inside. The place was dimly lighted. It was a large open room scattered with mattresses on the floor and a few short tables where several men in white lab jackets worked. Fumes in the room blinded McKnight instantly, making him drop to his knees to find cleaner air. The reporter started crawling from body to body. He noticed probably a dozen embalmers and assistants in white jackets scattered around the room. A quick yet primitive method of preserving the bodies was being used.

"They had galvanized buckets, like garden buckets, with a formaldehyde solution in them, and brushes sort of like large paint brushes, and they'd dip into that solution and just kind of swish it on those sheets [covering bodies]," McKnight recalled. "You could not identify any of those children. They were just terribly mutilated. I got on my knees and crawled around those lines because the formaldehyde solution was just blinding, and I got down about half of the first row and one of the guys in charge came over to me and wanted to know who I was and he said, 'Well, we have work for you.'"

The reporter realized that he was being commandeered for another stint of disaster work and that it would do no good to protest. McKnight was assigned a job of retrieving fresh buckets of formaldehyde from a place in another part of the hall, lugging them back into the main room, and distributing the buckets among the undertakers. "About every two or three minutes, they'd take me to the door and stick my head out, and stick theirs out, too, so we could restore our eyesight. Tears were streaming down our faces and we just couldn't see."

While McKnight was caught up with his bucket work, he had the freedom to roam about the room and count bodies. It was a gruesome and tedious process. Toward sunrise, the AP could report a more accurate death count than the initial estimates by the Red Cross and Texas Rangers. The total dead would not reach five hundred—maybe not even four hundred. It began to look as though the total would be higher than three hundred but fewer than four hundred, McKnight and other reporters realized.

The embalmers, including J. Raymond Meissner and C. B. McBride from Shannon Funeral Homes in Fort Worth, worked on sawhorses with one-inch-by-ten-inch planks thrown across them. "There was no drainage and bed sheets were thrown down on the floor to partially absorb the great amount of blood," Meissner recalled. "Many bodies were decapitated or crushed beyond resemblance of a human face. I made efforts in many cases to hurriedly rebuild features, but in most instances it helped but little."

Meissner and McBride had started for the disaster by car around 6 p.m., after catching one of Ted Hudson's radio appeals for undertakers needed at the catastrophe site. At first, they knew only that the disaster was some-where in East Texas; later they heard Hudson on the car radio giving direc-tions to the New London school in Rusk County.

"I've been there," Meissner told McBride. "I know the way. Last summer I went to New London to visit my very close friend, L. R. Butler." Meissner wouldn't learn for days that Lemmie Butler was killed instantly when the school exploded.

When McBride and Meissner reached Tyler, every road leading to the east was blocked with official barricades or hopelessly clogged with mas-sive traffic jams that would take hours to untangle. Highway patrol officers on motorcycles offered to escort the embalmers to the makeshift morgue in Overton. They arrived shortly before 11 p.m. The morticians unloaded embalming equipment and hurried inside to set up their stations.

"The scene in this American Legion Hall and skating rink was beyond description," said Meissner, who was then twenty-six. "The enormity of the task was evident when you realized that more than two hundred bod-ies passed through the hall during the next eighteen hours."

Meissner embalmed twenty-five children, and other licensed morti-cians around him worked at the same brisk pace. Funeral homes, relatives, and friends were taking the bodies away soon after they were identified.

"I worked so hard and fast, I scarcely knew what was going on around me," Meissner said. "I do remember there was almost no outward emo-tion, even when a mother recognized the body of her child. People seemed dazed, dry-eyed and submissive."

"Yes, that's her," a man said. And then the man and his wife passed quietly out of the building, holding the body of their child, without saying another word, Meissner recalled.

"Many parents identified a son or daughter without even seeing the body," he added. "When we embalmed a body we stacked the clothing on top of a sheet that covered the lifeless form, and parents seeing familiar articles of wearing apparel would at once recognize it. I worked all night and part of the next day without rest until the bodies were all embalmed.

"It was pitiful how the people had to make identification. Those with children missing had to make all the rounds."

Meissner got word to officials at Shannon Funeral Homes that funeral coaches in East Texas were far too scarce to handle the disaster's aftermath. A pair of Shannon hearses left Fort Worth early Friday morning and headed toward East Texas.[1]

McKnight and Rives were taking turns helping the embalmers and counting bodies. "I counted for a while and the last time they let me go to the door for air, I took off," McKnight said.

While his partner set out to find a fresh story angle for afternoon newspapers, Rives stayed at the morgue to continue the body count. In a short while, he heard an argument break out between one of the roughneck supervisors and a woman reporter. In notes he made of the incident, Rives didn't identify the woman, but his description of her nicely fit Sarah Mc-Clendon, the Tyler reporter who'd been helping McKnight and Rives cut through local red tape.

The woman was demanding that people in charge of the morgue provide the news media with the names of the dead—those with positive IDs. She explained that the public has a right to know such information as soon as possible after a disaster. The man in charge, who apparently had lost a child himself, was in no mood to discuss the finer points of journalistic rules. The argument grew heated and loud, and the man threatened to throw the reporter out of the building.

"Go ahead. I dare you," the woman said, putting her glare as close to the roughneck's face as she could without bumping his nose. He backed off but continued to argue his points as the reporter followed him through the room, bickering from behind.[2]

Using the distraction as a shield, Rives crept quietly among the bodies, lifting sheets and taking notes.

Walter Cronkite felt like he was stuffed inside a press box at a major bowl game. The small Western Union building in Overton had been converted overnight into a makeshift newsroom to accommodate all the reporters from outside East Texas. Journalists and photographers had been arriving in a steady trickle since midnight, and now groups of reporters were showing up—all trying to get a spot in the Western Union office. The explosion was not just the hottest story in the nation; it was being followed around the globe. A front-page story in the *London Times* in England on Friday morning grabbed readers with a chilling headline:

Explosion at U.S. School

———

Hundreds Killed

———

Walls and Roof Collapse

———

Children Buried Under Ruins

By noon on Friday, scores of reporters were buzzing in and out of the Western Union office, where coffee tables, end tables, and apple crates were being used to supplement the dozen regular desks in the room. The reporters were sharing typewriters. Just as soon as one ended his story, snatched up his copy, and took it to a teletype operator, a competing reporter plopped down at the vacant typewriter and began pecking out a story. About forty Western Union operators were on the job. The small office was as noisy as a big city newsroom on an election night. Nearly everybody in the room—reporters and telegraph operators—was smoking—cigarettes, cigars, pipes—and the office swirled with bluish-gray smoke. The only rule about it: do not under any circumstances ignite a fire because a room so clogged with cheap copy paper and strips of teletype tape will burst into flames immediately.

Henry McLemore had written much of his copy out in longhand as he waited for a typewriter. When he finally got one, he quickly spun out the first few paragraphs of the story he was writing for the afternoon daily newspapers: "NEW LONDON, Texas, March 19—The radio voice told of Royal Mail's victory in the Grand National, gave the winners of the exhibition baseball games, and price of crude oil, and then—without a change of feeling, said:

"'Will someone go to . . . street and sit with Mrs. . . . She has been unable to locate her two children, Timmy, aged 9, and Francine, aged 11. They went to school Thursday morning and have not returned.'"

McLemore notes that he went to the address—"a little box house in the richest oil fields in the world, and the woman was almost too tired to answer my ring." He explained that she was one of the first mothers who waded into the giant pile of rubble in search of her children, yanking absurdly at boulders and beams it would take heavy equipment to move. Then she hurried to the nearest temporary morgue—"a frame building with a ragged sheet hung over the door—and tiptoed from cot to cot afraid of what she might find.

"But Tommy and Francine weren't there," McLemore wrote. "She made the tragic rounds in Overton, Tyler, Henderson, Kilgore, and all of the other neighboring towns to which bodies were carried in that frantic hour after the explosion. She was a member of the quiet shuffling crowds that sightseers saw standing in the front of the funeral homes and the hospitals."

The woman turned and faced McLemore, looking him in the eyes. "They must be somewhere, my babies. But I am so tired and there is nowhere else to look," she told him.

"She was right," McLemore wrote. "There was no other place, and there was no other place for others like her; she was not alone. Scattered over the oil fields, in the little houses pitched in the forests of derricks were more than one family who could hope for no trace of the children they sent off to school that morning."

School officials already were suggesting that all the victims may not be found, as such, McLemore said.

"With the blast went the school records, and 14 of the teachers. No one knows exactly who was in what classes, how many children were in the building at the time of the detonation. I saw steel filing cabinets and their contents, hundreds of yards from the site of the blast. I saw bits of clothing, books, and desks, scattered over far away tennis courts and play fields. Blackboards, with lessons chalked upon them, sailed blocks from the building. Gray steel lockers with clothing hanging from their sprained doors littered the campus."

Officials have good reason to be skeptical about finding all the victims, the reporter noted. "For some of the pupils were literally blown to bits when the gas in the basement, ignited and, striking upward and outward, shattered the building. No one knows the actual number of the dead," McLemore wrote. "No one ever will."[3]

Even before he sent the copy onto Dallas, Kansas City, and New York, the puckish Georgian was pretty sure he had just crafted a report packed with emotional dynamite.

"Dynamite!" somebody shouted across the Western Union office. "They've found dynamite in the ruins."

Every reporter in the room dropped what they were doing and scrambled to be the first out the door. This was a potentially sinister new angle— explosives that might have been planted and detonated to intentionally raze the school and kill as many children as possible. The few reporters who stayed behind typed out briefs about the discovery of several bundles of dynamite located under the stage in a part of the ruins where the auditorium had stood.[4] The bulletins were coded to ring bells in teletype machines at every newsroom in the country and many across the world.

By the time the mob of reporters reached the school grounds, though, the dynamite story had fizzled. It wasn't quite a dud, but neither was it an incendiary blast of news that would shake the world.

It was true: several sticks of dynamite were located in a storage cabinet beneath the stage. A custodian quickly came forward and explained why dynamite was there. When he and other janitors had been working on the football field the previous summer, they had used dynamite to blast boulders out of the playing field area, to make the field as smooth as possible. Somebody had clumsily stored the leftover sticks of dynamite in an inappropriate location. "A stupid location," somebody said. So the information about the dynamite stored casually within the school, where it might have caused a disaster, but didn't, just deepened skepticism among reporters, parents, and others about whether the school campus was being administered in ways to keep the children safe. Superintendent Chesley Shaw's painstakingly constructed reputation began to unravel.

Back in the makeshift newsroom, Cronkite found a vacant workstation and plopped down in a wooden swivel chair to start on his afternoon dispatch for late-breaking afternoon newspapers and the a.m. dailies. An old-fashioned Remington typewriter missing a keypad here and there sat on the desk. It was part of the discarded supplies and material that had been dug out of the attic and backroom of the Western Union office. Cronkite felt lucky to have any kind of typewriter at all. He lit his corncob pipe, took a couple of tentative puffs, and started pecking the typewriter's keyboard.

"NEW LONDON, Texas, March 19 (UP)—A few parents, still hopeful that they would find their children, even if only in death, clung to the ropes surrounding the New London school site Friday night," Cronkite wrote.

He had spent much of the day at the explosion site, taking notes as the recovery mission drew to a close. Parents still at the scene had spent what must have been the most miserable night of their lives, the reporter surmised. "By daybreak most of them had visited every morgue in the vicinity," Cronkite wrote. "They returned to the scene of the holocaust, startled to find that workers nearly had completed the demolition."

In less than twenty-four hours, three thousand volunteers had removed so much rubble from the blast zone to several piles on the perimeter of the campus that now it looked as though the ground where the school had stood was only a shadow of its former self—swept clean by a giant broom. Countless tons of debris had been hauled out by the men of the peach-basket brigades. The accomplishment was an unparalleled engineering feat in modern times.

The roar of trucks, generators, cranes, and other heavy equipment used in the night had gone silent by midmorning. "It seemed that the last hope had faded from the surviving onlookers when the last loose stones and girders were pulled from the site," Cronkite wrote. "But within a few minutes workers returned to dig in four feet of silt that filled the subbasement to ground level." No more bodies were found. "Morticians, ambulance drivers and nuns packed suitcases and left to return, in some cases, hundreds of miles to their homes."

"Despite efforts of workmen to clear away the gruesome debris," Cronkite wrote, "Friday's visitors found morbid souvenirs of the tragedy. Bits of musical instruments, blasted into tiny pieces; blood-stained books and assorted rags, once adornment on Rusk County school children's backs, were acquired."[5]

In another corner of the makeshift newsroom, Felix McKnight pounded away on a typewriter with his third rewrite since daybreak of the day's main news story. A group of fresh Associated Press reporters had arrived during the night; they were out working with Bill Rives on new material. The reporters eventually brought all their findings back to McKnight at the Western Union building, so he could weave their notes into the day's main story or set it aside as material for a sidebar.

The Alvin Gerdes story made a poignant sidebar. McKnight hammered out a quick two-paragraph brief that he could follow later with more details:

"New London, Texas—The name Alvin Gerdes, no stranger to print, appeared again today but it drew no cheers—only bowed heads."

"Hero of the district champion London football team and considered a brilliant college prospect, he was one of the blast victims."[6]

Gerdes, a senior about to graduate and captain of the football team, was killed along with his younger brother Allen. Allen, sixteen, also played for the London Wildcats football team but had yet to make a name for himself as an athlete. He was a Boy Scout, a member of Jack Fentress's New London Troop 217, and had been close friends with the scoutmaster's son, Jack Jr., who also died in the explosion. One of the troop's favorite events had occurred during May of a previous spring, at the Camp-O-Ral. Scoutmaster Fentress and Scoutmaster William Mote of London's Troop 219 together escorted their boys over to Henderson for the weekend. There they joined eight troops—two hundred boys, all told—from Rusk and Panola Counties for two days and nights of scouting.

*The encampment rose on the grounds of the Henderson Junior High School. Scores of olive green pup tents sprouted quickly in regimented lines and divisions. Allen, Jack Jr., and other boys pitched their tents near where the flag for Troop 217 waved in the early summer air. They helped erect the troop kitchen, and after the evening meal, their patrol squad marched with the rest of their troop to the center of the camp, where all the uniformed scouts congregated for a ceremonial lighting of the bonfire and Indian benediction. As the fire licked a tall yellow-red flame against the dusky sky, the boys sang a soft vesper. A lone bugler played taps, and the Grand Council concluded with a prayer. The boys reorganized into patrols and troops and marched back to their camp-sites. Just outside the tents, crickets sang in the dark grass. The front tent flaps were open, allowing an evening breeze into the canvas enclosure, and stars sparkled brightly in the patch of sky visible from the tent's doorway beyond stands of pine. The boys had talked for hours, of hunting and fishing and last year's football season; of baseball, and the New York Yankees and St. Louis Cardinals; of the next day, which would include cooking contests and first-aid drills and signaling and starting fires with flint stones and constructing rope fences with elaborate knots, and they talked on into the night about school and their favorite teachers and most despised teachers and about what they planned to do when they were finally grown up and finished with school. And they spoke of girls, until finally, the talk dwindled and the boys drifted off to sleep, lulled by the harmony of the crickets and sheltered by the shimmering stars.*[7]

The wire services dispatched sidebars about the death of New London's pretty music teacher, Mattie Queen Price. Queen had been one of those people that everyone, children and adults alike, just loved. She also was society editor for the *Overton Press.*

As McKnight worked on his rewrite, a man who had been helpful with tips on a number of other stories rushed into the newsroom and approached the reporter. He asked in a whisper whether AP might be interested in a very unusual telegram offering condolences. At first McKnight was leery. A mishmash of information—telegrams from dignitaries, notes from officials announcing scholarship funds, and such—tended to clog up the main story, and often such correspondence was not meaty enough for a sidebar. At best they could be turned into briefs.

"Tell me who?" McKnight said, offering his ear to his source.

"Adolf Hitler," the man whispered.

"I'll take it," McKnight said quickly.

This was fascinating, the reporter thought. The harsh little man with a postage-stamp mustache had seized dictatorial control of Germany and become a frightful character on the world stage by spring 1937. His regime was rearming Germany in violation of the Treaty of Versailles. Talk of a new war, incited by Hitler, was sweeping Europe. Now, he was expressing sorrow about the deaths of American schoolchildren. Hitler's propaganda man must be working overtime tonight, McKnight thought. He wrote a two-paragraph brief about the telegram, noting it was an "AP exclusive."

It was approaching noon when Marvin Dees finally made it home. The roughneck took his boots off outside on the porch and tried as best he could to brush some of the loose dirt from layers of filth on his shirt and pants. His wife, Floy, met him in the front room and hugged him for a long, long time without talking. Finally, she said she was going to make him a hot meal.

"You probably haven't eaten since yesterday," Floy said.

"I'm not hungry," Marvin said.

"You've got to be hungry," she insisted.

"No. Not now."

Marvin went to the bedroom, peeled off his clothes, and lay down across the foot of the bed. He was exhausted but not sleepy. His mind was whirling with scenes from the rescue mission, turning again and again like some kind of bizarre carousel in the haunted house at a carnival. He tried to think about other things. Each time his thoughts started in the direction he aimed them—such as the last time he'd been fishing, or the first time he rode a bicycle—the haunted house carousel would quickly swirl back into view, full of mangled bodies. "I knew right then it was going to be something you just lived with for the rest of your life," Marvin Dees said in an interview for this book.

Felix McKnight's local tipster returned late Friday afternoon, this time with a solemn look on his face. "Big news," he whispered in McKnight's ear. "Superintendent Shaw has killed himself."

McKnight drew back. "Are you sure about this?"

The man nodded and shrugged his shoulders at the same time.

"Is that a yes or a no?"

It comes from a normally reliable source, the man said.

McKnight grabbed Bill Rives by the shoulder and whispered in his ear. "There's a rumor Chesley Shaw has committed suicide. Leave the newsroom as casually as possible and go check it out."

In a moment, Rives pulled a sheet out of the typewriter he was using, laid it face down on the desk, and strolled out of the office. McKnight said good-bye to his source and turned back to his typewriter

Not five minutes had passed when his phone rang. It was Fred Dye in Dallas, wanting to know, "What in the hell is going on down there?!"

"Excuse me?" McKnight said.

Dye told him there was a bulletin on a competing wire service saying Superintendent Shaw has committed suicide. "How'd we get beat on this?" Dye demanded.

"It's unconfirmed. I've got Rives over there right now checking it out."

"Well, since it's out there, we've got to say something."

McKnight thought about it for a moment. "How about this: The superintendent of a school that exploded, killing hundreds of students, has committed suicide, according to an unconfirmed report."

"Not bad, but don't use suicide."

"We are reporting on their report, right?"

"It works for me. File it," Dye said.

McKnight filed the short bulletin about Shaw's supposed death.

It wouldn't surprise me a bit, given what the man has been through, McKnight thought. Now rumors were spreading that some of the rougher elements in the community were trying to stir up a lynch mob—with Chesley Shaw as its primary target.

About ten minutes later Rives appeared, smiling. "Not true," he told McKnight.

"Are you sure?"

"I just spoke with the man. He's at home, sitting in his living room."

McKnight killed the bulletin about Shaw.

Sarah McClendon was walking out of the disaster site, her legs coated with mud up to the knees, when she saw a truck driver sitting in the cab of his truck, going nowhere. His arms were draped around the steering wheel, and his face was down against his arms. She tapped him on the shoulder. "What's the matter?"

The driver looked up, his face smeared with grime. "Nothing, lady. I've just been sick for the last two nights."

McClendon quickly found a ride to Tyler, went straight to the news-room, and began an afternoon story for the *Courier-Times*. She noted that some officials suggested a mass burial might be needed to lower the risk of an epidemic from the large number of unburied bodies. Parents from all over crushed the idea immediately, saying they would have no part of a mass burial. They all wanted their children to receive the traditional cer-emonies for the dead, even if the funerals were abbreviated and hurried. The children, they argued, should have at least a semblance of dignity be-fore they went to eternal rest.

McClendon reported that coffin factories were working overtime to meet the needs of the East Texas catastrophe. Embalmer supplies were running low, and some bodies already were beginning to decay, she wrote.

"David Frame, general superintendent of the Humble [Oil] Company at Houston, directed relief efforts from that camp," McClendon reported. "Three men at the Humble Headquarters office sat with one grief-stricken family of company employees after another dealing out company money to defray funeral expenses."

McClendon said most undertaking establishments reported funeral ar-rangements still pending.[8]

The *Tyler Courier-Times* carried a short piece that afternoon stat-ing that Superintendent Chesley Shaw speculated it was "quite possible" natural gas from the oil field on which the school was built had somehow seeped into the basement and caused the explosion.

The architect who designed the school, T. Roy Ainsworth of Houston, told the Associated Press that no ordinary blast could have destroyed the school that his firm designed in 1931. The structure—254 feet long and 146 feet wide—was framed with steel, using hollow tile for walls within the building and a brick exterior with stone trim. Roof trusses were steel, covered with concrete slab and then roofing tile.

"The entire structure was fireproof," Ainsworth said.

It was designed to be steam-heated from a properly ventilated central boiler that burned oil, he added.[9]

*Houston Post* reporter John Mortimer finagled a typewriter in the Overton Western Union office and sat down to write his piece for Saturday.

"The aftermath of the New London catastrophe came Friday—an after-math of stark pathetic silence when the hour came to count the score," Mortimer wrote. The reporter had detected "something in the faces of those men which was not good to see.

"Cold staring eyes—something had gone out of them," he wrote. "There was an absence of tears. But not of suffering."

As he went about trying to interview those who had worked in the res-cue and recovery operation, including some who had lost children, Mor-timer confronted "a belligerent, repelling silence. They did not want to talk about it. The early frenzy had passed. They had begun to realize the extent of the tragedy, and they wanted to share their grief alone."

He asked about a relief program set up to help with hospital and funeral expenses. "We don't want money. We just want to be left alone," a rescue worker told him.[10]

Bill Rives wandered over to the Overton city hall, which had become a clear-ing house for information about the victims. He overheard a woman speak-ing to a clerk. "Bobby was wearing a brown shirt, corduroy pants, and brown shoes," she said. "He was such a little boy. Weighed about a hundred ten pounds."

People were using every phone in the building. Rives didn't intrude, but he got close enough to hear bits of their conversations, and he jotted notes as he listened.

"We have found Mary, mother," a woman said. "No, I don't think she suffered much. Her face had a sort of smile on it."

Near her, on another phone, a man said, "Can you come tomorrow, Tom? They haven't found the boy yet."

Rives headed back to the Western Union office to feed McKnight some of the material to use in the wire service's next dispatch.

McKnight, picking up on every poignant detail he could locate, even those close at hand, added this line to the story he was about to send: "Kin and friends of the dead packed the telegram office to send messages as scores of newsmen beat a steady clatter on a battery of typewriters."[11]

Henry McLemore was on a roll. He'd crafted another brilliant opening and solid story that could run Saturday or Sunday. Or the editors could switch his earlier story to a Sunday piece, since it was so pent up with emotion, and run this story for tomorrow. McLemore didn't care when they ran them; he just wanted to keep writing as quickly as the material presented itself. He had started his latest piece with one of the most powerful lines of any of the thousands of stories that were filed during a week of intense news coverage.

"London, Rusk Co. Texas, March 19—The richest little school district in the world became the poorest."

The opening was a balled fist, packed with bitter irony, designed to smack a reader on the chin. As the reader sits back and decides he's got to know what this means, McLemore explains, "This tiny place sprawls over almost the exact center of what men have called the richest strip of earth in all the world. Beneath it, bubbling and gurgling, crawls a river of black gold that is oil.

"Twenty-five thousand derricks, each a marker for a well, lift their gaunt ends in and about it. Twenty-five thousand sand flares, each a guarantee that the well over which it sheds a crimson light is flowing, burn day and night.

"But Friday night the derricks stood out as symbols of fabulous wealth" converted to "markers for the dead," and the flares "were funeral torches for the hundreds of children who died in the schoolhouse catastrophe which has no equal in the United States.

"Oil town folk are hard folk. Literary realists have portrayed them many and many a time as the hardest of folk. They're big and tough, and they live the same way. Oil towns are notorious for their hell-for-leather, rip-roaring times; for their anything-goes-anytime spirit.

"And Friday night is always a gala night in an oil town. Because Friday night is payday and tomorrow is Saturday, when all the joints are open—wide open.

"You should have been in this oil town Friday night. The only places where there were crowds were the telegraph companies ('Try and be there by twelve stop Bobby will be buried in early afternoon'), the funeral homes ('No, it ain't her. My God!'), and the hospitals ('Be as quiet as you can, please').

"The crowds that stand dumbly around these places in London have duplicates in thirteen other East Texas towns."

McLemore spoke with every survivor he could locate. "There was Evelyn Hudkins, 16, pretty. She crawled through a twisted tangle of girders and dragged behind her the torn body" of a boy.

"He was my sweetheart," she said. "I've gone around with him ever since I can remember, and I couldn't leave him there . . . though I knew he was dead."

McLemore met a man who identified himself as an Englishman. "I went through four years of the war, and this is the first time I ever saw anything that was worse," the Englishman told the reporter.

"For one-quarter of a block there was nothing but ruin. It was as if a tremendous cathedral had been struck dead by a bomb," McLemore wrote.

"Four tractors fastened their cables to the entire side of a wall that had fallen in, sealing a classroom. The ten-ton slab was yanked aside, and three little bodies removed. A blackboard, miraculously intact, still had arithmetic inscriptions chalked on the board.

"Mothers and fathers superintended the crow-barring of the children's lockers. It was almost more than one could bear as they were handed sweaters, baseball gloves, tennis racquets, and books. Some of the lockers were half a block away from the building—half buried in the muddy red clay.

"I talked to a mother and father whose little girl, having forgotten her coat when she left school early, returned and was halfway up to the wall leading to the main entrance when the building went straight up in the air. Somehow, nothing struck her.

"I talked to the school plumber who, two minutes before the blast, missed a needed tool and walked outside to his truck to fetch it.

"I talked to parents who, earlier in the day, had whipped their children for playing hooky. They cried with joy as they told me of the punishment they had meted out.

"But there were more than 400 I didn't talk to. And that's why the richest school district in the world is the poorest."[12]

Carolyn Jones went with her mother and stepfather to the funeral home in Henderson to make arrangements for Helen's and Paul's bodies to be shipped to Oklahoma. "I was told to wait in the car," Carolyn recalled.

By that time, night had fallen.

"The day before a carnival set up its rides on a vacant lot near the Court House square in Henderson, and I could hear the tinny music of the merry-go-round calliope," Carolyn said. "Growing tired of waiting, I climbed out and walked to the door of a nearby sheet iron shed or garage. Standing in the open door, I saw on makeshift tables row upon row of bundles wrapped in bloody sheets. I hurried back to the car."

As she waited, the calliope music danced up over the dark trees and evaporated into the black sky.[13]

# Part III. **Aftermath, March 20–29**

# 26
## Coffin Train

Ted Hudson was still on the radio, more than thirty-six hours after he first took the mic and started talking. He asked for volunteers to go to the railroad depot in Overton to help unload coffins arriving from Dallas.

Even if Hudson had an opportunity to sleep, he would have had a hard time shutting his eyes and letting himself sink toward unconsciousness. Too many images were swirling in his head. Like many of those who worked for long hours in the rescue and recovery mission, he didn't feel as though he ever wanted to sleep or eat again.

Felix McKnight had now gone more than forty-eight hours without sleep. He had barely moved from his typewriter all night, listening intently to all the chitchat buzzing across the Western Union office, just in case he caught something he'd missed. He hadn't missed much.

But he and the other reporters had reported a couple of things wrong. The early death toll estimates were too high. That happens in disasters. Numbers are high at first, when everybody is in a panic and people are having a hard time locating their loved ones. The actual death toll was somewhere between 300 and, perhaps, 350. The goof about Shaw's alleged suicide was bad—terrible, considering everything the man had been through yesterday. Wire service reporters had put up a brief that a grieving mother died of a heart attack after locating the body of her daughter in a morgue. The story was lifted from a local newspaper and regurgitated without anyone double-checking the facts. It was wrong. Mother and daughter were alive and doing okay. McKnight put a correction on the wire to kill the earlier brief.[1]

McKnight called home and spoke briefly with his wife. Baby Joan was doing fine, Lib said. She asked him to please take care of himself and try to get some rest.

"Rest, sure," McKnight promised, but in his mind it seemed as though time had entered some new demarcation when the school exploded—before and after the school disaster. He doubted that he would ever look at life the same way again.

Bill Thompson was so restless he could scream. All night and all day people had stopped at his bed, asking him questions about the explosion. "Did you sleep well last night?" a nurse asked.

"I wasn't here last night," Bill said—meaning the night before last, since he hadn't really slept any in the past twenty-four hours. The past two days seemed as though they made one day.

A reporter listening in on the nurse and her patient wrote a story for the next day that indicated Bill was not even aware he was in the hospital. That was wrong. He knew where he was; he'd just lost track of time. Events surrounding the explosion were beginning to seem fuzzy, almost unreal.

A nurse drifted into the room to check his bandages and take his temperature. His brother, Laverne, was sitting in a nearby chair, asleep.

The bed in which Arliss Middleton had died now contained another badly hurt child.

Henry McLemore obtained a copy of a list somebody had made of all the funerals taking place that day. It was fascinating to read—though heartbreaking at the same time—so many services in so few churches, all happening Saturday afternoon. Many more were being scheduled for Sunday. Some of the children were being buried in the new clothes their parents had bought for them to wear to church on Easter—the following Sunday. McLemore underlined some details he wanted to include in his next piece.

The railroad depot was a center of action Saturday morning because many of the transient oil-field families were shipping bodies home for burial. Also, a shipment of new coffins was expected to arrive by freight train. McLemore was beginning to realize that he could use a railroad motif or theme in his article—that might work.

He made some notes—funerals taking place on back-to-back schedules sounds like a train schedule of arrivals and departures. He jotted down a line on notebook paper:

"When the hearses and trucks moved slowly away the crowd outside the church didn't disperse. Children of other friends were to have funerals this afternoon. Like train schedules, the services were scheduled for 2 p.m., 3 p.m., 4:30 p.m., and 7 p.m."

That paragraph works exquisitely, McLemore decided. Now he needed an opening line that would be unlike the many others written today; most reporters were blobbing the whole story, or at least half of it, into the opening paragraph, choking the readers with words. McLemore wanted something simple, sharp, and aimed straight for the heart of every person who picked up the newspaper and scanned the stories. He thought about it deeply for a moment, with his eyes closed. And then he wrote a line on a scrap of notepaper:

"This grief-torn community today began the sad job of burying its dead."[2]

That's it. It says just enough, punches the story home whether you read the second paragraph or not. He was about ready to write but decided to go out and stroll around Overton for a while. He was an artist of sorts and hoped to spy a new color in the spectrum.

At an intersection along Commerce Street in Tyler, a traffic cop saw an ancient pickup truck with a crude, hand-lettered sign on the hood that read, "Funereal." A rough pine box, tied with rope, protruded from the bed. A man and a woman, both looking weary, sat inside. The policeman turned his car in behind the sooty black truck and drew alongside the driver's door.

"Where to?" the cop asked the driver, whose face was creased with wrinkles, the stub of a cigarette hanging from his lips.

"West Texas," the roughneck said.

"Was it . . . the explosion?"

"Yep."

"And . . ."

"I'm taking her home."

The cop tipped his hat.[3]

The Smoot family was planning a double funeral for Helen and Anna. Their four older brothers, all roughnecks, had worked in the rescue operation from immediately after the explosion on Thursday until the last shovel of debris was cleared Friday afternoon. The two oldest—Greg and Wayne—went from morgue to morgue until they had identified the bodies of both their sisters.

Scores of the girls' friends, including many of the students who had made Helen and Anna the presidents of their respective classes, streamed up the steps to the Smoot home's front door all day Saturday and knocked, quietly, respectfully, for permission to come inside and visit with the family.

Mr. Smoot had ordered an oblong granite headstone that was being inscribed with the girls' names and a poignant epitaph: "Side by side in the sunshine, side by side in the rain."[4]

Carolyn Jones journeyed with her mother and stepfather to Ardmore, Oklahoma, to attend the funeral and burial of her sister Helen and her Uncle Paul. When her father, Walter Jones, arrived, he confronted his former wife, angrily blaming Eula for Helen's death because Eula had wanted to get the divorce and take the children with her. Eula, stunned, said he was being absurd to make such a wrongheaded and hurtful accusation.

"Helen was there because you decided to put her in that school," he said, bitterly.

"We would all have starved to death if it had been up to you," she fired back.

The Old London Baptist Church was packed with mourners—well more than the two hundred people the sanctuary was designed to seat. The room was stuffy and a little too warm, even though the windows were open and five-bladed fans droned above the funeral congregation. Henry McLemore stood near the back, behind all the rows of pews that led to the altar, and had just made a note that the five coffins at this funeral were each no more than five feet long.

"The caskets rest on cane back chairs, in front of the brightly varnished pulpit," he wrote. "Probably fifth-graders."

Sunlight streamed through the windows, brightening the flowers amassed atop the caskets. As McLemore heard mention of the families whose children were being eulogized, he noted the family names—Hasbrook, Willis, Lambert, Ragsdale, and Stearns. Between eulogies, the sanctuary rang with bedrock Protestant hymns, including "Rock of Ages." Those who knew the song by heart let their voices lift it to the rafters. Others hummed the melody behind the words:

Rock of Ages, cleft for me,
Let me hid myself in Thee;
Let the water and the blood,
From Thy wounded side which flowed,
Be of sin the double cure,
Save from wrath and make me pure.

Five ministers spoke during the hour-long service. An American Legion commander then took the podium, requesting that only immediate family members accompany the deceased to graveside services at the Pleasant Hill Cemetery, about four miles away.

"The roads are choked with funerals today," he said. "The highway patrol has asked that friends do not attend. So, please, the families only."

McLemore watched as most of the crowd receded against the walls while men and boys carried the coffins, one by one, out the church door, down the steps, and out to the curb. Two were placed in a pair of hearses. The other three were put on mattresses in the backs of delivery trucks that had been washed and polished for the occasion. "Each truck carried a bouquet on the partition behind the drivers' seats," the reporter noted. "There were not enough hearses to serve this town today."

The crowd outside the church didn't disperse after the hearses and trucks departed for the graveyard. Another round of funerals was slated to begin shortly at this church and other nearby churches across New London. Many more were scheduled for the next day.[5]

Laborers at a coffin factory in Dallas had been working around the clock since shortly after the explosion because in all of Texas there were too few child-size coffins to meet the need caused by the catastrophe. This was not a gross oversight on the part of the undertaking business. Funeral homes and casket makers generally based the number of coffins they kept ready for use on a historical pattern of demand. Each year adults typically died in larger numbers than children and teenagers. The New London school explosion threw the traditional supply-and-demand formula off kilter.

Many of the caskets needed to bury children killed in the explosion were paid for by the oil companies the children's fathers worked for. Private donors and the Red Cross also helped out. Some of the grieving parents, though, considered this sort of help a form of charity, and they refused to accept pricey caskets for no charge. Some would accept only the crude pine coffins that volunteers such as Graften Ferguson constructed in the explosion's immediate aftermath.

Dressed in his best clothes, Joe Davidson stood at the ticket window in the Overton railroad station and bought five tickets to Brazoria—two roundtrip and three one way.[6] The roundtrip tickets were for Mary and him. The other three were for the coffins bearing the remains of Helen, Anna, and Wheeler.

It's not known why Joe and Mary decided to bury their children at a cemetery in Brazoria, down around Houston. Possibly, it was because the children were born there and had developed their first sense of home in that region near the Gulf of Mexico. Joe and Mary were taking them home. Or, it might have been because Brazoria County reminded Joe Davidson of his childhood home in southern Louisiana. He had spent a lot of time in boats on the Gulf and on the open seas and already was thinking of joining the merchant marines when his time in the oil fields played out. Or, perhaps Joe and Mary wanted to put some space between themselves and the horribly scarred earth where the New London school had stood. Catching a train was a sure way to do that.

Before they left, Joe and Mary checked on Marilla, their only remaining child, at Mother Frances Hospital in Tyler. The doctors felt Marilla had survived the crisis period of her injuries and eventually would recover—

though it would take months of hospital care and a lengthy rehabilitation even after she returned home. According to her prognosis, she would more than likely walk with a limp for the rest of her life.

Comparing your own misfortune with something worse that happened to others was a phony consolation, Joe Davidson thought. Even so, it seemed a blessing that Marilla was alive at a moment when some New London parents had no children left and that she was expected to some day walk again, even with a slight limp, considering that Elbert Box, a New London student in a hospital room near Marilla's, was going to have a leg amputated.

Joe settled back and watched the Texas scenery roll by as the train headed south toward the coast. Mary didn't seem to see any of it.

# 27
## Reckoning

Governor Allred declared martial law shortly after news of the explosion reached Austin. He ordered National Guard troops and aid workers to the site and instructed his commander, Maj. Gaston Howard, to form a military court of inquiry. Less than forty-eight hours after the blast, the court—six military officers, State Senator Joe Hill, and a pioneering chemical engineer, Dr. Eugene Paul Schoch—convened in a small, wood-paneled building a few steps from the ruined school, in a room full of the weary, the angry, and the reporters.

Following is an excerpt of Capt. Zachariah Ellis Coombes's examination of Daniel Kolb Morgan during the military court of inquiry in New London, Texas:

Q:  Mr. Morgan, when did you first come on this location after the accident occurred, the explosion?
A:  To the best of my knowledge it was around 5:30 in the evening.
Q:  You are one of the men who helped remove the debris and search the ruins?
A:  Yes, sir.
Q:  You are an employee of the Gulf Oil Company?
A:  Yes, sir.
Q:  You were present when the part of the building that was blown completely apart, when they were using some acetylene torches for cutting material?

A:  Yes, sir.

Q:  Will you tell the court what peculiar circumstances you noticed at that time?[1]

*Mangled claws of bent steel arched from the concrete and terra-cotta remains. Morgan picked his way toward the nearest crew carefully, on thick boots and shaky knees. The sun, an hour from slipping beyond the yawning sky, lit girders wrapped around great shards of cement. The men, some weeping, pulled with futile, bone-bending effort. Others, staring blindly down, scrabbled at the pile and left their skin on the rocks. The twisted steel hugged the mess to itself. Morgan pulled, and pulled, and stopped.*

*"We need a torch."*

*"A torch! Get a torch up here!"*

*A man gripping the long metal nozzle in one of his gloved hands arrived. Two tubes slung over his shoulder led back to tanks of oxygen and acetylene. Morgan and the others stood back as the scared man's eyes passed over the jumble, looking for a safe place to cut. He moved sideways, straddling a row of exposed steel reinforcements, and planted each foot on an angled concrete slab. He spun one wheel on the nozzle and acetylene hissed through his fist. He spun another and oxygen breathed behind it. A squeeze of the igniter. A spark. A flame, wielded.*

*The blue tip of the inner cone of flame, burning hotter than six thousand degrees Fahrenheit, touched the first steel rod. A fountain of orange sparks arced away from the torch man. White-hot oxygen and carbon curled around the steel, cutting a metal valley and falling into the crevice below in a stream of slag. The men caught their breath and listened for a scream. One by one, the supports parted for the fire until the concrete slab tilted, scraped, shifted, and tumbled away from the crew. The torch man pulled back, and Morgan descended into the gap.*

*Below were leaves of paper spread around a thin spine of cracked earth, six or seven feet long. Morgan saw blue flames leaping out of it, setting fire to the fluttering paper. He began kicking dirt over the vein of fuel the torch had ignited in the ground. Morgan knew at once what fed the vein. No one had shut off the gas.*

The court convened on the morning of March 20, 1937. Dr. Eugene Schoch, sixty-two, tall, with a swimmer's lean build, sat beside Major Howard at a plain wooden table. He held the first civil engineering degree ever granted by the University of Texas and founded the school's Bureau of Industrial Chemistry.[2]

Rumors had circulated that the explosion had been caused by dynamite, which had been stored in the school's basement and used to clear rocks from the athletic fields. Schoch knew before the hearing began—knew just by walking past the wreckage—that the rumors were wrong. No school would have this much dynamite.

J. L. Downing had drafted the plans for this ruined marvel, and he was the court's first witness. The young Downing's architectural firm was based in Henderson, ten miles away. Downing dated his plan for the main building July 1, 1932, and wrote on them "London Independent School District of Rusk County, Texas." The main building would rest on a foundation of poured concrete and would look from above like an E with the points facing east. To the west was Main Street. The wings looked as though they were one-story tall from the road, but a gentle downward slope beginning close behind the longest wall added another story below and out of sight from the street.

Downing designed the building to have a central boiler. A radiator salesman named A. J. Belew convinced the school board to alter Downing's plan and install Gasteam radiators in every classroom. He told the board the building would need no costly redesigns; his radiators, he said, did not need vents to the outside.

Belew took the stand, and Schoch watched him slip through questions from the court's lead inquisitor, Captain Coombes. After twenty minutes of evasions and half answers, the only thing made clear to the court was that Belew had a slightly better grasp of gas composition and English than Coombes. Schoch could abide no more. Belew could dance around these other men, but not him. Whatever Belew might have read about the powder kegs he sold, Schoch or one of his students likely had something to do with crafting the text. Science is lucid and binary—yes or no, on or off, right or wrong. Nature's ambiguity is a human construct. The pull of science's certainty drew Schoch from his family's farm in Floresville, southeast of San Antonio, forty years before. His guiding premise was that an answer existed, regardless of its visibility. Science needs no salesmen. Belew's pitch was over.

Schoch leveled his head and glared through the black, circular rims of his glasses at the polished man. "Mr. Belew," he said. Generations of students would have shrunk at his tone. "I take it that you are what we would term a gas engineer, are you not?"

"I don't know that I would qualify."

"Don't know that you would qualify on that?"

"No."

"Let's be definite about this now." Schoch straightened and leaned toward the table. "What is the extent of your training? Will you tell us what your training is?"

"Well, like I said, some fourteen years selling experience."

Belew said he had no college degree but had studied on his own.

"You can calculate drafts," Schoch said. "And you understand the necessity for drafts. And you can analyze gases—"

"No," Belew cut in. "I haven't said I could analyze gases."

He'd said twice he wasn't an engineer, but this was not enough to quell Schoch's welling anger—not enough to quell the anger of anyone who'd seen the bodies just beyond the door. Schoch wanted to embarrass the salesman, to strip his credibility, to wound him. To witness the ruin was to be bound to this tragedy and its people, to their grief and exhaustion. Adrenaline had spent itself days before. Something darker had been seeping upward to take its place: a lust for the blood of someone who wasn't innocent.

The people of New London would not get it. The court found that Belew had done nothing wrong, and Schoch offered something of an apology the next day. It found no grounds for criminal charges against anyone—not the salesman who convinced the school board to change its design, the board that acquiesced, the state that required no inspectors and no oversight of any plans, despite what this building would house. According to the court's findings, the man-made tragedy had taken one of every four children from the town of New London, but no law had been broken.

The proceedings would claim a victim, however.

William Chesley Shaw testified during the court's second and final day of hearings. He had lost a son and a career in the explosion. Many parents blamed him for the catastrophe. Talk of a lynching continued. Captain Coombes spoke, instead, of a pipeline.

"Mr. Shaw, were you the man that gave the orders for the connection with the Parade Oil Company, or the Parade Gasoline Company pipeline?" Coombes asked.

"I was partly responsible, yes, sir."

"Were you the one who directed the janitor to make that connection?"

"Yes, sir."

The Parade Gasoline Company operated a refining plant in Rusk County. Oil from the rigs flowed into the plant for processing and was shipped to customers throughout the country. The refining process created waste gas that the company sent back to the rigs through a network of pipes segmenting Rusk County. With a lower methane content and higher concentration of butane, ethane, and heavy hydrocarbons, the gas could not be sold, and so the company included wording in the lease agreements that put the burden of disposal on the rig owners. Neither the company nor the roughnecks had any use for the gas. Most owners released it into the air through tall pipes, then set fire to it as it escaped, creating burning pillars that lit the East Texas night. The practice of tapping into waste gas lines was something of an open secret in the oil patch. Homeowners would weld valves onto the disposal lines and connect them to their gas-fired heaters through pipe they laid themselves. Municipal gas companies regulated the pressure of the gas they piped through town, keeping it to around two pounds per square inch. Waste gas, pouring from the refinery in bursts, could rush through pipes with twenty times as much pressure. Those who tapped into the lines had to attach their own regulators to their homes or risk having the heavier gas burst through the small nozzles inside their heaters, sink to the floor, collect, and wait for a spark. The gas had no odor and so gave no warning. With no one monitoring it, it came with no bill.

Somewhere in a Parade Gasoline Company office, tucked inside a desk drawer or filing cabinet, was the company's policy paper stating its opposition to unauthorized taps into its waste gas lines. Responsibility for enforcing the policy fell to the plant's superintendent, Earl Clover, who also oversaw the immensely complex and profitable operations for which the company existed—the acquisition and refining of crude in the busiest oil field in the world.

Four members of the school's seven-member board of directors—A. D. Blackwell, Judson Wyche, J. R. Kerns, and the board's president, E. W. Reagan—gave Shaw approval to tap into the Parade line in early 1937. The safety of burning waste gas did not come up. The men did not tell anyone and did not discuss it again but for a conversation between Shaw and Clover.

"You didn't want to get out and advertise the fact, and so you didn't mention it in your minutes?" Coombes asked Shaw, who shifted uncomfortably in his chair.

"No, sir," he said, wishing to God the photographers would stop taking his picture.

"It was one of those affairs then, I take it, that this gas was just going into the air, the officials of the Parade company had indicated that [Clover]—so far as he was concerned—he didn't care?"

"Far as them using the gas, they didn't care."

"But he didn't want the company compromised by giving you permission to use it. He had instructions, perhaps, not to give it away?"

"I should think, from the way he talked. That was my interpretation."

"Do you know whether Mr. Clover has returned from the funeral of his child?"

The crew had gone out in early January—a janitor, two bus drivers, and a welder the school had contracted to tap into the waste gas line about two hundred feet from the school. They dug a trench, welded a two-inch iron pipe to Parade's four-inch main, and buried the pipe. A. J. Belew came out to inspect the connection to the school. He told the men that the two regulators they'd installed between the Parade line and the school wouldn't be enough to hold back the pressure. He told them to add one more, and they did. Not long after, teachers and students began complaining of headaches.

No one returned to the Parade line tap until shortly after Daniel Morgan found blue flames flickering from the seven-foot crack in the earth beneath the rubble of the school. Thousands of people were crawling over the wreckage, lit by a setting sun. A man Morgan spoke to alerted United Gas Company, New London's natural gas utility. The company told the man they hadn't provided gas to the school since January. Word eventually reached the Parade refinery, and field foreman Delbert Leon Clark, that the company's waste gas was flowing beneath the ruin.

Clark had to act alone; his boss, Earl Clover, was among the swarm, looking for his two children and finding one. Clark sent out a line maintenance man to find the tap. After an hour or so, the man returned with nothing. Clark went out himself. Walking along his company's main line where it passed in front of the school, he saw a patch of overturned earth that, in the winter chill, had not grown over. Though he dug frantically through the hard dirt, long minutes passed before he could find the shutoff valve. They had attached it two feet from the main, welded it sideways rather than upright, then buried it.

The school used Parade's waste gas for one month before the explosion. The school district saved $250.84.

A flashbulb snapped. The questions seemed to come faster; Shaw's responses more haltingly. The tap. The regulators. The headaches. He sweated and twitched. Another flashbulb snapped.

"I don't know what they want to keep taking these pictures here for."

"Cut out the flashes until we get through with Mr. Shaw," ordered Gaston Howard.

But it was over. Coombes saw Shaw teetering on the edge of a nervous breakdown. Coombes looked to Howard, and Howard said, "Mr. Shaw, if you are not feeling all right, we can recess for a short while until you feel better." Two men helped him from his chair. He did not return.

"The superintendent appeared to have aged a dozen years since the worst American school disaster," wrote Tom Reynolds of United Press. "He was a man shattered, his legs wobbled and his hands trembled violently."[3]

Felix McKnight watched Shaw leave the room. The superintendent walked slowly with the assistance of a friend. "His face was the living definition of grief," McKnight recalled in an interview for this book.

Two long days of testimony—wrenching accounts by rescuers of shattered children, tempers flaring over company men protecting themselves, quiet answers from children with dried blood on their scalps—drew to a close. Few witnesses remained before Dr. Schoch rendered his judgment, that gas filled the basement and an electrical spark ignited it.

Steven Hawley, the chief engineer of the Texas Fire Insurance Department, took his seat before the court, and the first whisper of redemption came to New London. As the previous day's testimony cast light on the common practice of tapping into waste gas lines, Hawley had left the crowded makeshift courtroom and found a phone. He ordered his engineers to go to every oil-field schoolhouse in East Texas to test the air inside. Now he looked at the uniformed men, the senator, and his state's preeminent chemical engineer, and told them an inspector named Newsome, two hours ago and six miles away, found in the basement of the Carlyle School 720 cubic feet of natural gas. He told them of his search of state records and of how many schools used similar heating systems. He told them something must be done.

"You heard testimony before you this morning regarding the arcing of a switch. All right, if this installation had been made explosive-proof, there would not have been any arcing of that switch. That is not hearsay. That is a statement of fact. What else is indicated is [the need for] a state building code, a state electrical law, a state exit code, a state boiler safety code, and all other general safety measures giving to governmental agencies the right, power and authority to make them behave without fear of God or anyone else. Now, I don't want to be heroic about this thing, but I realize it is a matter of concern to many people. If that condition which was found within six miles of this place is typical, why, I think it is time to get busy. I don't believe I have anything else to say."

A local superintendent spoke up from the audience. "I would like to know what he means by the arcing of a switch."

"Well, in opening a switch, if you will notice—"

A photographer's flashbulb snapped.

"—there will be a flash. Just like that."

Coombes looked at the spent flashbulb and back at his witness.

"Thank you very much, Mr. Hawley."

The Texas Inspection Bureau conducted a separate investigation immediately following the disaster. The bureau, an investigative body representing fire underwriters, issued a report nine days after the explosion. Like the military court of inquiry, the organization laid no specific blame on school officials.

"No one individual was personally responsible," concluded H. Oram Smith, the bureau manager and an expert on the safety of gas and its dangers. "It was the collective faults of average individuals, ignorant or indifferent to the need of precautionary measures, where they cannot, in their lack of knowledge, visualize a danger or hazard."[4]

The school board that had stood behind Chesley Shaw in the hours and days following the disaster reversed itself and asked for his resignation. Several members said, privately, it was in Shaw's best interest to remove himself and his family from the spotlight, considering rumors of violence festering throughout the community.

Shaw resigned. He later wrote this letter for publication in the local newspapers:

> I do not bear any resentment against those who demanded my removal. It must be remembered that they were under an intense emotional strain, and regardless of the findings of the court of inquiry, they felt someone must be held accountable. Because of my position, I was the target.
>
> New London is and shall always remain my home. My people and my wife's people were reared in the community. Our ties of friendship date back to childhood. We could not be content anywhere else.[5]

With visible rage and threats of violence spreading across the community, the Texas Rangers and Highway Patrol sent armed guards to stay with Shaw and other school officials who felt they might need protection.

Nine-year-old Priscilla Kerns, who performed in the Mexican hat dance in the gym before the explosion, learned that some angry men with guns had congregated in front of her home and called out her father, J. R. Kerns, a member of the school board. He walked out into the yard, without a coat, and rolled his sleeves up to show bare arms. "I have no gun on me. I have no gun in the house," Kerns said. "I've never kept guns in the house. I will be glad to speak with you men, but it will be without guns."

A short while later, a pair of Texas Rangers arrived at the house, riding horses. It was mainly a precautionary measure, officials said, to keep the situation from escalating. Oil-field workers had a reputation for settling disputes with their knuckles. Even before the roughnecks arrived, Henderson and Rusk County had experienced lynch-mob violence.

Priscilla was excited to see the big horses. She watched them ride around the house, again and again, until it became too dark to see them anymore.

# 28

# Lament

She lay nameless and alone in a makeshift morgue in Overton. All the rest—those who had filled this morgue and all the others—had been claimed.

Thousands had shuffled past her, most of them peering at the child's disfigured face, seeking recognition and praying they wouldn't find it. Jessie and Luna Emberling looked not at her face but at the girl's feet. The night before the explosion, their ten-year-old daughter, Wanda, had had a party with her friends and pretended to be a grown-up, like the girls in high school. The girls had taken crayons, for lack of nail polish, and colored their toenails. Wanda chose red. This child's nails were the pale blue of the cold skin beneath, and one toe had a scar unfamiliar to the Emberlings. The lost parents moved on, through the hospitals, morgues, and funeral homes of East Texas.[1]

Three days after the explosion, someone finally suggested the child might be Dale May York, a ten-year-old, like Wanda. Dale May had missed several days of school because of an illness but had returned the day of the explosion.

"Impossible," said another. "Dale May has already been buried."

Word reached the Yorks, and although they had suffered through their daughter's funeral, they returned. They saw the scar, where Dale May had clipped her toe with a garden hoe, and it was almost too much to bear.

They exhumed the body they had buried. Jessie and Luna Emberling came, for there was nowhere else to go. They stood together and saw auburn grains of dirt, a miniature casket stained by the earth, and, inside, delicate toenails colored red. Luna Emberling, exhausted from three sleepless days and nights, was carried to and from the cemetery on a stretcher. Mr. and Mrs. York faced the heartbreak of a second funeral for Dale May.

"Please, Lord, don't let me faint," Mrs. York murmured, repeating the prayer again and again as her daughter's burial repeated.

Jessie and Luna placed their daughter in a grave with her own name in Pleasant Hill Cemetery. Later that day, their son, George, died from injuries he suffered in the explosion.[2]

Felix McKnight awoke on Sunday morning on a cot in an attic room above the Western Union office in Overton. Sunshine streaming through a small window startled him. McKnight's heart raced as he jumped up and started pulling on his clothes. The AP reporter had slept for just a couple of hours, but he was afraid that he might have missed some major part of the story.

In reality, he had nothing to worry about because the Associated Press now had enough reporters in New London to cover every aspect of the story while McKnight and Bill Rives took a much-overdue breather. In the wee hours of Sunday morning, McKnight had become nearly incoherent after three days and nights without sleep. Finally, he surrendered his typewriter to a fresh replacement and headed upstairs to rest. He had fallen asleep only after taking two long pulls from a half pint of Blue Roses whisky that somebody had gotten from an Overton pharmacy.

McKnight made plans to go out to Pleasant Hill Cemetery, where nonstop funerals were taking place all Sunday.

UP reporter Walter Cronkite also finally took a rest. His boss told him fellow UP staffer Henry McLemore had rented a room with twin beds at a small hotel in Overton. Cronkite could go there for a few hours. Also, McLemore had brought extra shirts. After he slept for a while, Cronkite could shave and put on a fresh shirt in McLemore's room.

Cronkite went to the room and tiptoed in so he wouldn't disturb McLemore, who was sound asleep in one of the beds. Early Sunday, Cronkite awoke refreshed. McLemore was already gone. Cronkite shaved, showered, and borrowed a clean shirt from McLemore's belongings. When he arrived at the newsroom in the Western Union office, Cronkite learned there had been a mix-up about the location of McLemore's room.

"I hadn't been in the UP room," Cronkite recalled many years later. "I had shared the room of the manager of the area's semipro baseball team. I never met him. I still don't know who he thought it was sleeping in his other bed that night, or if he missed the shirt."[3]

Felix McKnight freshened up and drove toward Pleasant Hill Cemetery. Leaving Overton, he noticed most of the businesses had the shades down on their front doors and crepe fluttering from the doorknobs. An officer stopped traffic to let men carrying coffins cross the street.[4] As McKnight drove through communities in the New London school district, he saw dozens of houses with bouquets of flowers tied with lavender ribbons affixed to the front doors. He followed a slowly moving funeral cortege toward the cemetery. McKnight parked near an old country church and hiked to the top of a rise overlooking Pleasant Hill Cemetery, a spot where he could observe graveside services without encroaching on the privacy of grief-stricken families saying good-bye to loved ones.

Dozens of open graves darkened the grassy turf across the graveyard. Men were shoveling dirt into some of them as pallbearers carried coffins toward others. Clusters of men, women, and children dressed in church clothes followed each. A quartet singing hymns moved from grave to grave. The words and melody of "Just a Closer Walk with Thee" drifted through the tall pines skirting the graveyard.

McKnight felt overwhelmed with sadness. He'd spent nights in rubble and days in cemeteries seeking the line between proximity and respect. Bottled-up emotions swam to the surface. He thought about his own daughter, Joan, at home with Lib—the blessings in his life—and life itself, which he suddenly treasured more than ever before.

A tale long-repeated by the Shaw family maintains that Walter Cronkite strode up to a car Chesley Shaw and his wife were sitting in and unabashedly asked whether he could ride with the family en route to graveside services for Sambo Shaw. Chesley Shaw said no, according to the legend.[5]

No information exists to suggest the story is anything but legend, possibly an embellishment that came about after Cronkite became world-famous as a CBS News anchorman. On the other hand, Cronkite, in his memoir, *A Reporter's Life,* wrote about Chesley Shaw as though he and the superintendent developed a rapport during the disaster's aftermath. It's not inconceivable that an aggressive reporter like Cronkite possibly asked to join the family on such a heartrending occasion, to better tell their story and honor the memory of Sambo Clifton Shaw. Questions, even when they seem insensitive or disrespectful, are a good reporter's best tool. Cronkite was a very good reporter. Unquestionably, Cronkite, like Felix McKnight, was deeply affected by the sorrow that engulfed an entire East Texas community in the early spring of 1937.

"You've got a job to do so you've got to keep thinking about that rather than thinking about the horror," Cronkite said in a 1987 television news interview. "The horror comes later. Driving back to Dallas I was overcome with grief. I had to drive off the road for a minute. It suddenly hit me."[6]

Felix McKnight returned from the cemetery to his desk in the Western Union office and worked into the evening, crafting the lead AP story for the morning newspapers.

Late that night, the door opened and five men came into the makeshift newsroom. One was holding the front page of a Shreveport newspaper, which had a headline that read, "East Texas Roughnecks Bury Their Kids Today." The man waved the newspaper in front of McKnight and demanded, "We want to see this guy—McLemore."

It was obvious they were upset about something Henry McLemore had written.

"You know where he is?" the man asked.

"Nah. I don't know where he is," McKnight said, although he knew McLemore was sleeping upstairs on an Army cot.

"Well, he works for you and you ought to know where he is," the man said.

"I work for the Associated Press and he works for the United Press."

"It's a damn lie. You know where he is and we want him."

Another reporter spoke up, telling the men there was no connection between McKnight and McLemore.

The group of angry men began a search of the building. They located the wooden steps going to the attic, and two of them stomped up the stairs. A moment later, they returned, pushing Henry McLemore in front of them. The men led the famed United Press writer outside, put him into a car, and drove away into the night.

McKnight learned the next morning the men had taken McLemore to the county line, put him out of the car, and told him never to return to New London. Although they worked for competing wire services, McKnight and McLemore had become friends after sitting side by side at various sports events they'd both covered. McLemore called McKnight early on Monday and said that he was okay, although he was obviously a bit rattled by the experience. He needed McKnight to contact the United Press staff to let them know he had hitchhiked to Tyler and needed somebody to send him over some clothes. All he had was the outfit he was wearing when the men roused him from his nap.

McLemore didn't say where he was going from there, whether he would chance returning to New London or look for a story somewhere else. The blue-eyed swashbuckler of a reporter was a good improviser. On an assignment once in Durham, North Carolina, McLemore found his style cramped when he discovered he couldn't buy a cocktail in the dry community. He left the hotel, roamed around for a while, and returned shortly with enough moonshine whiskey to last him the week.[7]

Such skill might have served him well on that day because Tyler was a citadel of prohibition sentiment and the dry gulch of the Bible belt.

# 29
# Amazing Grace

Schoolchildren in Cherbourg, France, conducted a drive to help children and parents stricken by the explosion in New London, Texas. They collected $8.74—among the first of many donations and expressions of sorrow from around the world.[1]

"Nothing makes us more sadly sensitive to the feelings of international solidarity than cruel catastrophes which suddenly plunge an entire country into mourning," said Jean Zay, the French minister of national education, in a message to Texas parents who lost their children.[2] "Every mother and father of French children mourn with the Texas parents in America," he added.

Elementary school children in Japan sent a sympathy telegram. A Girl Scout troop from a town in Kansas collected coins to send to New London. A five-year-old girl from Galveston sent the pennies she'd been saving for a new doll. The New London tragedy galvanized the attention and grief of people across the boundary lines of states, nations, and continents from America to Europe and Asia in a way that had not happened before the age of global radio and telegraphic communications.

On the Thursday after the disaster, one week after the explosion, a half-million students and teachers in Chicago stood, faced southwest, and participated in a one-minute silent observance for the lost students and teachers of New London.[3] The principal of a small rural school in North Dakota asked students there to pray for victims of the Texas disaster.[4] But nothing was more indicative of the human spirit reaching out to help those in crisis than the story of C. H. Crawford of Joinerville, Texas. He worked in the rescue mission in New London wearing a pair of borrowed overalls and canvas shoes, all the clothes he could muster because his home and all his belongings had been destroyed in a fire the day before.[5]

"It seemed as though the entire world was touched in but a few minutes," wrote the Reverend Robert L. Jackson, the New London Methodist minister who spoke at the school on the morning before it exploded and worked that afternoon in the rescue operation. "Every phase of our civilization sprang into action. The whole world listened with a sympathetic ear."[6]

The donations helped establish a fund to memorialize the children and teachers who perished. Within days, organizers laid out a plan for a monument at the site: a cenotaph, or empty tomb, to be carved from 120 tons of Texas granite and soaring to a height of thirty-four feet. At the crown of the impressive twin columns, the sculptor coaxed from rock a vivid circle of buoyant children and their teachers reaching out for one another. At its base, the names of most of the victims were inscribed on beveled tablets of granite.

Ministers tried their best to explain, in a wide-ranging variety of sermons, meditations, and funeral messages, how the concept of a loving, personal God can be reconciled with the devastation of a disaster that claimed mostly innocent children.

"We can't understand but we shouldn't question God's ways," proclaimed the Reverend W. T. Bratton, pastor of the New London Baptist Church. "Only last week these boys and girls were happy in their work and play in the community. We miss them but we must bless God that He gave them to us and remember his promise in the Fourteenth Chapter of St. John: 'Let not your hearts be troubled for I have gone to prepare a place for you.'"[7]

Many preachers, like Robert Jackson, gave uplifting sermons about Christian beliefs in life after death.

"Why?" asked the Reverend A. D. Sparkman, pastor of the Old London Baptist Church. "The fault is not God's. It is man's error."[8]

Many East Texans were deeply traumatized, oil-field historians Clark and Halbouty concluded. "These people felt that the lives of the innocent had been claimed in payment of spiritual debts piled high during the most sinful and reckless period of the boom. . . . God had slaughtered lambs."[9]

The idea of such a vengeful Creator—crushing to death little children to make a point—frightened some people and was dismissed as absurd by others.

John Lumpkin was one of the few people in East Texas rich enough to afford the luxury of a movie camera. He bought it for recreational use and to preserve family memories. He used it to film his son's funeral.[10]

During the service, Lumpkin dropped to his knees and asked God to help him through the loss of his boy, John Jr. The elder Lumpkin hadn't given much thought to religion before the explosion, but he found that praying soothed his spirit. He promised God that he would devote the rest of his life to helping the less fortunate. He bought a bus and began driving it around the community on Sunday mornings to pick up children who wanted to attend Sunday school, taking them to the church of their choice.[11]

The Reverend James Shera Montgomery, chaplain of the U.S. House of Representatives, reached for a place beyond the spirit, into the soothing calm of mystic light, when he opened a congressional session with this prayer the morning after the explosion: "O speak, mighty life, and let in the morning of hope and peace. Thou blessed Christ, whose love for little children was so divine that it would not let them go, take and keep them in the white light of the Father's Throne. Their shadow was love, their language was music, and their steps were a benediction."[12]

Carolyn Jones was picked for an immensely important task. In the wake of the disaster, the Texas legislature met to debate school safety issues, and East Texas lawmakers wanted a New London student who survived the explosion to speak before the House of Representatives. Nine-year-old Carolyn was chosen. Her father and his sister, Gladys Uhl, drove Carolyn to the state capitol in Austin. Carolyn and her Aunt Gladys wrote the speech after they arrived.

"Mr. President, members of the House of Representatives, and friends of schoolchildren, I'm here today as a representative of the London school and as a survivor of the school explosion that took the lives of nearly five hundred pupils, teachers, and parents," the speech began.

At the time, the death count being reported was still too high. School officials had concluded the actual number was probably closer to three hundred.

"Last Thursday afternoon, while my colleague and I were studying spelling for the interscholastic meet in which we were going to represent our school the next day," Carolyn continued, "our teacher Mrs. Sory saw some pictures fall from the wall and several vases crash from the desk.

"In an instant she had jerked open two nearby windows and said, 'Get out of here.' We were clinging to her when we heard the first awful rumble that in a few seconds caused the room to collapse."[13]

The passage of time would never erase that terrifying moment from Carolyn's mind.

Elbert Box lost a leg when the school came crashing down. It was still attached to his body, but it was useless now. The doctors had already said that if the infection didn't clear up soon, they would have to amputate.

First they cut off part of it, but that didn't help. So they told Elbert and his parents the rest of it had to go. Otherwise, the boy was going to die.

Getting your leg chopped off at eighteen is a rotten way to start your manhood, Elbert thought. The nurse patted his hand. It will be okay, her eyes told him. Elbert wasn't the kind of person to mope or complain, so he gave her a brave smile. Seeing her face each day, this lovely young woman in her nurse's cap and cape, gave him a sense of hope that offset the pain in his body and the emotional turmoil roiling in his mind because the school had exploded, nearly costing him his life and exacting one leg as the price for his survival.

Elbert soon felt he was falling in love with Louise McAdam. She was one of five professional nurses assigned to the daily medical care of seriously injured New London students who would be long-term patients at Mother Frances Hospital. Louise, as it turned out, was also falling in love with Elbert. An assistant nurse, one of the nuns at the hospital, noticed the giddy smiles and soft touches Elbert and Louise exchanged. The astute sister played cupid.

It's not known whether Elbert Box proposed marriage to Louise McAdam before or after his leg was amputated. What is known is her answer:

yes. The explosion cost him dearly, but he gained a loving companion for the rest of his life.[14]

Carolyn Jones had to stand on a chair to speak from the podium in the House of Representatives. The little girl thanked the Texas lawmakers and Governor Allred for the relief the government provided upon learning of the disaster. She asked the legislature to consider setting March 18 aside each year as a day for remembering those who died in the catastrophe.

"Let me urge you, our lawmaking body," Carolyn said, "to make laws of safety so it will not be possible for another explosion of this type to occur in the history of Texas schools.

"Our daddies and mothers, as well as the teachers, want to know that when we leave our homes in the morning and go to school, that we will come out safely when our lessons are over."

Wearing a cotton dress with a blue print and puffed sleeves, the child spoke with composure, only occasionally glancing at her notes, newspapers reported.[15]

"Out of this explosion," Carolyn said, "we have learned of a new hazard that hovers about some of our school buildings. If this hazard can be forever blotted out of existence, then we will not have completely lost our loved ones in vain. All of us who were spared will try to show our appreciation by striving to become the finest of citizens to carry on the work of this wonderful land of yours and mine.

"This is our plea. Thank you."[16]

The chamber thundered with applause.

Within a short time of Carolyn's remarks, Texas lawmakers passed the toughest law in the nation governing safety standards in schools and other public buildings. They also passed a law requiring an odor to be added to odorless natural gas used in homes and buildings so that dangerous leaks could be detected quickly. Soon similar laws were enacted in all states in the nation and in nations around the world.

The rotten egg smell added to natural gas today—an odor that has saved countless lives over seven decades—is a direct result of the Texas school explosion on March 18, 1937, and the deaths of more than three hundred students, teachers, and others.

As Carolyn Jones traveled with her father back to East Texas on a sunny day just one week after the explosion, the catastrophe was still too fresh in everyone's mind to think that any good could come of it. Many of the survivors, including those who escaped serious injury, bore deep psychological wounds. In those days, there were no grief counselors to meet with students, teachers, parents, and rescue workers struggling to come to terms, emotionally, with the shock of living through such an experience. Post-traumatic stress disorder was not yet a condition recognized by mental-health experts, although the condition was tentatively recognized during World War I under the broad category of shell shock. Ministers and fellow church members did their best to console and counsel those in grief and despair.

Some of the mothers who were at the PTA meeting the afternoon of the explosion noticed, within days, that their hair was turning prematurely gray, wrote Lorine Zylks Bright. "I know that many mothers suffered nervous breakdowns, and some fathers, too," she added. Bright told of one woman who, after losing her only child in the disaster, became reclusive and essentially starved herself to death.[17]

On the third day following the explosion, F. M. Herron and his wife sat next to the hospital bed where their daughter Inez lay bandaged and unconscious. Inez, twelve, had been transported to Mother Frances Hospital by ambulance soon after she was found alive in the ruins. Surgeons immediately operated to remove a piece of her skull that was cracked in such a way they felt it endangered the child's survival. Then they could only wait to see whether the girl would come back from the unconscious state she'd been in since her classroom disintegrated around her.

Although hundreds of parents and others streamed in and out of Inez's room to take a glimpse of her, nobody could identify the girl on Friday and most of Saturday. Mr. Herron had located the body of his oldest child, Juanita, fourteen, soon after the explosion, and he found his son, F. M. Herron Jr., ten, unharmed. But the whereabouts of Inez remained unknown for agonizing hours and days. On an erroneous tip, the father first visited a hospital and funeral homes in Shreveport. Then he followed another rumor that she was in either Longview or Marshall, but she was in neither place.

On Saturday, F. M. Jr. caught a ride to Tyler and found his sister at Mother Frances Hospital. Now her parents and brother waited beside her, praying that she would wake and be okay. Sunday dragged into Monday. Early Monday morning, Inez's eyes opened.

"Inez, don't you know me?" her mother said.

The girl nodded and then turned her heavy-lidded eyes toward her father.

"Daddy," she whispered.[18]

# 30

# Survivors Assembly, March 29

A cluster of children stood near the narrow country road, waiting for a bus that would take them to school for the first time since the explosion. Several wore bandages on their heads, and all were bundled in sweaters and coats. The sunny spring weather that had blessed East Texas recently had given way to raw winter again—it was a blustery, cold, and damp Monday morning beneath a gray overcast. Lower clouds scudded against the sky like streaks of chalk.

The students were instructed to report to the wooden gym behind the empty patch where the high school used to stand and find their homeroom teachers. If their teachers were deceased, they gathered with surviving classmates from their homerooms and sat as a group. The first day back was scheduled to last just an hour or two—time enough for the principal to call roll and determine who would be returning to school and who would not, and to help authorities firm up the death toll. Classes were supposed to resume Tuesday in the gym, the home economics cottage, and a building formerly used for band practice. During the rescue and recovery operation, the band room had served as a makeshift first-aid station and, later, a temporary morgue. Several small buildings were being moved to the campus to function as classrooms until school was over in May. Plans already were in the works to construct a new high school in time for the start of the fall semester. It would be even bigger and more modern than the structure that exploded; the district would spare no expense to make it one of the safest schools ever built. The school board had approved the project just six days after the disaster. It was designed with a similar look—beige bricks for the outer walls and red tile on the roof, with a large auditorium in the center—and would occupy the same site as the previous school.

Senior High School Principal Troy Duran gazed across the gym and estimated the attendance. Fewer than half the students enrolled in the combined junior-senior high school had showed up, Duran calculated. Missing were the dead, the wounded, the children of families who'd fled New London, and those whose parents simply would not allow them to return to this broken place. When Duran started calling the roll alphabetically, some students answered "here" or "present." For others, teachers and classmates answered. Names of children killed in the blast quickly popped up: Boyd Abercrombie, fifteen; Evelyn Bonnie Adams, twelve; Almita Allman, twelve; Allene Anderson, twelve; and her sister, Lillian Anderson, fourteen.

"Betty Ruth Apple," Duran said.

"She was killed," somebody answered.

"Wayne Scott Arnold."

"He is dead," a tense, quiet voice said.[1]

"Arden Barber."

Dead.

"Ollie Barber."

Dead.

Bus driver Lonnie Barber, Arden's father and Ollie's uncle, stood in the back of the gym listening intently to the roll call. He knew many of the children, and his heart sank each time he recognized one of the dead. This was a never-ending tragedy—fresh tears glistened in Barber's eyes and on faces throughout the crowd—eleven days after the explosion.

"Murvin Barton."

Dead.

Barton, seventeen, was a starting guard for the London Wildcats and described as quick and tough by his football teammates. The football and basketball teams, the track and field squad, the high school band—all were decimated. The 120-piece band had been scheduled to leave for a concert in Jacksonville when classes ended on the day of the explosion.[2]

Some band members were spared because they already had gone to the band room behind the high school. Shortly before the explosion, Charles Dial realized he'd forgotten to bring his band uniform to school, so he got permission to leave class and run home to retrieve it. The band was also preparing for a big thirty-band festival at Kilgore the weekend of March 27–28. Instead, the festival was dedicated to the London Wildcats marching band.[3]

Football players who were killed included the Gerdes brothers, Alvin and Allen; Forrest Coker; Joe Gordon; Paul Greer; and Arliss Middleton. Starting end Elmer Rainwater survived but lost three siblings—Aubra, fifteen; Evelyn, thirteen; and Helen, eleven. Evelyn Rainwater was the girl who survived the explosion but died after jumping from a second-floor window and crashing into a lower window. Ray Smoot, a tackler on the football team in a previous season, was not in the explosion, but he lost two sisters—Helen and Anna, presidents of their respective classes.

Ardyth Davidson, a member of the girls' champion softball team, was killed. One of her teammates, Marilla Davidson (no relation) survived, although she was seriously injured and lost three siblings—Joe Wheeler, Helen, and Anna. Marilla and at least two dozen other students were still recovering in hospitals. On April 18, the one-month anniversary of the explosion, twenty-one students remained hospitalized.[4] Marilla Davidson wouldn't be released from Mother Frances until June.

Nearly everybody involved with the school lost somebody—a brother, sister, teacher, homeroom classmate, teammate, boyfriend, girlfriend, son, or daughter. The children of school board members died. The janitors who helped make the school sparkle and kept its machinery operating smoothly lost sons and daughters.

Boys' basketball lost its star power: Sambo Shaw, Alvin Gerdes, and Forrest Coker. Girls' basketball lost Helen Smoot and Melba Lee Hughes, girls who controlled the ball with snappy passes back and forth until the other team grew frustrated and fouled one of them. Helen and Melba tossed their free throws through the basket with a sassy switch.

The drama club lost Irma Hodges, Philo Stephens, Annie Marie Milstead, and Miss Katie Mae Watson, the club's sponsor and one of fourteen teachers who died. Philo had become a good stage manager, and Irma Hodges was quite talented as a makeup artist.

When Duran reached last names starting with "D," Ledell Dorsey listened carefully for her name to be called. She didn't want to miss it and have anyone think that she had been killed. Ledell was at school that morning only so she could tell her friends and classmates that she'd survived. Returning to the site of the explosion filled her with dark dread. After the assembly was over, she planned to beg her father not to force her to return to the school ever again.[5] Being in the place where all those others, including two of her sisters, had perished was just too hard.

"Alice Dorsey," Duran said.

"She was killed."

"Ethel Dorsey."

"She is dead."

Bill Thompson, sitting with several of his homeroom classmates, looked up when he heard someone say Ethel had been killed. Bill was stunned. He didn't know Ethel was among the dead. The boy suddenly felt in his heart that he had caused her death because Ethel had switched seats with him and she was in Bill's place when she was killed. He imagined everybody in the gym must be looking at him, blaming him, although, in reality, no one but Bill knew this secret. This fear, this shame, would not leave him until he became a limping, creased man, sixty years later.

Others at school that day and throughout the community were sorting out emotions associated with the disaster that would affect the rest of their lives. Some, like Bill Thompson, felt guilty because they had survived while others perished. Geneva Elrod, recovering at Mother Frances from multiple bone fractures and internal injuries, was also suffering from the heartbreak of losing two siblings she cherished—a brother, Edwin, and sister, Juanita. Edwin, the youngest, had wanted to play hooky the day of the explosion, but Juanita and Geneva ordered him to school. Geneva felt guilty about that for a long time.[6]

Sixth-grader James Kennedy gazed around the gym and suddenly realized how hard the blast had hit the sixth-grade class. Four classrooms of sixth-grade students had dwindled to just one because eighty-seven sixth graders had been killed, thirty-three boys and fifty-four girls.[7] The fifth grade, which lost sixty-seven students, was the second hardest hit.

The first night after he survived an explosion that instantly killed classmates all around him, Kennedy was so upset that he slept with his mom and dad, even though he was thirteen. "You have dreams about it," he said.[8]

Other students in the gym that morning were experiencing nightmares of their own when they tried to sleep. Seventh-grader William Follis, thirteen, had witnessed unthinkable sights. As he struggled to free himself from the debris, the boy saw a girl who was nearly cut in half, still conscious, and aware that her clothes had been stripped from her body. She was desperately trying to cover her breasts. He tried to save another girl who was choking on dirt the blast had forced into her mouth and throat. Their eyes made contact before she died.

"It still haunts me to this day," Follis said more than seventy years later in an interview for this book.

The assembly ended after about an hour, and the students filed outside and onto waiting buses. Snow began to fall, silently covering the giant scar left on the earth where the high school once stood.

# Part IV. **Epilogue**

# 31

# Reunion

A cluster of white-haired men and women, several on walkers and in wheelchairs, gaze at a monument with twin fluted columns towering thirty-four feet above Memorial Drive in New London, Texas. They are surviving members of a student body and schoolhouse at the center of a massive explosion on March 18, 1937.

A dwindling number of survivors gather for reunions every two years at the site of the disaster that killed more than three hundred students, teachers, and others. Most spend some time in front of the monument, quietly scrolling through names inscribed across pink granite along the base of the cenotaph. Each survivor has a distinct and harrowing recollection of that day, but their collective memory conveys an overlapping constancy of sorrow. They are bound by a grief that never quite healed, many will tell you.

"You just couldn't believe your eyes," says one old man, leaning on his cane. "I climbed out from under the bricks and boards, and ran around here—to a spot right yonder—and the school was just gone."

Most are willing to spill their souls about it, even to a stranger, though with pain still in their voices and tears in their eyes after nearly seventy-five years. In the weeks, months, and years following the tragedy, however, parents, teachers, and students—the entire community—were silent about what had happened. The nation moved on, its attention attracted by the Hindenburg's explosion in Lakehurst, New Jersey, less than two months after the New London disaster; a continuing depression; and a growing threat of war in Europe. Because talking about the tragedy was taboo among New Londoners the memory slipped from American consciousness, and the affected families sought relief through their silence. Shunning any reminders of the catastrophe, some parents refused to have their children's names inscribed on the monument.

An event in New London recognizing the first anniversary of the disaster focused on the future, not the past, wrote Robert M. Hayes of the *Dallas Morning News* in a March 1938 story. After a brief service, the community returned to its "never-ending struggle to blot out the terrifying picture of the world's worst school tragedy."[1]

For decades, curious outsiders were unable to lift the veil of mourning that shrouded the town. "It was such a terrible, terrible thing that nobody could talk about it," said survivor Priscilla Kerns Joffee, whose father was a member of the school board when the school exploded.

A *Houston Chronicle* reporter ventured to New London in March 1956 for a story that appeared on the nineteenth anniversary. "They don't talk about that day of doom in 1937 anymore," wrote Pete Gilpin. "'We'd prefer to forget,' the townspeople agree and back it up with a marked reticence to any inquiry."[2]

John Davidson was a student at the high school in New London when the 1956 story appeared. He was born May 12, 1940. His parents lost their only child, Ardyth, in the explosion, and John was conceived to take her place. It was a tall order. Ardyth was fourteen when she died, a pretty girl with exuberant spirits, a good student, a softball standout, a budding dancer, and the radiant center of her parents' universe. But John grew up knowing little about her.

"I knew her name, but they were very reluctant to talk about her," he recalled.

Like many of his classmates, John Davidson walked past the cenotaph each day on the way into school, scarcely aware that the monument was anything more than an architectural adornment. That changed one afternoon when he made an unsettling discovery in a storeroom behind his home. The curious teenager pried the lid open on a dusty old wooden box and was startled to find the clothes Ardyth wore the day she was killed.

Her diary was tucked between her coat and partially burned dress. The box had been nailed shut at the funeral home.

"I knew what it was the moment I saw it," John said. "I closed it up as soon as I saw the death clothes."

He was embarrassed to have meddled with a precious object his parents had chosen to leave undisturbed. But opening the container finally gave John Davidson a true link with a sister he would hold dear for the rest of his days.

The New London story resurfaced abruptly in 1961, when a former student claimed he rigged a death trap that caused the explosion. After being arrested in Oklahoma City on a $38 robbery charge, William Estel Benson blurted a shocking "confession" to Oklahoma authorities. Benson wrote a statement saying that as a seventeen-year-old student, he had deliberately loosened pipe connections under the school, letting gas escape and accumulate in the basement. The act was revenge for punishment he had received for smoking in the schoolyard, he said.[3]

"It is a cruel turn in a story that has been buried in silence these 24 years," wrote Felix McKnight, who by then had become executive editor of the *Dallas Times Herald*.[4]

"I stole two 18-inch wrenches to take loose the unions which connected the gas line under the school," Benson said.[5] "I broke both loose and waited for two weeks to see what would happen."

A guilty conscience made him confess, he told the United Press International.

"I haven't been able to live with myself until last night. Last night was the first time I have slept in 24 years," Benson said. "Just check it out and you will find I am not lying."[6]

A lie detector test Benson took in Oklahoma City showed inconclusive results, but a second test administered in Dallas indicated his confession was a fake. Benson was transferred to a jail in Henderson, Texas, while Texas authorities investigated his claim. His mother, Helen Curlee, described her son as a "mental patient" obsessed for many years with the catastrophe that killed his fourteen-year-old sister, Betty Lou. William Benson had spent time in several mental health facilities for treatment of alcoholism.

"His mind is bad and he doesn't know anything else because he has thought about this explosion so long," Helen Curlee told the *Tyler Courier-Times*.[7]

Thirty-six hours after his arrest, Benson retracted the confession, saying he'd made it up to get attention, and he apologized for lies that reopened so great a wound. William Ferguson, the local district attorney, said the second lie detector test and a thick file of previous false confessions convinced him that Benson's tale about sabotaging the school was fabricated. The only charges brought against him were for burglarizing two coin-operated laundries when he lived in Rusk County—part of Benson's confession the lie detector test showed was true.[8]

The furor prompted by the confession abated soon afterward, and memories of the worst school disaster in history drifted back into silence.

A group of survivors, including some who had not seen each other in forty years, finally held a reunion in New London in March 1977. They exchanged hugs and handshakes, prayed together, shared stories of their experiences that day, listened to gospel singers, and paid homage to those who had perished in the explosion.

H. G. White, then fifty-two, had last seen the teacher who helped him out of the rubble, Ann Wright, when he was a twelve-year-old fifth grader. "Do you remember falling into the hole where I was?" he asked her at the reunion.

"I certainly do."

"I didn't know what had happened. I was trapped. I remember somebody screaming real loud," White said.

"That was me," she said.

"I was such a kid I thought you were an old lady."

"I was twenty-two and in my first year as a teacher," Wright recalled with a smile.

Many survivors who had kept their painful memories bottled up for decades experienced catharsis by talking about what had happened to them. The gathering was such a success that the group decided to reunite every two years. At later reunions, especially those marking the fiftieth, sixtieth, and seventieth anniversaries, news reporters showed up in increasing numbers, looking for fresh angles in a story that had shocked the world when it happened but that had been largely forgotten in the years since the explosion. The former students and teachers swapped stories about how life had turned out for themselves and others involved in a disaster that had deeply affected their lives.

L. A. "Tiger" Mathis and his brother, Donald, both joined the Marines in World War II. L. A., the rescue worker in the peach-basket brigade, and Donald, who was in the explosion but survived, landed at Normandy in the same wave of troops. Donald was shot dead. L. A. lived to be an old man.

Ted Hudson was recognized as a folk hero for his ingenuity and quick thinking to establish a radio broadcast from the disaster site that helped direct emergency personnel and enabled the nation to listen in as the tragedy unfolded. When his story was featured in the national *Kiwanis* magazine, Hudson said he deserved no special recognition; he was merely doing what needed to be done.[9] In November 1946 Ted Hudson, then forty-one, was killed in the crash of a small airplane he was piloting.

Elbert Box received his high school diploma in the hospital, during his long recovery from a leg amputation and various other injuries. He adapted quickly to life with an artificial leg. Soon after being discharged from Mother Frances Hospital, Box married his nurse, Louise McAdam, whom he called "Tweetie Pie," and went to work for the Texas Company, later Texaco, which paid for his college education. He retired from Texaco in 1976, after nearly forty years on the job, and died ten years later. His "Tweetie Pie" lived until 2006.[10]

Lonnie Barber, the farmer and school bus driver who saw the school explode with his four children inside, continued to farm and work for the school district. Always a shy man, he received unsolicited publicity on the tenth anniversary of the explosion when Robert Hayes of the *Dallas Morning News* described Barber as "typical of the unsung heroes" of the disaster.

At the wheel of a bus loaded with grade school children, Barber "felt that his first duty was to the frantic parents of the children in his charge," Hayes wrote. "He saw that they were all safely home before returning to check on the safety of his own. He found that three had escaped, but the youngest, Arden, had been killed."[11]

Lonnie Barber kept his thoughts to himself about it all. His father never talked much about the explosion, then or later, L. V. Barber said.

James Kennedy, the boy who was so terrified after living through the explosion that he slept with his parents that night, overcame his fears, became a U.S. Marine, and later attended Stephen F. Austin University on the GI Bill. He spent his entire career as a teacher and school administrator, retiring in 1985 after seventeen years as principal of an elementary school in Kilgore, Texas.

Jimmie Jordan, the little girl saved and protected by her older sister, Elsie, in the aftermath of the explosion, had Elsie watching over her for the next sixty-one years, until Elsie died in 1998. "She was always protective of her little sister," Jimmie Jordan Robinson said in a 2010 interview for this book.

Bobby Clayton, the boy who survived because he sat near the back of his classroom and a bank of lockers shielded him from being crushed, had another near-miss with death in 1970. On a road trip with his wife, Arlene, Bob was critically injured in a head-on collision. He typically spurned wearing a seat belt but had one on that day because of Arlene's insistence. He recovered after a twenty-eight-day stint in the hospital. The physician told Clayton he survived only through the grace of God, his will to live, and the seat belt. In his eighties, while living near Pittsburgh, Pennsylvania, he overheard a discussion on an early morning radio talk show of a book being written about the New London school explosion. He could hardly believe his ears. He later agreed to being interviewed on KDKA radio in Pittsburgh to share his memories of that tragic day.

Bobbie Kate Myers, the sister of Perry Lee Cox, said her father's "heart never mended" from whipping her brother and taking him to school that morning. "It so grieved my dad that in 1939 my parents separated and divorced," she said in a 2002 interview with the *Overton Press*.[12] Her mother remarried but her father didn't.

"They became the dearest and sweetest friends," Myers said. "Their desire was to be put next to my brother at Pleasant Hill. So that's what I did."

Marilla Davidson—Joe and Mary Davidson's only surviving child—married John Dial, the boy who witnessed Lemmie Butler flip the switch that set off the explosion.

Mary Davidson never recovered emotionally from losing her other children, according to those who knew her well. Joe Davidson reenlisted in the navy when World War II erupted. He retired from the navy as a lieutenant commander and returned to work in the oil fields.

"Neither one of them got over their three children being killed," said Charles Dial, Marilla Davidson's brother-in-law. "I really don't think any of the parents of children killed in the school explosion, including my dad and mother, ever got over it." Charles Dial's younger brother, Travis, died in the blast.

Dial's father had had blood in his eyes in the aftermath of the disaster, which he blamed on human error and poor judgment. "My dad was very, very upset, and he was going to hurt somebody," Dial said. "Me and a couple of guys he worked with got together and talked him out of it, but he was very mad."

After Chesley Shaw was forced to resign as superintendent, he took a job teaching at the school in Minden where he'd previously been the headmaster for more than twenty years. Shaw needed to teach two more years to qualify for a state pension, and the Minden job, where his boss was one of his former students, enabled him to do that.[13] Some of the bereaved parents filed lawsuits against the former superintendent and the school district, alleging school officials were to blame for the deaths of their children. A circuit court judge, however, ruled that Shaw and the school board were not at fault because lax laws regarding the use of natural gas allowed conditions that caused the explosion. Chesley Shaw slowly descended into dementia; he relived the disaster again and again for the rest of his life.

Ronnie Gaudet, Shaw's nephew, said time seemed to stand still for his uncle, fixed on March 18, 1937. Decades later, Chesley Shaw talked about the explosion—as though it had just happened—every time he sat down for coffee at a café in New London. One day in 1967, while Gaudet was a student at the high school in New London, he saw Shaw wandering through a hall.

"I said, 'Uncle Chesley, are you lost or something?' and he said, 'Nah, I'm just up here at the school.' I said, 'Well, doesn't anybody know you are up here?' and he said, 'Nah.' He was mumbling, a little bit incoherent," Gaudet recalled. "I went down and told our superintendent the situation and he told me to go on to class and he would take care of it."

Chesley and Leila Shaw were buried at Pleasant Hill Cemetery near their son, Sambo, and more than a hundred others who died in the explosion.

Fannie Rayford Shaw, Leila's sister who had married Chesley's brother, died a similar death to the child she lost in the explosion, Dorothy Oleta. On an early January day in 1942, nearly five years after the school disaster, Fannie accompanied her son Wylie and his wife to a house that the young couple was getting ready to occupy. After the trio entered, Wylie struck a match, and the house instantly exploded. Somehow, natural gas had accumulated inside while the house sat empty. Wylie and his wife were burned on their hands and faces; Fannie Shaw was burned over much of her body. An ambulance rushed her to Mother Francis Hospital, but her injuries were too serious for her to survive. She died on January 6, 1942. Reverend A. D. Sparkman, who preached at dozens of funerals after the school explosion, officiated at Fannie's services in New London. She was buried beside her daughter at Pleasant Hill.

Carroll and Mildred Evans retired after long careers as public school teachers and fulfilled many of the dreams they shared as lovesick newlyweds at the start of the Great Depression. Carroll continued to be fondly known as Boxhead to his many friends and former students until his death in 1991 at eighty-three. Mildred passed away when she was ninety-one in 2004.

For nearly sixty years, Bill Thompson kept as his own secret the identity of the girl who traded seats with him. The burden of guilt he felt seemed unbearable at times because he believed in his heart he was responsible for his friend's death. He lives on a New London side street, just around a corner from the memorial. "Every time I walked up to that monument and saw Ethel's name there, I thought it should be mine."

Finally, after speaking with members of Ethel Dorsey's family and receiving warm assurances that they in no way held him responsible, Thompson stood at the sixtieth anniversary reunion and talked about it, publicly stating Ethel's name and breaking into tears. His misplaced guilt finally lifted.

Walter Cronkite, late in life, still considered the New London explosion the most tragic peacetime story in his long and storied career as a journalist.

After his stint with the AP, Felix McKnight became managing editor at the *Dallas Morning News*, executive editor and copublisher at the *Dallas Times Herald*, and president of the American Society of Newspaper Editors. Colleagues called him the "dean of Texas journalism." McKnight returned to New London on several anniversaries of the disaster to write news columns based on his memories.

"Fifty years ago today—the day the whole world cried—a tiny East Texas community lost a generation in a boiling flash of fire that lasted only a few seconds," McKnight wrote in his *Dallas Times Herald* column for March 18, 1987. "The world's richest independent school district suddenly and violently became the poorest with the pull of a switch in a basement manual training classroom." He'd written nearly identical lines in one of his first dispatches from the disaster site.[14]

"There have been few days in those 50 years that I have not thought of the children of New London," McKnight said.

Henry McLemore received the prestigious National Headliner Award for his coverage of the New London disaster. When he died in June 1968 at sixty-one, the once-famous sportswriter was remembered in his obituaries not only for his sports coverage, but for the heartrending stories he wrote in New London, Texas, over four hectic days in March 1937.[15]

Sarah McClendon established her own news bureau in Washington, D.C., and covered the White House during the administrations of eight presidents. "This was a story I will never forget," she said in a March 1987 news interview about her coverage of the school explosion.

"I think of it every year at this time. It was equal to war," McClendon said.[16]

At the 2005 reunion of survivors of the New London school explosion, Carolyn Jones Frei stood in a museum of artifacts from the disaster and read the same words she'd spoken to the Texas legislature in 1937, when she was a little girl who needed a chair to reach the podium. At the reenactment, Carolyn stood next to an early model of the mechanism used to inject the foul smell into odorless natural gas—now a museum piece. The device, invented by a man who witnessed the explosion's aftermath, represents one of the sweeping reforms that came about, in part, because of nine-year-old Carolyn Jones's urgent plea for safer schools and as a direct result of the New London catastrophe.

At the reunion in 2009, an elected representative spoke on the subject. "The explosion was no one's fault," he said. Afterward, while photos were being snapped, he asked Carolyn, "You do agree with me, don't you?"

"I was too shocked to answer," she said later in an interview for this book. "Of course, no one meant for anyone to die. But they were carried away by their appetite for wealth, their pleasure in the oil money that was accumulating. That's what happens when people lose sight of what is important," she said. "And in retrospect, did anyone ever ask what happened to all that money?"

The bitter lessons of the explosion—human mistakes, oversights, and imprudence that created a massive, hair-triggered bomb ready to detonate beneath hundreds of innocent children—lost their urgency over time. Few people alive today have any clue about why gas from their ovens and furnaces smells so noxious when the pilot light goes out. Most have never heard of the New London, Texas, school explosion.

Carolyn Frei downplays any personal credit, saying reforms enacted by the Texas legislature would have passed in the wake of the catastrophe regardless of her plea. Even so, her testament must have had a profound impact on the lawmakers and given calls for reform unstoppable momentum.

She went on to chart a life for herself as a teacher, wife, and mother. She had three children with her first husband, Bert Morris, who died in an accident. Her daughter, Helen McKenzie, works as an academic at the University of Idaho. Twin sons, Richard and Ronald, are a tax attorney and family physician, respectively. She has nine grandchildren.

Early in her career, after receiving a college degree in elementary education, Carolyn taught fifth grade and elementary reading. She later received a master of teaching degree, and for eighteen years she taught high school students language arts—English literature, grammar, journalism, and speech. She loved coaching debate. She credits her mother with instilling in her a love for education.

Carolyn never developed a close relationship with her father, Walter Jones, although he came in and out of her life at various times over the years. She loved him, but . . . and she never really finished that sentence. She was a dutiful daughter and took care of her father as he lay dying.

She and her second husband, Ray Frei, live in Lewiston, Idaho, where Carolyn enjoys doing volunteer work, reading, and writing poetry. She has written several poems in recent years that have dealt with the school explosion. One recaptures the terror she felt:

Cold Morning
(March 18, 1937)


The night of the disaster, no one slept.
Sirens ripped darkness with doom.
Dogs howled in Greek chorus.
After the bodies were found,
we tried sleep, staring at the dark
ceiling, transfixed by scenes
we could never escape or soon describe.
Fatigue broke our grip on consciousness;
we slipped into a dark pool, floated
face down below the surface, until
water merged with gray dawn.

Rising, we forced leaden feet to the terrible task:
caskets, the unctuous minister, the exhausted
emergency worker. In a garage next
to the mortuary, makeshift tables held
the remnants of lives, shrouded in bloody sheets.

Rituals were forgone. No neighbors stood
in doorways bearing plates of cake.
Those not bereaved avoided our eyes,
terrible as gorgons.

Friday's March morning warmed
to the trills of mockingbirds. Gulf breezes
rushing inland tossed new bluebonnets.
Saturday was a cottonmouth under a stone.

A second poem is Carolyn's peace offering to her sister, Helen, who was killed before they had a chance to sort out hard feelings between them as a result of their parent's divorce.

### Begging Your Pardon

First born, first grandchild, your place
secure before our parents' marriage died,
you were never soft, never a coquette.
Armed with a cutting tongue,
        you disputed Mother.

I learned from you the futility
of war; as the middle child,
I appeased, swallowed rebellion
        until I choked.

We would have made peace
in time. You never
held the child I named
for you. Did you hover
over her cradle? Shadow
        my way west?

When I was fifty, you opened
a door at Ashlawn, a Colonial
miss, dressed in mobcap;
another year I saw you
in a cousin's face.

Had you lived, you'd be
nearing ninety, Welsh locks
white as your forebears',
your wit perhaps still keen.
Now eternally fourteen, budding

Womanhood wrapped in a
a crimson sheet. Forgive
my submission, my failure
to conspire.

The only period in his life that Bill Thompson spent much time away from East Texas was during World War II. Even during the war, it was impossible for him to escape the past.

Thompson enlisted in the navy in 1943 and became an ordnance specialist in the Naval Air Corp. His job was keeping the guns and ammunition ready for action, and he was required to go up with one of the pilots on maneuvers.

On one of his first flights, he sat behind the pilot in a fighter plane. The pilot took the aircraft high up into the sky and suddenly began making barrel rolls through the clouds. A remarkable flash registered in Thompson's brain, taking him back to the instant the school exploded. He was rolling through space. Years before he had felt only that sensation, nothing more, before he awoke covered with debris.

After the war, Bill and millions of other GIs returned home and set out to claim their stake in the American dream. Bill and his sweetheart, Margaret, were married in 1947. Bill used the GI bill to attend Kilgore College. After college, he seized a business opportunity in New London and established a profitable dry cleaners, housed in a storefront directly across from the high school that was built to replace the one that had exploded. The new school is still in use today. Occupying the same gentle slope, it is a handsome structure of a style and design similar to the previous schoolhouse. The front window of Thompson's dry-cleaning business looked out on the monument that bears the names of his lost classmates.

Bill and Margaret bought a modest, three-bedroom house with a carport and a shady lot on a side street in New London, less than a hundred yards from the cleaners. There they set about the arduous task of raising four sons.

The building that housed his cleaners now contains the London Museum and Tea Room and is located across from the high school on Memorial Drive. The museum faces an island in the road on which the towering cenotaph stands as the town's solemn centerpiece.

Before a recent summer when the pain in his hip became so acute it limited his physical activities, Thompson frequently walked from his home to have his morning coffee in the museum he helped establish. Molly (Sealy) Ward, another survivor, spearheaded the drive for the museum. Visitors at the museum sometimes make the walk to Bill's house and have coffee with him. The conversations are hit and miss because, even with the assistance of a hearing aid, his hearing is fading. Life at home is more lonesome now, he will tell you. Margaret had become so fragile she had to move to an assisted-living facility in Henderson. Bill spends his days there but always likes to come home to his own bed at night. His grown boys have encouraged him to move into the facility with Margaret. "I'm not quite ready yet," he says.

If his legs and hips are up to a stroll, Thompson might take you for a walk to a narrow ravine across from his house. It is thick with summer brush. He pulls back some of the weeds and points. "There it is—that old black pipe. That's part of the old Parade line that took residue gas down to the school," he says, matter-of-factly. Bill Thompson's life is as entwined with the school explosion that happened when he was twelve as this section of pipe is wrapped in vines that have held it, inert, for more than seven decades. Bill doesn't mind talking about the past

The old man shifts his position on the kitchen stool, takes a sip from the coffee that he's let get cold, and stares out the back screen door with a wistful gaze.

"My family had been intact for a long time," he says. "I hadn't lost any brothers or sisters that I knew. There was one I didn't know. They were all healthy. Had healthy families. No tragedies until 1968; my oldest son was killed in a tragic car accident. He never regained consciousness."

Rodney was nineteen and preparing to start his second year in college. "My father died about the same time. I grieved for them both."

"What brings you out of grief is another grief," Thompson says. "Two years later, my younger son, Greg—he was fifteen—was riding a motorcycle on Sunday evening before sunset. A couple of brothers were out on a regular Sunday evening drinking party and racing cars. They were racing down the highway on a stretch that was kind of curvy, and my son was coming home from Overton, and they were coming west, side by side, and they couldn't miss my son."

A doctor in Overton stopped Greg's profuse bleeding and stabilized him for an ambulance ride to a Tyler hospital. Bill Thompson rode in the back of the ambulance.

"He was kind of thrashing around, except one side wasn't moving," Bill recalls. "They rolled him into the emergency room, and when they pulled the sheet back, I saw why one side was still. His foot was gone and all that was left of his leg was a bare bone all the way up to his hip.

"I shouldn't have had to see that," Thompson says, breaking into tears, and then quickly regaining control of his emotions.

"They said it was a miracle he lived. He lost over half his blood, but he survived and he's doing well today. He went to Kilgore College and became a mechanic and owner of an automobile repair shop.

"So, one tragedy leads to the next. Relating back to the families that lost children, through the years when tragedies started hitting my family, my siblings and children, I would think about the families that lost them all at one time. The thought of my losing a son, compared with losing all, saved me some grief; I say it did, because I still had the comfort of having three boys left, one not whole, but he's still happy.

"We celebrate many reunions over and over—the ones that lived before us, the ones that left in their childhood in the explosion, will be waiting for our next and final reunion, which will not be on this earth. That's my thoughts. As long as I'm living I'll be trying to make the reunions with people I knew and loved and went to school with, knowing I've overcome the loss of those in the past. In the end, we'll all be a part of one whole. From the other side, we'll look back and understand all of this."

In June 2010 Bill Thompson slipped in his bathroom and cracked one of his hips beyond repair. That July he became the oldest person to receive a hip replacement at Mother Frances Hospital in Tyler.

The survivors, though dwindling in number, gather still.

# 32

# A Final Word

Of all the personal articles combed from the rubble—the bits and pieces of the many lives shattered on March 18, 1937, in New London, Texas—none can rend the heart more, nor serve a higher purpose, than the small autograph booklet one of the children had been passing among her classmates.[1] Contained within are wishes, flirtations, silliness, exhortations, and notes of friendship. Above all, this meager book is a remembrance, the touchstone of our divinity. What physics and time conspire to erase, we resurrect with memory.

"Dear Betty Joe," Rachael wrote. "Roses are red, violets are blue, pickles are sour, and so are you (Ha! Ha!)."

Other notes followed on pages of alternating pink, yellow, and green.

"Dear Betty Joe,

"When you slide down the banister of life may there be no splinters."—Ethel.

"Dear Betty Joe,

"When you get married, and live across the flat, send me a kiss by the old tom cat."—Donald.

"Dear Betty Joe,

"It gives me great pleasure to write in your little book. I enjoy having you in my room. You are so sweet and help me with my lessons. Always remember me as your friend."—Ruth.

But for one more note, the rest of the pages were blank, smudged with dirt and dimpled where drops of rain fell from the heavens. The note ended with a vow of dedication—"Yours always"—from Gene.

"Dear Betty Joe,

"When I am dead and buried, and all my bones are rotten, this little book will tell you my name, when others have forgotten."

# In Memoriam

**Pleasant Hill Cemetery, Rusk County**

| Name | Status | Name | Status |
| --- | --- | --- | --- |
| Almita Fae Allman | 5th grade | Martha Jean Gandy | 5th grade |
| Lillian Anderson | 7th grade | Harun David Gunn | 6th grade |
| Allene (Myrtle) Anderson | 6th grade | Valieda Frances Hankins | 6th grade |
| Betty Ruth Apple | 8th grade | Betty Joe Harrington | 5th grade |
| Arden Leon Barber | 5th grade | Mary Ellen Harrington | 6th grade |
| Ollie B. Barber | 5th grade | James W. Harris | 5th grade |
| Donald P. Barrett | 5th grade | Charles Edward Hasbrook Jr. | 9th grade |
| Edward T. Barrett Jr. | 7th grade | Juanita W. Herron | 6th grade |
| Pauline Barrett | Postgrad | Margretta Hogue | 6th grade |
| Mary Frances Bennett | 5th grade | Bessie Estelle Holland | 5th grade |
| Sybil Dell Braden | 6th grade | Charles Porter Hunt | 5th grade |
| Bobbie Lorene Brown | 9th grade | Lena J. Hunt | Teacher |
| Elaine W. Brown | 6th grade | Ruby Francis Hunt | 6th grade |
| Murray Dixon Choate | 6th grade | Kenneth Johnson | 5th grade |
| Perry Lee Cox | 5th grade | Mary Lois King | 5th grade |
| Annie Belle Crim | 8th grade | Robert Austin Lambert | 6th grade |
| Zana Jo Curry | 6th grade | Mary Emily Lloyd | 8th grade |
| Winnifred Melvene Drake | Student | Virginia Allene Loe | 6th grade |
| George Lee Emberling | 5th grade | John A. Lumpkin Jr. | 5th grade |
| Wanda Louise Emberling | 5th grade | Doris Manck | 7th grade |
| John Arnold Ford | 7th grade | Blondell F. Maxwell | 7th grade |
| Myrtle Marie Freeman | 5th grade | Henry Maxwell | 6th grade |

## Pleasant Hill Cemetery, Rusk County *(continued)*

| Name | Status | Name | Status |
|------|--------|------|--------|
| Louise Maxwell | Senior | Dorothy Oleta Shaw | 6th grade |
| R. Donald McChesney | 5th grade | Joe Marvin Shaw | 8th grade |
| Carroll Evaughn Miller | 5th grade | Sambo Clifton Shaw | 10th grade |
| Sebe C. Miller Jr. | 10th grade | Robert Wayne Shoemaker | 6th grade |
| Annie Marie Milstead | 10th grade | Sammie Lee Shoemate | 6th grade |
| Marjorie Louise Myers | 6th grade | Anna Maude Smoot | 9th grade |
| Shirley Elizabeth Myers | 6th grade | Helen Smoot | Senior |
| Jack Nail | 8th grade | Geraldine Sterns | 6th grade |
| Aubry L. Netherton | 9th grade | Philo Stephens | Postgrad |
| Orrin N. Newell | Senior | Howard Lee Stone | Postgrad |
| Lewis Malernee Payne | 9th grade | Mildred Louise Thompson | 5th grade |
| James Henry Phillips | Visitor | Annie Morine Walker | Student |
| Twillia Ruth Phillips | 5th grade | Euda Alice (Bynum) Walker | Visitor |
| Virgil B. Phillips | 7th grade | Herman Lawrence Walker | Student |
| Hazel Marie Pierson | 6th grade | S. J. Warthan | Student |
| John Henry Propes | Teacher | Mary Lou Willis | 6th grade |
| Gabe Ragsdale | 6th grade | Thomas Malcolm Woolley | Student |
| Curtis B. Reams | 7th grade | Dale May York | 5th grade |
| Thomas Blanton Rogers | 10th grade | | |

## Lakewood Memorial Park, Henderson

| Name | Status | Name | Status |
|------|--------|------|--------|
| John Adran Blackerby Jr | 5th grade | Geneva Lucille Jolly | 7th grade |
| Elvin Neale Blackford | Senior | Billie Patterson Moore | Visitor |
| Mildred Louise Clair | 6th grade | Mary Ethel Neal | Teacher |
| Travis Hardy Dial | 6th grade | Betty Mozell Norton | 8th grade |
| Emaloyd Francis | 5th grade | Vester Allen Norton | Senior |
| Margine Francis | 5th grade | Marie Patterson | Secretary, |
| Carl Hamilton Frey Jr. | 7th grade | | HS |
| Yvonne Jackolene Hathaway | 9th grade | Forrest Lavon Person | 6th grade |
| Betty Jo Hodges | 5th grade | Billy Roberts | 10th grade |
| Jesse Elinor Holt | 6th grade | Rose C. Van Haverbeke | 8th grade |
| Mary Frances Hooten | 7th grade | | |

## Overton City Cemetery, Overton

| Name | Status |
| --- | --- |
| Betty Lou Benson | 6th grade |
| Nellene Bishop | 6th grade |
| Chloe Ann Carr | 10th grade |
| Kenneth Durward Corrie | 5th grade |
| Jimmy Wilmot Crumbley | 6th grade |
| Alice Dorsey | Senior |
| Ethel Dorsey | 5th grade |
| Mary Ellen Forman | 8th grade |
| Oscar Grady Hall Jr. | 5th grade |
| Irene Emma Hall | 10th grade |
| Imogene Houser | 5th grade |
| Laura Lee Houser | 5th grade |
| Martha Ellen Houser | 6th grade |
| Charles Goodall Jones | 6th grade |
| Claudell Kilgore | 5th grade |
| Louise E. Martin | 6th grade |
| Billie J. Morefield | 6th grade |
| Norma Wayne Roberts | 5th grade |

## Rose Hill Cemetery, Tyler

| Name | Status |
| --- | --- |
| Holly Jo Ellison | 5th grade |
| Betty Kathryn Holleyman | 6th grade |
| Anna Maxine Rogers | 6th grade |
| Robert Henry Sallee | Senior |
| Anna Bell Waggoner | 6th grade |

## Shiloh Cemetery, Brachfield

| Name | Status |
| --- | --- |
| Nellie Barnes | Teacher |
| Aubra Rainwater | 9th grade |
| Evelyn M. Rainwater | 8th grade |
| Helen Jo Rainwater | 5th grade |
| Louise Rowell | Senior |

## Mount Hope, Joinerville

| Name | Status |
| --- | --- |
| Graham Keith Henson | 8th grade |
| Florence Ruby Lee | 8th grade |
| Willie Ruth Roberts | 7th grade |
| A. W. Stubblefield | 6th grade |

## Oakwood Cemetery, Waco

| Name | Status |
| --- | --- |
| George Atmon Bonner | 7th grade |
| Oneita Bonner | 6th grade |
| Allen T. Gerdes | 9th grade |
| Alvin Augustus Gerdes | Senior |

## Pirtle Baptist, Pitner Junction

| Name | Status |
| --- | --- |
| William Polk "Billy" Childress | 5th grade |
| Maxine Jacobs | 5th grade |
| (Nellie) Florene Warren | Student |
| Doris Wyche | Student |

## Crims Chapel, Henderson

| Name | Status |
| --- | --- |
| Laverne Barton | 7th grade |
| Elijah M. Hudson | 6th grade |
| Esther Fay Rucker | 6th grade |

## Ebenezer Cemetery, Arp

| Name | Status |
| --- | --- |
| Louise Arnold | Teacher |
| Raymond Briton O'Neal | 5th grade |
| Dorothy Mae Richardson | 8th grade |

## New Brazoria Cemetery, Brazoria

| Name | Status |
| --- | --- |
| Anna "Annie" Laurie Davidson | 6th grade |
| Helen Adams Davidson | 7th grade |
| Joe Wheeler Davidson Jr. | 8th grade |

## Breckenridge Cemetery, Breckenridge

| Name | Status |
| --- | --- |
| Wayne Scott Arnold | 5th grade |
| Maudine Ray Kelly | 6th grade |

## Joaquin Cemetery, Joaquin

| Name | Status |
| --- | --- |
| David Willard Scott | 7th grade |
| Earl Jefferson Scott | 7th grade |

## Memory Park, Longview Heights

| Name | Status |
| --- | --- |
| Holton Dean Roberts | 6th grade |
| R. B. Roberts | 5th grade |

## Mt. Tabor Cemetery, Caviness

| Name | Status |
| --- | --- |
| Helen Cole (d. March 20, 1937) | Senior |
| Ardyth Davidson | 8th grade |

## Sipe Springs Cemetery, Sipe Springs

| Name | Status |
| --- | --- |
| Marion Wayne Mote | 8th grade |
| Patty Anna Mote | 6th grade |

## Tennessee Cemetery, Simpson

| Name | Status |
| --- | --- |
| Henry Bryan Bowlin | 6th grade |
| Edna Ruby Peace | 5th grade |

## Thornton Church Cemetery, Glendale

| Name | Status |
| --- | --- |
| Homer Clint Latham | 9th grade |
| Walter Dumont "W. D." Latham | Senior |

## Tyler Memorial Park, Tyler

| Name | Status |
| --- | --- |
| Evelyn Jo Mayhew | 5th grade |
| William Floyd Meador Jr. | 5th grade |

## White Oak Cemetery, White Oak

| Name | Status |
| --- | --- |
| Kenneth Wayne Davis | 5th grade |

## Alto City Cemetery, Alto

| Name | Status |
| --- | --- |
| Velma Earline "Ruby" Reed | Senior |

## Bethel Cemetery, Appleby

| Name | Status |
| --- | --- |
| Doris Ray Melton | 8th grade |

## Cedar Hill Cemetery, Rusk

| Name | Status |
| --- | --- |
| Tom Howard Guinn | 8th grade |

## Center Ridge, Maud

| Name | Status |
| --- | --- |
| Mary Jo Webb | Student |

## Corinth Cemetery, Timpson

| Name | Status |
| --- | --- |
| Glenn Turner Wood | 5th grade |

## Creekmore Cemetery Cass County

| Name | Status |
| --- | --- |
| Naoma Bunting | Senior |

## Eastland City Cemetery, Eastland

| Name | Status |
| --- | --- |
| Delores Ray | 8th grade |

## Eastview Memorial Park, Vernon

| Name | Status |
| --- | --- |
| Mozelle Young | 5th grade |

## Elderville Cemetery, Rusk County

| Name | Status |
| --- | --- |
| Fedelia Lee Jones | 6th grade |

## Elmwood Cemetery, Bowie

| Name | Status |
| --- | --- |
| Kenneth Wayne Davis | 5th grade |

## Fairview Cemetery, Center

| Name | Status |
| --- | --- |
| Lloyd Garland "Lonnie" Pride | 5th grade |

## Fairview Church Cemetery, Nacogdoches

| Name | Status |
| --- | --- |
| Doris Lucile Wells | Student |

## Greenpond Cemetery, Como

| Name | Status |
| --- | --- |
| Forrest E. Coker | Senior |

## Greenwood Cemetery, Garrison

| Name | Status |
| --- | --- |
| Laura Elizabeth Bell | Teacher |

## Hamilton Beeman Cemetery, Retreat

| Name | Status |
| --- | --- |
| Rachel Mae Knotts | 7th grade |

## Highland Cemetery, Deport

| Name | Status |
| --- | --- |
| Marshall Starks | 7th grade |

## Holly Springs Cemetery, Montalba

| Name | Status |
| --- | --- |
| Glyndell Sutherlin | 6th grade |

## Huffines Cemetery, Atlanta, Texas

| Name | Status |
| --- | --- |
| Mary Inez Walker | Student |

## Indian Creek Cemetery, Mineral Wells

| Name | Status |
| --- | --- |
| Charles Harrel O'Neal | 8th grade |

## Johnson City Masonic Cemetery

| Name | Status |
| --- | --- |
| Marcelyn Carol Gibson | 7th grade |

## Kemp City Cemetery, Kemp

| Name | Status |
| --- | --- |
| Mary Ellen Lehew | 7th grade |

## Kingsbury Cemetery, Sequin

| Name | Status |
| --- | --- |
| Lataine Parchman McQuaid | 5th grade |

## Loving Cemetery, Loving

| Name | Status |
| --- | --- |
| Wanda Joyce Dickenson | 6th grade |

## Lynch Chapel Cemetery, Alto

| Name | Status |
| --- | --- |
| Arzell Lloyd | 6th grade |

## Macedonia Cemetery, Caddo

| Name | Status |
| --- | --- |
| Jackie Mae Newham | 5th grade |

## Maple Grove Cemetery, Minden

| Name | Status |
| --- | --- |
| Melba Lee Hughes | Senior |

## Melrose Baptist Church Cemetery, Nacogdoches County

| Name | Status |
| --- | --- |
| Lizzie Ella Thompson | Teacher |

## Mostyn Cemetery, Montgomery County

| Name | Status |
| --- | --- |
| Jane Damuth | 6th grade |

## Mount Calm Cemetery, Limestone County

| Name | Status |
| --- | --- |
| Johnnie Marie "Purcell" Nelson | Teacher |

## Nocona Cemetery, Nocona

| Name | Status |
| --- | --- |
| Irma Elizabeth Hodges | Senior |

## Oak Grove Cemetery, Graham

| Name | Status |
| --- | --- |
| Mattie Queen Price | Teacher |

## Oak Grove Cemetery, Kerens

| Name | Status |
| --- | --- |
| Doris Nell Etheredge | 10th grade |

## Oak Grove Cemetery, Nacogdoches

| Name | Status |
| --- | --- |
| Mazel Lorene Hanna | Teacher |

## Oakwood Cemetery, Corsicana

| Name | Status |
| --- | --- |
| Rose Smith Sammie Jr. | 7th grade |

## Old Palestine Cemetery, Alto

| Name | Status |
| --- | --- |
| Ruben Abner "R. A." Goff Jr. | 6th grade |

## Peatown Cemetery, Lakeport

| Name | Status |
| --- | --- |
| Katie Mae Watson | Teacher |

## Plainview Cemetery, Madison County

| Name | Status |
| --- | --- |
| Maudine "Nida" Sevens | 5th grade |

## Reilly Springs Cemetery, Reilly Springs

| Name | Status |
| --- | --- |
| Joyce Genelle Payne | 5th grade |

## Rock Church Cemetery, Tolar

| Name | Status |
| --- | --- |
| Harvey Edwin Grigg | 7th grade |

## Rogers Cemetery, Rogers

| Name | Status |
| --- | --- |
| Mary Lynn Clark | 7th grade |

## Salem Cemetery, Troup

| Name | Status |
| --- | --- |
| Evelyn Bonnie Adams | 6th grade |

## Savannah Cemetery, Jefferson

| Name | Status |
| --- | --- |
| Norris Thurston Hale | 8th grade |

## Sonora Cemetery, Fairlie

| Name | Status |
| --- | --- |
| John Robert Buzbee | 5th grade |

## Stag Creek Cemetery, Sidney

| Name | Status |
| --- | --- |
| Mary Elizabeth Vines | 8th grade |

## Stanford Chapel Cemetery, Waco

| Name | Status |
| --- | --- |
| Virginia Rose Blanton | 10th grade |

## Stong Cemetery, Henderson

| Name | Status |
| --- | --- |
| Willie H. Tate | Teacher |

## Sweetwater Cemetery, Decatur

| Name | Status |
| --- | --- |
| Charles Ray Taylor | 6th grade |

# Burial Sites Outside Texas

## Bethel Cemetery, Bethel, Louisiana

| Name | Status |
| --- | --- |
| William Conley McLawchlin | 6th grade |

## Bethel Cemetery, Lillie, Union Parish, Louisiana

| Name | Status |
| --- | --- |
| Owen Byrom | Student |

## Bethleman Cemetery, Claiborne Parish, Louisiana

| Name | Status |
| --- | --- |
| Ida Maxine Maddry | 6th grade |
| J. E. Maddry | Senior |

## Shreveport, Louisiana

| Name | Status |
| --- | --- |
| Mary Priscilla Carney | 7th grade |

## Central Cemetery, Robeline, Louisiana

| Name | Status |
| --- | --- |
| William Edward Sowell | 10th grade |

## Cooper Cemetery, Leesville, Louisiana

| Name | Status |
| --- | --- |
| Walter M. Thompson | 6th grade |

## East Mt. Olive Cemetery, Bienville Parish, Louisiana

| Name | Status |
| --- | --- |
| Boyd Anderson Abercrombie | 9th grade |

## Fairlawn Cemetery, Oklahoma City, Oklahoma

| Name | Status |
| --- | --- |
| Anna May Lechtenberg | Senior |
| Helen Lechtenberg | 7th grade |

### Gracelawn Cemetery, Edmond, Oklahoma

| Name | Status |
| --- | --- |
| Robert Basil Salyer | 6th grade |

### Morris Cemetery, Morris, Oklahoma

| Name | Status |
| --- | --- |
| Forrest Eugene Eakes | 6th grade |

### Mount Gilead Cemetery, Vivian, Louisiana

| Name | Status |
| --- | --- |
| Aubry Williams | Student |
| Doris Dean Williams | Student |
| Erma Gene Williams | Student |

### Rock Creek Cemetery, Duncan, Oklahoma

| Name | Status |
| --- | --- |
| William Artice Ketchum | Senior |

### Rose Hill Cemetery, Ardmore, Oklahoma

| Name | Status |
| --- | --- |
| Helen Charlotte Jones | 8th grade |

### Shiloh Cemetery, Provencal, Louisiana

| Name | Status |
| --- | --- |
| Dessie Lometer Morre | 6th grade |

### Hillcrest Cemetery, Weleetka, Oklahoma

| Name | Status |
| --- | --- |
| Coy Dee Harrelson Jr. | 5th grade |

### Wilton Cemetery, Wilton, Arkansas

| Name | Status |
| --- | --- |
| Betty Kathryn Gordon | Postgrad |
| Joe Curry Gordon | 6th grade |

### Woodberry-Forest Cemetery, Madill, Oklahoma

| Name | Status |
| --- | --- |
| Jacqueline Knight Cuvelier | 5th grade |
| James Pickney Tatum Jr. | 7th grade |

### Woodford Cemetery, Woodford, Oklahoma

| Name | Status |
| --- | --- |
| Paul Greer | Senior |

### Woodland Cemetery, Kentwood, Louisiana

| Name | Status |
| --- | --- |
| Edna Elizabeth Powell | 6th grade |

# Probable Burial Sites Based on Research

| Name | Status | Site |
|---|---|---|
| Murvin Harland Barton | Senior | Rapides Parish, Louisiana |
| Margaret Louise Baucum | 8th grade | Pleasant Hill Cemetery, unmarked |
| Eloise "Powell" Brister | 9th grade | Woodland Cemetery, Kentwood, Louisiana |
| Lemmie R. Butler | Teacher | Commerce, Texas |
| Byron Clover | 5th grade | Medill, Oklahoma |
| Charles Russ Collins Jr. | 7th grade | Oakwood Cemetery, Comanche, Texas |
| Marcella Cummings | 6th grade | Shawnee, Oklahoma |
| June Davis | 5th grade | Hamilton, Texas |
| Dorothy Ann Dearing | 6th grade | Pine Bluff, Arkansas |
| James Alfred Duncan | 9th grade | Pearland, Texas |
| Vera Virginia "Sue" Duncan | 7th grade | Pearland, Texas |
| Edwin Zone Elrod | 5th grade | Concord, Tyler, Texas |
| Juanita Elrod | 10th grade | Concord, Tyler, Texas |
| James Patrick Fealy | 6th grade | Lockhart, Texas |
| Jack Fentress Jr. | Senior | Arlington, Texas |
| Mary Elizabeth Ford | 5th grade | Houston, Texas |
| Eddie Herman Gauthreaux | 3rd grade | Woodville, Texas |
| Carl Hamilton Jr. | Student | Henderson, Texas |
| Laneta Fae Hardy | 6th grade | Turnertown, Texas |
| Earnestine Hogue | 6th grade | Pleasant Hill Cemetery |
| Hubert Hudson | 7th grade | Pleasant Hill Cemetery |
| Ernest Knipe | 6th grade | Overton, Texas |
| Robert L. Krause | 6th grade | Enid, Oklahoma |
| Vincent Harold McClure | 6th grade | Troup, Texas |
| Larry Oliver "Lanny" McCune | 6th grade | Shelby County, Texas |
| George "Jack" McGovney | Senior | Pleasant Hill Cemetery |
| James McGovney | Senior | Pleasant Hill Cemetery |
| Arliss Ray Middleton | 10th grade | Springridge Cemetery, Shreveport, Louisiana |
| Sarah Jane Mills | 5th grade | Winnsboro, Texas |
| Alma Louise Monday | 5th grade | Rylie, Texas |
| James Roy Petty | 6th grade | Houston, Texas |
| Rose Ann Phillips | 6th grade | Greenwood Cemetery, Fort Worth, Texas |
| Christine Platt | 6th grade | Kilgore, Texas |
| Anna Ray Purcell | 8th grade | Woodville, Texas |

| | | |
|---|---|---|
| James Basel Rhodes | 6th grade | Overton, Texas |
| Betty Jane Rider | 6th grade | Shawnee, Texas |
| Charles Oliver Rider | Senior | Shawnee, Texas |
| Abner Lavelle Smith | 10th grade | Pleasant Hill Cemetery, unmarked |
| Bobbie Jean Smith | 5th grade | Steppville, Alabama |
| Mattie Mae Smith | 6th grade | Pleasant Hill Cemetery |
| Ruth Willien Smith | 5th grade | Pleasant Hill Cemetery |
| Carl Francis Staggs | Student | Lone Oak, Arkansas |
| Henry Lee Steele | 8th grade | Pirtle, Texas |
| Lawrence Swift | 8th grade | Kilgore,  Texas |
| Marjorie J. Thiebaud | 8th grade | Lamar, Missouri |
| Billy Tipp | 5th grade | Farmerville, Louisiana |
| Louis Waller | Teacher | Pickton, Texas |

## Uncertain Burial Sites

| Name | Status |
|---|---|
| Edwin Bassett | Student |
| G. W. Gipson | Student |
| Mrs. John Gore | Teacher |
| Martin Krauss | Student |
| Laura Lee | 5th grade |
| John Worthy Neil | 8th grade |
| Shirley Parchman | Student |
| Harvey Pinkerton | Student |
| Maudine Stevens | Student |
| Ammie Lois Watkins | Student |
| Dorothy J. White | Student |
| Bernice Womack | Student |

Different spellings are shown on various lists for many of the victims named here. We made a diligent effort to find sources for correct spellings. We apologize for any spelling errors that still occurred.

# Interviews

This book derives its form and heartbeat from interviews with scores of survivors, witnesses, rescue workers, and others who either experienced the New London school explosion in person or had direct knowledge about it from family members who lived through the disaster. Other interviews were conducted for background with people who had direct knowledge of experiences in the oil fields of East Texas, the Great Depression, and the historical background of the story's setting. To all those who shared their stories, we say thank you from our hearts; without you no book of this scope and depth would have been possible. An audio copy of all taped interviews was presented to the London Museum in New London, Texas, for preservation and the use of future researchers. Principal interviews that shaped the story include the following:

Carl Barber, Henderson background; L. V. Barber, survivor*; Clinton Barton, survivor; Anna (Smoot) Brannon, relative of Helen and Anna Smoot; J. B. Downs, witness, background on Kilgore; Ledell (Dorsey) Carpenter,

---

\* Various definitions of "survivor" have developed over the years among those who lived through this disaster. For some, a survivor was someone who was in the building and escaped with his or her life; the term "campus survivor" developed for the many children who were outside and spared death from falling debris. Here we use "survivor" to include all those who were in the building and on the campus, plus those who would have been in the building except for a twist of fate, such as Charles Dial, who should have been in a classroom but rushed home at the last minute to get his band uniform, which he had forgotten to bring with him that morning. The band had planned to perform a concert after school. After the explosion, the band, as such, no longer existed.

survivor; Robert "Bobby" Clayton, survivor; Hazel (Shaw) Cobb, teacher, survivor, daughter of Chesley Shaw; Doris Brown Cooper, background, growing up in the Great Depression; Finis J. Cooper, rescue worker; Clyde Cowen, rescue worker; Preston Crim, survivor; John Davidson, explosion and family background; Everett Davis, East Texas background; Marvin Dees, rescue worker; Charles Dial, survivor; Jim Dickeson, Rusk County background; Lamone Dickeson, witness; John Dulin, East Texas background; Stanley Dzimitrowicz, Great Depression background; Ronnie Gaudet, nephew of Chesley Shaw; Carroll "Boxhead" Evans, teacher, survivor; Mildred Evans, teacher, survivor; Glenda Fleming, relative of victims; Graften Ferguson, rescue worker; William Follis, survivor; Sandra (Anderson) Florence, sister of Lillian and Allene Anderson who were killed in the explosion; Walter Freeman, survivor; Carolyn (Jones) Frei, survivor; Jack Gainey, survivor; Ellie Goldberg, advocate for children and school safety; A. L. Green, rescue worker; Avis Griffin, friend of Shaw family, former student of Chesley Shaw; Mary Hall, Tyler background; Myrtle (Meador) Hayes, survivor; Alvis Henderson, East Texas background; C. H. Hicks, witness; Jola (Rainwater) Hicks, survivor; Merle (Davidson) Hinchee, niece of Joe Wheeler Davidson Sr.; Max Holleyman, survivor; Georgia Lorine Bright "Darwin" Hoff, survivor, daughter of Lorine Bright, author of a memoir about the school explosion; Paul Howard, witness; Jean (Emerson) Howard, daughter of rescue worker Harold Emerson; Priscilla (Kerns) Joffe, survivor; Johnny Johnson, East Texas background; Margie (Gilstrap) Johnson, survivor; Otis Jones, witness; Virginia Knapp, historian, Rusk County; Claude Joseph "Joe Bo" Kerce, survivor; Joan Lloyd, explosion background; Grace Mathis, explosion background; L. A. "Tiger" Mathis, rescue worker; Carolyn McClain, daughter of first-responder Dr. J. T. McClain; Joan (McKnight) McIlyar, Felix McKnight's daughter; Felix McKnight, reporter and rescue worker; Ben Meador, witness; Ira Joe Moore, survivor; Barbara (Moore) Page, survivor; Ezzie Poole, witness; Olen Poole, survivor; Mary Lou (Hudson) Powell, daughter of radio-man Ted Hudson; Douglas Reeh, explosion background; Jimmie (Jordan) Robinson, survivor; Arthur Shaw, survivor, nephew of Chesley Shaw; Charles Shaw, witness, son of Chesley Shaw; Marjorie Shaw, great-niece of Chesley Shaw; Barbara (Keeling) Smart, daughter of a school board member; M. A. Smith, New

London background; Bill Thompson, survivor; Tina Todd, relative of nurse who worked in rescue mission; Miles Toler, director, London Museum and Tea Room; Felton Waggoner, junior high principal, survivor; Mrs. Felton Waggoner, teacher, witness; Molly (Sealy) Ward, student, survivor, leading advocate for the museum; Billie (Anderson) Watson, survivor, sister of Lillian and Allene Anderson who were killed in the explosion; H. G. White, survivor; Sam Wooley, witness.

# Notes

## Chapter 1. 3:16 p.m

1. Numerous news stories mentioned the warm, spring-like weather in East Texas on March 18, 1937, which backed up memories of that day among survivors interviewed by the authors. The temperature in the region reached at least 70 degrees by mid-afternoon, reported Janice Talley Marsh, "Learning From Disaster," *Tyler Life*, March 1985.
2. The opening is based on interviews with Bill Thompson and other survivors who were in Miss Wright's classroom, including Preston Crim and Claude Joseph "Joe Bo" Kerce. Subsequent passages throughout the book based on personal interviews conducted by the authors will not be cited routinely in separate endnotes, except when a citation is needed to clarify the source of information or to add another source outside of the interview; readers may rely on the book's list of people interviewed as the source of all quotes and story lines involving those individuals or family members directly affected by the disaster, not otherwise cited.
3. Carolyn (Jones) Frei and Barbara (Moore) Page, interview by the authors, conducted with Frei in October 2009 and February 2011 and with Page on July 23, 2009; and Carolyn (Jones) Frei, unpublished memoir of childhood.
4. Military Court of Inquiry Report, New London school explosion, March 23, 1937, Texas State Archives, Austin, TX, 150–51.
5. Various newspaper accounts in the aftermath of the explosion reported James Henry Phillips's dash into the building, including, "700 Children Thought Dead as Blast Razes Rusk County School Building," on the front page of the *Dallas Morning News*, March 19, 1937.
6. Associated Press story about the explosion, March 19, 1937.
7. Time line of events before, during, and after the explosion, London Museum and Tea Room, New London, TX.
8. Zana Jo Curry obituary, *Henderson Daily News*, March 28, 1937.
9. Robert L. Jackson, *Living Lessons from the New London Explosion* (Nashville, TN: Parthenon Press, 1938), 53.

10. Carroll Evans, interview by the authors, March 5, 1990; and Military Court of Inquiry Report, 364–65.
11. Bud Price interviewed by London Museum and Tea Room official Ronnie Gaudet, August 8, 1997, notes on file at the London Museum and Tea Room.
12. Military Court of Inquiry Report, 310–14

### Chapter 2. Daybreak, March 18

1. Joe Davidson's dream was widely reported in the aftermath of the explosion, including an Associated Press story, "Pathos and Tragedy in Texas School Explosion," *Mansfield (OH) News Journal,* March 19, 1937, among numerous publications, and an AP year-in-review story that ran in client newspapers, including Dale Harrison, "Dream Warns Of Tragedy To New London Children," *Waterloo (IA) Sunday Courier,* December 12, 1937. Early AP stories had his name as George Davidson, which was corrected in other dispatches.
2. Except for his brief time in the news media spotlight after the school disaster, Davidson was not a public figure, so very few records exist to document his existence. It was possible, however, to develop a reasonably accurate profile of him using news reports and public records associated with the school explosion; a death certificate; U.S. census data on Davidson, his wife, and his children; and interviews and correspondence with members of his extended family and others who knew him, including New London explosion survivors Bill Thompson and Charles Dial.
3. No biography of Columbus Marion Joiner is available, although plenty of information about him can be sifted from the works of oil-field historians. The profile of him here and later in the text was drawn from news stories and an assimilation of details and insights about Joiner from James A. Clark and Michel T. Halbouty, *The Last Boom* (New York: Random House, 1972); Walter Rundell Jr., *Early Texas Oil: A Photographic History, 1866–1936* (College Station: Texas A&M University Press, 1977); Ruth Sheldon Knowles, *The Greatest Gamblers: The Epic of American Oil Exploration* (Norman: University of Oklahoma Press, 1978).
4. The physical description of Joiner is from Clark and Halbouty, *Last Boom,* 9.
5. A. D. "Doc" Lloyd's profile relies on numerous details assembled from the works of the same oil-field historians who wrote about Joiner. Essentially, the pair became locked at the hip regarding the discovery of the mammoth East Texas oil field, as historians and newspaper stories recorded it.
6. Clark and Halbouty, *Last Boom,* 7, 18, 19.
7. In 1910, when Joiner was living in Ardmore with his wife and seven children, the U.S. Census lists his occupation simply as real estate agent.
8. Roger M. Olien and Diana Davids Olien, *Wildcatters: Texas Independent Oilmen* (Austin: Texas Monthly Press, 1984), 56.
9. Clark and Halbouty, *Last Boom,* 110.
10. News clip in vertical file at the Rusk County Library, attributed to Joiner by H. L. Hunt, Joiner's protégé, during Hunt's speech at the October 3, 1965, dedication of a monument honoring Joiner's discovery. Hunt developed his own vast wealth after buying Joiner's stake in the Black Giant.
11. Clark and Halbouty, *Last Boom,* 123.

12. *Fifteenth Census of the United States—1930* (Washington, D.C.: U.S. Government Printing Office, 1931).
13. Roger M. Olien, "Oil and Gas Industry," *Handbook of Texas Online* (accessed April 2011), http://www.tshaonline.org/handbook/online/articles/doogz.
14. Merle Weir and Diana J. Kleiner, "West Columbia, TX," *Handbook of Texas Online,* (accessed April 2011), http://www.tshaonline.org/handbook/online/articles/hgw03.
15. Weather forecast for East Texas, March 18, 1937, National Weather Service, *Henderson Daily News*, daily weather report and forecast, March 17, 1937.

**Chapter 3. The Superintendent**

1. Junior high principal Felton Waggoner, testimony recorded in the Military Court of Inquiry Report, 139; Lorine Zylks Bright, *New London 1937: One Woman's Memory of Orange and Green* (Wichita Falls, TX: Nortex Press, 1977).
2. D. C. Saxon, testimony in Military Court of Inquiry Report, 156.
3. Barbara (Keeling) Smart, interview by the authors, July 27, 2009. Barbara's father, Jason William Keeling was a member of the school board at the time of the explosion. Keeling and other school board members met Shaw before the start of classes and walked the entire length of the high school, looking for evidence of what might be causing headaches in the building, according to Smart, who said she personally remembers her father talking about their excursion.
4. Norfolk Notes, *Rusk County News,* June 20, 1900, July 25, 1900, January 2, 1901.
5. Several news stories before and after the explosion, including reports written by Felix McKnight of the Associated Press and Henry McLemore of the United Press, referred to the school district as the wealthiest rural district in the nation. Our research never came upon evidence of a study or survey of all rural districts in the country during this period that verified claims that the London Consolidated School District was the richest in the United States. This possibly was anecdotal information picked up by newspapers and passed, like a virus, from one to the other. Nevertheless, it was a very wealthy district, undoubtedly among the richest during the Great Depression.

**Chapter 4. Sweet Chariot**

1. Towns such as Henderson, Kilgore, and Tyler had electricity long before rural areas in Texas. In 1937 less than 3 percent of residential dwellings in Texas, including the area surrounding New London, had no power lines supplying electricity, hence the use of oil-burning lamps and lanterns was still prevalent. Norris G. Davis, "Rural Electrification," *Handbook of Texas Online* (accessed February 2011), http://www.tshaonline.org/handbook/online/articles/dpr01.
2. In interviews with former students, Propes and Hunt frequently were described as stern; Propes was mentioned in various editions of the weekly *Rusk County News* as an election official who counted votes.
3. Frei, unpublished memoir.
4. Paul F. Lambert and Kenny A. Franks, eds., *Voices from the Oil Fields* (Norman: University of Oklahoma Press, 1984), 24, 29, 70, 95, 192, 222, 230. This book was based on interviews conducted in the late 1930s by workers for the Federal Writers Project.
5. "London Well Still Burns," *Henderson Daily News,* July 26, 1931, 8.

## Chapter 5. Pleasant Hill

1. Texas historical marker at Pleasant Hill Cemetery, near New London, TX.
2. Cleburne Huston, *Towering Texan: A Biography of Thomas J. Rusk* (Waco, TX: Texian Press, 1971), 1.
3. Weather reports from *Overton Press,* January 15 and January 22, 1937; *Kilgore Daily News*, February 2, March 15–17, 1937.
4. Helen Smoot, "Snowflakes," London Museum and Tea Room, New London, TX.

## Chapter 6. American Dreams

1. Dixon Wecter, *The Age of the Great Depression, 1929–1941* (New York: Macmillan, 1948), 35.
2. Ibid., 27, 40, 49, 62.
3. Gene Smith, *The Shattered Dream: Herbert Hoover and the Great Depression* (New York: William Morrow, 1970), 15.
4. Ibid., 105.
5. Wecter, *Age of the Great Depression,* 39.
6. Mildred Evans, "The Life and Times of Carroll and Mildred Evans," comp. Kevin C. Evans (unpublished manuscript, 1986), 8.
7. Ibid.

## Chapter 7. Wildcats' Pep Rally

1. Jackson, *Living Lessons*, 13.
2. "Interscholastic League Banquet Attracts Many Educators," *Henderson Daily News*, March 17, 1937, 12, covered the Interscholastic League's annual banquet the night before. Shaw was the keynote speaker at the banquet and discussed the history of the contests from his perspective as a former student, teacher, and school official over nearly sixty years.
3. News brief, *Overton Press,* January 15, 1937.
4. Jackson, *Living Lessons,* 13.
5. Associated Press, "Pathos and Tragedy."
6. Joanne Rosamond and Walter Fields, comps., "The Gaston Story," (unpublished manuscript, West Rusk County Consolidated Independent School District, New London, TX, May 1989), 14.
7. Ibid., 14–15.
8. This italicized segment is based on New London's last football game of 1936, in which Gerdes was a star for the Wildcats. Comments from the game announcer are hypothetical but derived from a careful reading of sports stories covering the Wildcats games and knowledge of football lingo in use at the time.
9. Kenneth Holtzclaw, "Wildcats Win District 19-B Title, Beating Red Devils," *Henderson Daily News*, November 22, 1936, 7; "Wildcats Primed for Bi-District Clash; Alvin Gerdes Unable to Play," *Henderson Daily News,* December 3, 1936.
10. "Football Player Dies of Injuries," *Henderson Daily News*, November 25, 1936.
11. "Center 6, London 0," *Henderson Daily News,* December 5, 1936.
12. Data on the Gerdes family from *Fifteenth Census of the United States—1930*.
13. "Bulldog and Ranger Quintets Beat London and Stanolind Here," *Kilgore Daily News*, January 8, 1937, a basketball game in which Alvin Gerdes was high scorer in London's losing effort.

## Chapter 8. Farmer's Boy

1. Information in this chapter is based almost entirely on interviews with Bill Thompson and the family's genealogical history, Nadine Thompson Heaberlin and Sam J. Heaberlin, comps., "Ancestors and Descendants of Alvin A. and Bonnie Freeman Thompson" (unpublished manuscript, 1989).
2. Temperatures in Texas were above normal in June and August 1936, and the state's record high is 120 degrees, recorded on August 12, 1936, at Seymour, according to the U.S. National Climatic Data Center. Data available through *USA Today* weather website (accessed September 26, 2011), http://www.usatoday.com/weather/wheat7.htm, cites U.S. National Climatic Data Center.

## Chapter 9. The Black Giant

1. Clark and Halbouty, *Last Boom*, 79–80.
2. Ibid., 77.
3. Knowles, *Greatest Gamblers*, 253–54.
4. Dorman Winfrey, *A History of Rusk County, Texas* (Waco, TX: Texian Press, 1961), 91.
5. Olien and Olien, *Wildcatters*, 56.
6. Clark and Halbouty, *Last Boom,* 80.
7. Photo on file at the London Museum and Tea Room, New London, TX.
8. Clark and Halbouty, *Last Boom*, 81.
9. Knowles, *Greatest Gamblers*, 260.
10. Clark and Halbouty, *Last Boom*, 123–29.
11. William T. Jack, *Gaston High School, Joinerville, Texas, and a Boy Named Billy Jack* (Campbell, TX: J & N Press, 1989), 69–71.
12. Centennial Celebration Publication, October 1950, First Presbyterian Church, Kilgore, TX.
13. "Too Many Oil Wells Spoiled Good Farmer But Brought to Light Good Café Man," *Henderson Daily News,* March 20, 1931.
14. Clark and Halbouty, *Last Boom*, 142.
15. Knowles, *Greatest Gamblers,* 262–64.
16. Olien and Olien, *Wildcatters*, 57.
17. Lambert and Franks, *Voices from the Oil Fields*, 201–3.

## Chapter 10. Lunchtime

1. Parts of Mattie Queen Price's teaching scrapbook are on file at the London Museum and Tea Room, New London, TX.
2. Price interview.
3. *Henderson, Texas City Directory—1935–36* (Springfield, MO: Interstate Directory Co., 1936).
4. Carolyn (Jones) Frei distinctly remembers a carnival set up and ready to open on Friday, the following day. Alvin Thompson likely would have noticed the carnival on his way to and from work, as carnivals and fairs in the 1930s were set up at a designated location—Fair Park—on the fringe of downtown Henderson. In an era before television, news of such attractions coming to town spread rapidly, typically with no more advertising than handbills posted throughout the region.

### Chapter 11. Fateful Afternoon

1. *London Times*, student newspaper, March 18, 1937, London Museum and Tea Room, New London, TX.
2. Jackson, *Living Lessons*, 52.

### Chapter 12. Last Dance

1. A haunting snippet of the film is on file at the London Museum and Tea Room, New London, TX.

### Chapter 13. 3:17 p.m.

1. Military Court of Inquiry Report, 311.
2. Jackson, *Living Lessons*, 41.
3. Ibid., 53; Steve Blow, "A Lost Generation," *Dallas Morning News,* March 1, 1987, story about the fiftieth anniversary of the explosion quoting Helen (Beard) Sillick.
4. Clipping in the Evans scrapbook, *Dallas Times-Herald*, March 19, 1937, 2.
5. Jackson, *Living Lessons*, 49.
6. "Boy Tells Of School Blast," *Tyler Courier-Times*, March 19, 1937, front page.
7. Jackson, *Living Lessons*, 43; the lesson page with Juanita Gibson's broken circle is displayed in a frame at the London Museum and Tea Room.
8. Steve Blow, "A Lost Generation," *Dallas Morning News*, March 1, 1987; also, Joe King describes his experience in great detail in Janice Talley Marsh, "Learning From Disaster," *Tyler Life*, March 1985.
9. "Teacher Saves 95 By Having Pupils Hide Under Desk," clipping in Mother Frances Hospital Memory Book, a scrapbook of newspaper clippings the sisters collected as a remembrance of the disaster and the opening of the hospital. It is kept in the hospital's archives.
10. Jackson, *Living Lessons*, 52; Kenneth Dean, "68th Anniversary Stirs Memories of Tragedy," *Tyler Morning Telegraph*, March 18, 2005, front page.
11. Military Court of Inquiry Report, 151.
12. "Sisters Helen Sillick and Marie Challis Remember Tragedy," special supplement, *Overton Press*, March 13, 1997.
13. *Herald-Examiner* (Chicago), undated clipping from news coverage immediately following the explosion, in Carroll and Mildred Evans's scrapbook.
14. "Jests of Cut-ups Stopped By Blast, Lucky Girl Avers," *Dallas Morning News*, March 22, 1937.
15. Bright, *New London 1937*, 36–40.
16. Undated *Henderson Daily News* clipping from news coverage immediately following the explosion, with Cletis Wells recounting her story, Carroll and Mildred Evans's scrapbook.
17. "Men, Trucks, Supplies, and Food Rushed To Scene of Explosion After Calls Made Over Radio," *Kilgore Daily News*, March 19, 1937; Jackson, *Living Lessons*, 40.
18. Jackson, *Living Lessons*, 42.
19. "Boy Tells Of School Blast," *Tyler Courier-Times*, March 19, 1937.
20. Jackson, *Living Lessons*, 39
21. Associated Press dispatch reviewing the New London school explosion, October 20, 1985.

22. Undated clipping in scrapbook of newspaper coverage immediately following the disaster, on file in the library at West Rusk High School.
23. Jackson, *Living Lessons*, 50.
24. J. B. Dial's super feat of strength, moving a slab of concrete to let a child escape, was among numerous reports of adrenaline-driven feats that became legendary over the years since the explosion. Some undoubtedly happened; others may have been exaggerations or the product of excited imaginations. We let the story of J. B. Dial's Herculean show of strength stand because it seems logical; he was a powerful roughneck frantically searching for his sons under the rubble.
25. Military Court of Inquiry Report, 141.

## Chapter 14. Thunder on a Clear Day
1. Jackson typically dressed in a coat and tie and frequently wore a white fedora; it is speculation he was wearing the hat when the school exploded, but it seems like a good guess. As near as he was to the school, the percussion from the blast almost certainly would have sent the fedora sailing.
2. Believe It Or Not, *London (TX) Times*, November 13, 1937.
3. London School Notes, *Henderson Daily News*, November 24, 1936.
4. Mrs. Bud Sanders, "Lest We Forget," *Kilgore News Herald*, March 18, 1970, front page, an anniversary story about the explosion.
5. Bright, *New London 1937*, 57.
6. William T. Rives, Associated Press story, March 19, 1937, 17.
7. Jackson, *Living Lessons*, 62–63.

## Chapter 15. Newshounds
1. United Press wire dispatch, March 18, 1937. This was prior to a merger that changed the wire service's name to United Press International.
2. "Girl Killed in Subway Leap," *New York Times*, March 19, 1937. The woman, Betty Schwartz, a twenty-one-year-old stenographer from Pittsburgh, Pennsylvania, had lived in New York one week before jumping in front of the subway train. She died at Bellevue Hospital a few minutes before the New London school explosion in Texas.
3. Henry McLemore, "Today's Sports Parade," United Press column, March 18, 1937.
4. Sarah McClendon, *My Eight Presidents* (New York: Simon & Schuster, 1978), 13.
5. Sarah McClendon, *Mr. President, Mr. President! My Fifty Years of Covering the White House*, with Jules Minton (Los Angeles, CA: General Publishing Group, 1996), 126, 127.

## Chapter 16. Holy Sisters
1. "New Hospital In City Seen As Big Move To Progress," *Tyler Morning Telegraph*, March 19, 1937, report on Rotary luncheon.
2. C. C. McDonald, *Medicine in Our Town* (Fort Worth, TX: Branch-Smith, 1975), 25. Unless otherwise noted, quotes and biographical information about C. C. McDonald in this chapter are from this memoir.
3. Congregation of the Sisters of the Holy Family of Nazareth, "God's Ways Are Not Our Ways," *Reflections* (newsletter) 18, no. 4 (October 1996).

4. Mother Frances Hospital, special section, *Tyler Courier-Times*, March 14, 1937.
5. Sisters of the Holy Family, "God's Ways."
6. Ibid.

## Chapter 17. Radio Man

1. Ted Hudson's profile is based on an interview with Mary Lou (Hudson) Powell, his daughter, newspaper clippings about his work in the rescue operation, an article in the national *Kiwanis* magazine in June after the New London explosion detailing his activities at the disaster site, a synopsis of his life in one book, a news story about his death, and his obituary.
2. Wecter, *Age of the Great Depression*, 229–31.
3. "Radio: NBC is 10 Years Old," *Life*, November 23, 1936.
4. Vincent Terrace, *Radio's Golden Years: The Encyclopedia of Radio Programs 1930–1960* (New York: A. S. Barnes, 1981), 167.
5. Ibid., 216.
6. Garland R. Farmer, *The Realm of Rusk County* (Henderson, TX: Henderson Times, 1951), 140.
7. "Ted Hudson, Les Dublin Killed by Plane Crash near Corsicana," *Henderson Daily News*, November 25, 1946.
8. Radio station KOCA network programming schedule for March 18, 1937, *Kilgore Daily News*, March 18, 1937, was used to note what was on the air at various times as Hudson's day progressed.

## Chapter 18. Into the Ruins

1. E. D. Powell, "Father of Two Blast Victims Says World War Horrors Are Nothing Compared to Explosion," International News Services, reprinted in London Museum and Tea Room souvenir edition by the *Overton Press*, March 1997.
2. "One of First To Reach Scene Finds his own Tot," wire dispatch, *Charleston Gazette*, March 19, 1937.
3. "Sillick and Challis Remember Tragedy," *Overton Press*.
4. "Three-Day Quest for Missing School Girl Ends at Hospital, When Inez Herron, 12, Speaks," unmarked newspaper clipping (probably from *Tyler Morning Telegraph* or *Tyler Courier-Times*), March 23, 1937, in "Memory Book March 1937–August 1949," Mother Frances Hospital, Tyler, TX.
5. "Sight of Victims Kills Arp Man 63," United Press dispatch, March 18, 1937, reprinted in London Museum and Tea Room souvenir edition of *Henderson Daily News*.
6. Marsh, "Learning from Disaster," 26; Jackson, *Living Lessons*, 53.
7. Jackson, *Living Lessons*, 49.
8. Price interview.
9. Ibid.

## Chapter 19. Newsflash

1. Segments involving Felix McKnight, including his quotes and the quotes from people McKnight spoke with, are derived from an interview with McKnight conducted by David M. Brown, November 20, 1990, unless otherwise explained in an endnote. The exact wording of his first short newsflash about

the explosion was not located in our research; the version here is based on McKnight's memory of what he wrote.

2. Walter Cronkite, interview by KHOU-TV, Houston, TX, March 1987. This was a special program about the explosion broadcast for the fiftieth anniversary of the tragedy.

3. Don Douglass, "A Kiwanian Broadcasts London, Texas, Tragedy," *Kiwanis*, June 1937, 348.

4. "Henry McLemore, Former Columnist," *New York Times*, June 24, 1968, obituary.

5. Henry McLemore, "McLemore Uses Old Speakeasy Card at Berlin and It Takes Him Inside of Dressing Room," United Press sports column, *Kilgore Daily News*, August 4, 1936, 8.

6. Henry McLemore, "McLemore Finds That Prague Taxi Drivers Make American Speedsters Look Like 'Pikers,'" United Press sports column, *Kilgore Daily News,* August 25, 1936, 7.

7. Henry McLemore, "Today's Sports Parade," United Press sports column, *Reading Eagle,* January 9, 1937.

8. Henry McLemore, "McLemore Tries His Hand At Art of Mountain Climbing But Quits After No St. Bernards Answer His Calls," United Press column, *Kilgore Daily News*, September 2, 1936, 10.

9. McLemore, "Today's Sports Parade."

10. Walter Cronkite notes McLemore was instructed to bring extra shirts in Walter Cronkite, *A Reporter's Life* (New York: Alfred A. Knopf, 1996), 65.

11. Ibid., 63.

12. Ibid., 61.

13. McClendon, *Mr. President, Mr. President!*, 127.

14. Ibid.

15. Ibid.

16. William T. Rives quote, AP 28, Writings about the Associated Press, Series IV, Reporters' Recollections, Oliver Gramling Commissions, AP Corporate Archives, New York, NY.

17. Ibid.

18. Felix McKnight quote in ibid.

## Chapter 20. A Blue Patch of Sky

1. Carroll Evans, interview in *The Day a Generation Died*, directed by Jerry Gumbert, KLTV-TV, Tyler, TX, March 1987. This documentary was filmed and broadcast for the fiftieth anniversary of the disaster.

2. Evans, "Carroll and Mildred Evans," 37–38.

3. "Three-Day Quest."

4. Price interview.

5. Ibid.

6. Letter from Jewel Lewis about her uncle and his son finding Queen Price, on file at the London Museum and Tea Room, New London, TX.

7. Charlotte Heldenbrand, "Family Torn by Young Son's Death," *Overton Press*, March 12, 2009, reprint of a story that originally appeared in the *Overton Press* on March 14, 2002.

**Chapter 21. Valley of Death at Sundown**

1. Frei, unpublished memoir.
2. "Call National Guard To Take Charge At Blast," Associated Press, *Tyler Courier-Times,* March 19, 1937.
3. Walter Cronkite, interview in Gumbert, *The Day a Generation Died.*
4. Ibid.

**Chapter 22. Mother Frances**

1. Jeannette Freeman Martin, interview by the authors, September 29, 2011.
2. Rhiannon Meyers, "A Day Before Opening, Mother Frances Hospital 'Was a Miracle,'" *Tyler Morning Telegraph,* March 18, 2007.
3. Charlotte Heldenbrand, "Schoolmates Emerge from Blast Rubble to Become Soulmates," *Overton Press,* March 15, 2007.
4. Frei, unpublished memoir.
5. McKnight quote, AP 28 Writings about the Associated Press, Series IV.
6. Ibid.
7. McKnight's dialogue with the phone operator is based on a combination of details from the interview he gave for this book and information in his AP notes in ibid.
8. Sisters of the Holy Family, "God's Ways."
9. McClendon, *Mr. President, Mr. President!,* 127.
10. Martha Harris, Associated Press dispatch, March 18, 1937.
11. Charlie Clair, United Press dispatch, March 18, 1937.
12. Heldenbrand, "Family Torn by Young Son's Death."
13. McKnight quote, AP 28 Writings about The Associated Press, Series IV.
14. Hudson segment, not knowing he was on national hookup, Don Douglass, "A Kiwanian Broadcasts London, Texas, Tragedy," *Kiwanis,* June 1937, 348.
15. "Mrs. Roosevelt Says 'Something Must Be Done,'" *Tyler Courier-Times,* March 19, 1937.
16. Heldenbrand, "Family Torn," 2002.
17. "Six Injured in Hospitals Here May Die," *Tyler Courier-Times,* March 19, 1937. The article includes a list of patients at Mother Frances Hospital and their conditions.

**Chapter 23. Midnight of the Soul**

1. McKnight, Associated Press dispatch, March 18, 1937.
2. Tom Reynolds, "Rain Steadily Beats Down On Scene Of Blast," United Press dispatch, March 19, 1937; clipping in Mother Frances Hospital "Memory Book," without note of specific newspaper.
3. Associated Press dispatch, March 19, 1937.
4. Associated Press, "Arms Clasped, Two Children Are Found Alive In Blast Ruins," *Daily Herald* (Big Springs, Texas), March 20, 1937.
5. William T. Rives, Associated Press dispatch, March 18, 1937.
6. "Blast Cleans Human Bones," *Tyler Courier-Times,* March 19, 1937.
7. William T. Rives, Associated Press dispatch, March 18, 1937.
8. Miscellaneous news article, apparently clipped from *Henderson Daily News,* March 19, 1937, reprinted by the London Museum and Tea Room.

9. *Dallas Times Herald*, March 19, 1937, clipping in Evans's scrapbook without headline or byline.
10. William T. Rives, Associated Press dispatch, March 18, 1937.
11. Jan Isbell Fortune, "Mass Burials Set for 300 Children in Rusk," *Henderson Daily News*, March 19, 1937.
12. *Henderson Daily News,* March 19, 1937, a list with descriptions of dead children, their clothes, etc., to help identify them, as sidebar to main front-page story.
13. Overton morgue quote from clipping in the Evans's scrapbook, dated but without a title, *Herald-Examiner* (Chicago), March 20, 1937.
14. Ibid.
15. Ibid.
16. Henry McLemore, "McLemore Writes of London Blast and Experiences," *Henderson Daily News*, March 19, 1937. McLemore began the piece he wrote with hearing about the woman on the radio.
17. Evans, "Carroll and Mildred Evans," 37–38.
18. London School Notes, *Henderson Daily News*, November 24, 1936.
19. Joe Davidson's comment was widely reported in local newspapers and by the wire services.
20. Jackson, *Living Lessons*, 54.
21. Associated Press, "700 Children Thought Dead as Blast Razes Rusk County School Building," *Dallas Morning News*, March 19, 1937.
22. Our research indicated McLemore had never covered any story of this magnitude, nor anything as tragic.
23. Davidson's comments were widely reported.

## Chapter 24. Dawn, March 19
1. Jimmie Donahue, "Grief-Stricken Mothers Carry on Ceaseless Search For Children," *Tyler Courier-Times*, March 19, 1937, front page.
2. Clipping in Evans's scrapbook without headline or byline, *Dallas Times-Herald*, March 19, 1937, 2.
3. Pat McNealy Barnes, *Houston Post*, March 20, 1937.
4. An Associated Press dispatch on March 19, 1937, reported Wesley H. Pitken, a thirty-eight-year-old oil-field worker in the Raccoon Bend oil field, "became demented" while listening to coverage of the New London school explosion on the radio and held a loaded double-barrel shotgun on his family, while threatening to kill them and himself.
5. Steve Blow, "A Generation Lost," *Dallas Morning News*, March 1, 1987.
6. Clipping in Evans's scrapbook, missing headline and with no byline, *Dallas Times Herald*, March 19, 1937.

## Chapter 25. Hard News
1. "Raymond Meissner, Embalmer, Helps at New London Disaster," *Fort Worth Star-Telegram*, undated newspaper clipping (clearly published soon after the explosion). The article detailed Meissner's experience and included copious quotes from him.
2. William T. Rives notes, AP 28 Writings about the Associated Press, Series IV.
3. Henry McLemore, "McLemore Writes of Blast and Experiences," United Press dispatch, *Henderson Daily News*, March 20, 1937.

4. Charles Saulsberry, "Spectators Sickened as Shattered Bodies are Removed in Baskets," *Dallas Morning News*, March 20, 1937.
5. Walter Cronkite, "Bereaved Parents Cling To Fragile Threads Of Hope," United Press dispatch, March 19, 1937, clipping in Mother Frances Hospital archival "Memory Book" of newspaper coverage collected mainly from the *Henderson Daily News, Kilgore Daily News, Tyler Morning-Courier, and Dallas Morning News.* The Cronkite clipping does not have a notation of which newspaper it was from.
6. Associated Press, "Pathos and Tragedy."
7. The scene is based on a detailed schedule of events for the Camp-O-Ral, "200 Boy Scouts Expected To Take Part in Camp-O-Ral," *Henderson Daily News*, May 17, 1935, 7.
8. Sarah McClendon, "Helpers at First-Aid Station Are Dead Tired as They Round Up 20 Hours on Duty," *Tyler Courier-Times*, March 19, 1937.
9. Associated Press, "Gruesome Task of Diggers is Ended," *Ironwood (MI) Daily Globe*, March 19, 1937.
10. John Mortimer, *Houston Post,* March 20, 1937, an article contained in the Evans's scrapbook without a headline.
11. An Associated Press dispatch, March 19, 1937, included the quotes Rives overheard.
12. Henry McLemore, "'Richest Little Town' Poorest After Tragedy," United Press dispatch, *The Salt Lake Tribune,* March 20, 1937.
13. Frei, unpublished memoir.

**Chapter 26. Coffin Train**
1. An Associated Press correction dated March 20, 1937, said Alma Stroud and her daughter Helen were not dead, as widely reported the day before; even so, the dramatic tale of a mother dropping dead upon finding the body of her child became urban legend in East Texas and is often repeated to this day.
2. Henry McLemore, "Henry McLemore Describes Terrible Carnage Of Blast; Noted Sports Writer Dips Pen in Different Color of Ink to Give Unusual Story of Tragedy," United Press dispatch, *Henderson Daily News*, March 20, 1937.
3. Undated news clipping, likely from the *Tyler Morning Telegraph* or *Courier-Times*, in a scrapbook kept by Carroll and Mildred Evans of news coverage of the explosion and aftermath.
4. Information from the cutline of a picture of the Smoot brothers, London Museum and Tea Room; Anna (Smoot) Brannon, interview by the authors over several telephone calls in August 2010.
5. Details in this segment derived from Henry McLemore's March 20, 1937, dispatch about the funerals.
6. Copies of receipts for train tickets Davidson purchased are on file at the London Museum and Tea Room, New London, TX.

**Chapter 27. Reckoning**
1. Unless otherwise noted, the information in this chapter was obtained from the Military Court of Inquiry Report. Military Court of Inquiry Report, 123–26.
2. Biographical information collected by the University of Texas Chemistry Li-

brary, Austin, TX, http://www.lib.utexas.edu/chem/history/schoch.pdf (accessed spring 2011).

3. Tom Reynolds, United Press dispatch, March 21, 1937.
4. Texas Inspection Bureau, "Report of the High School Explosion and the Disaster of London, Texas" (Austin, TX, March 27, 1937).
5. Robert M. Hayes, "Lest London Forget, Brief Service Slated March 20 to Mark Blast's Anniversary," *Dallas Morning News*, March 13, 1938.

## Chapter 28. Lament
1. Bright, *New London 1937*, 64–67.
2. Robert Nieman, "Impossible. It Can't Be Dale May York," *Overton Press*, undated newspaper clipping, London Museum and Tea Room, New London, TX.
3. Cronkite, *Reporter's Life*, 65–66.
4. Associated Press dispatch, March 20, 1937.
5. Shaw family interviews and correspondence with the authors.
6. Gumbert, *The Day a Generation Died*.
7. McLemore, "Today's Sports Parade."

## Chapter 29. Amazing Grace
1. "French Tots Send Aid To New London," Associated Press, reprinted by the *Overton Press*, March 1996 as souvenir edition for the London Museum and Tea Room.
2. Wire dispatch summary of foreign response to the disaster, March 22, 1937, reprinted in the *Overton Press*, March 11, 1987.
3. Clipping in the Evans's scrapbook without headline or byline, *Herald-Examiner* (Chicago), March 20, 1937.
4. New London explosion anniversary edition, *Overton Press*, March 21, 1985, contains brief with comment that Dr. George Hamm, then president of the University of Texas at Tyler, was a student in the North Dakota school when the principal asked students to pray for the children in the Texas disaster.
5. Newspaper clip in Evans's scrapbook, no headline, *Dallas Times-Herald*, March 19, 1937.
6. Jackson, *Living Lessons*, 61.
7. Miscellaneous news clipping in the Evans's scrapbook.
8. Ibid.
9. Clark and Halbouty, *Last Boom*, 257.
10. The film of John Lumpkin Jr.'s funeral is on file at the London Museum and Tea Room.
11. Jackson, *Living Lessons*, photo cutline in unnumbered picture section; the John Lumpkin story is on file at the London Museum and Tea Room.
12. Wire Service reports, March 19, 1937, on remarks of the chaplin of the U.S. House of Representatives concerning New London disaster.
13. Carolyn Jones, speech given to the Texas House of Representatives, March 25, 1937. Speech can be found online at *Lessons of the 1937 Texas School Explosion*, "Set Aside a Special Day Each Year as a Memorial," blog entry by Ellie Goldberg, March 12, 2010, http://lessonsofthe1937texasschoolexplosion .blogspot.com/2010/02/set-aside-special-day-each-year-as.html.

14. The story of Elbert Box and Louise McAdam is on file at the London Museum and Tea Room.
15. United Press dispatch, "Child Pleads With Legislature For Safety In Schools," March 25, 1936, reprinted by the *Overton Press* as a souvenir newspaper for the London Museum and Tea Room.
16. Carolyn Jones, March 25, 1937 speech; Dawson Duncan, "Public Not Aware of Peril In Use of Gas, Expert Says," *Dallas Morning News*, March 26, 1937.
17. Bright, *New London 1937*, 63, 68.
18. "Three-Day Quest."

### Chapter 30. Survivors Assembly, March 29
1. The soft-spoken lines "He is dead" or "She was killed" were repeated time and again as the roll was called, according to Bess Stephenson, "Pupils Troop Back through Chill Air to London School and Their Studies," *Fort Worth Star-Telegram*, March 30, 1937.
2. "New London Band Was To Play Here," *Overton Press*, article reprinted for special edition marking 60th anniversary of the explosion, March 1997, 7.
3. "Kilgore Music Festival To Be Dedicated to Henderson Band," *Kilgore Daily News*, March 23, 1937.
4. J. W. Harris, "21 London Blast Victims Still in East Texas Hospitals," *Henderson Daily News*, April 18, 1937.
5. Ledell Dorsey's father would not force her to return to school in New London, although he had her enroll in a different school. Later she told him that going to any school filled her with dread, and he allowed her to drop out and get a job. Ledell (Dorsey) Carpenter, interview by the authors, June 10, 2010.
6. Geneva Stovall, "New London Blast—March 18, 1937: Death of a Generation," *Texarkana Gazette*, March 18, 2010. Geneva Stovall is the daughter of Geneva Elrod, who survived the explosion.
7. Breakdown of numbers killed in each class in the London Museum and Tea Room.
8. Charlotte Heldenbrand, "Sixth-Grade Class One of Hardest Hit," *Overton Press*, March 12, 2009.

### Chapter 31. Reunion
1. Hayes, "Lest London Forget."
2. Pete Gilpin, "Day of Doom," *Houston Chronicle Rotogravure Magazine*, March 18, 1956.
3. Joe Davenport, "Man Says He Caused New London Blast; Loosened Gas Pipes, He Claims," *Tyler Courier-Times*, July 18, 1961.
4. Felix McKnight, copy without title of story written for the Associated Press for release July 19, 1961, in McKnight's personal files, made available to the authors by his daughter, Joan (McKnight) McIlyar.
5. Davenport, "Man Says He Caused New London Blast."
6. "First Lie Test Fails In New London Case," United Press International, *Dallas Morning News*, July 19, 1961.
7. Davenport, "Man Says He Caused New London Blast."
8. Associated Press and United Press International dispatches, July 20, 1961.

9. Douglass, "Kiwanian Broadcasts London, Texas, Tragedy."
10. Elbert Box file, London Museum and Tea Room.
11. Robert M. Hayes, "London Would Forget School Disaster," *Dallas Morning News*, March 16, 1947.
12. Heldenbrand, "Family Torn," 2009.
13. Hayes, "Lest London Forget."
14. Both McLemore of the United Press and McKnight of the Associated Press used the "richest-poorest" approach in their different stories on the tragedy, just as both wire services used a similar line that March 18, 1937 was the day "a generation died."
15. "Ex-reporter dies in Florida," *Dallas Morning News*, June 24, 1968, United Press International obituary.
16. Gumbert, *The Day a Generation Died*.

**Chapter 32. A Final Word**

1. "Tiny Autograph Booklet Tells of Broken Lives," *Henderson Daily News*, March 19, 1937.

# Selected Bibliography

**Books**

Bright, Lorine Zylks. *New London 1937: One Woman's Memory of Orange and Green*. Wichita Falls, TX: Nortex Press, 1977.

Clark, James A., and Michel T. Halbouty. *The Last Boom*. New York: Random House, 1972.

Cronkite, Walter. *A Reporter's Life*. New York: Alfred A. Knopf, 1996.

Farmer, Garland R. *The Realm of Rusk County*. Henderson, TX: Henderson Times, 1951.

*Henderson, Texas City Directory—1935–36*. Springfield, MO: Interstate Directory, 1936.

Horan, James D. *The Desperate Years: A Pictorial History of the Thirties*. New York: Crown Publishers, 1962.

Huston, Cleburne. *Towering Texan: A Biography of Thomas J. Rusk*. Waco, TX: Texian Press, 1971.

Jack, William T. *Gaston High School, Joinerville, Texas, and a Boy Named Billy Jack*. Campbell, TX: J & N Press, 1989.

Jackson, Robert L. *Living Lessons from the New London Explosion*. Nashville, TN: Parthenon Press, 1938.

Knowles, Ruth Sheldon. *The Greatest Gamblers: The Epic of American Oil Exploration*. Norman: University of Oklahoma Press, 1978.

Lambert, Paul F., and Kenny A. Franks, eds. *Voices from the Oil Fields*. Norman: University of Oklahoma Press, 1984.

*Londona*. (The first New London High School annual.) New London, TX, 1935.

*Londona*. (The second New London High School annual.) New London, TX, 1936.

McClendon, Sarah. *Mr. President, Mr. President! My Fifty Years of Covering the White House*. With Jules Minton. Los Angeles, CA: General Publishing Group, 1996.

———. *My Eight Presidents*. New York: Simon & Schuster, 1978.

McDonald, C. C. *Medicine in Our Town*. Fort Worth, TX: Branch-Smith, 1975.

McElvaine, Robert S. *The Great Depression: America, 1929–1941*. New York: Times Books, 1984.

McKay, Seth S., and Odie B. Faulk. *Texas after Spindletop: The Saga of Texas— 1901–1965*. Austin: Steck-Vaughn, 1965.

Olien, Roger M., and Diana Davids Olien. *Life in the Oil Fields*. Austin: Texas Monthly Press, 1986.

———. *Wildcatters: Texas Independent Oilmen*. Austin: Texas Monthly Press, 1984.

Rundell, Walter, Jr. *Early Texas Oil: A Photographic History, 1866–1936*. College Station: Texas A&M University Press, 1977.

Rusk County Historical Commission. *Rusk County History*. Dallas: Taylor Publishing, 1982.

Smith, Gene. *The Shattered Dream: Herbert Hoover and the Great Depression*. New York: William Morrow, 1970.

Steen, Ralph W. *The Texas Story*. Austin: Steck, 1948.

Terrace, Vincent. *Radio's Golden Years: The Encyclopedia of Radio Programs, 1930–1960*. New York: A. S. Barnes, 1981.

Webb, Walter Prescott, ed. *The Handbook of Texas*. Austin: Texas State Historical Association, 1952.

Wecter, Dixon. *The Age of the Great Depression, 1929–1941*. New York: Macmillan, 1948.

Winfrey, Dorman. *A History of Rusk County, Texas*. Waco, TX: Texian Press, 1961.

### Journals, Reports, and Manuscripts

Evans, Mildred. "The Life and Times of Carroll and Mildred Evans." Compiled by Kevin C. Evans. Unpublished manuscript, 1986.

Frei, Carolyn (Jones). Poems and unpublished memoir.

Heaberlin, Nadine Thompson, and Sam J. Heaberlin, comps. "Ancestors and Descendants of Alvin A. and Bonnie Freeman Thompson." Unpublished manuscript, 1989.

Military Court of Inquiry Report, New London school explosion, March 23, 1937, Texas State Archives, Austin, TX.

Rosamond, Joanne, and Walter Fields, comps. "The Gaston Story." Unpublished manuscript, West Rusk County Consolidated Independent School District, New London, TX, May 1989.

———. "The London Story." Unpublished manuscript, West Rusk County Consolidated Independent School District, New London, TX, March 1989.

Texas Inspection Bureau. "Report of the High School Explosion and the Disaster of London, Texas." Austin, TX, March 27, 1937.

*Tyler Life,* March 1985.

U.S. Bureau of Mines. "Explosion in School Building, New London, Texas, March 18, 1937." Federal report, serial 3365, December 1937.

### Film and Video

Cronkite, Walter. Interview by KHOU-TV, Houston, TX, March 1987.

"Dances of the World." Film of PTA meeting, New London School, March 18, 1937, London Museum, New London, TX.

*The Day a Generation Died*, directed by Jerry Gumbert, KLTV-TV, Tyler, TX, March 1987.

Lumpkin, John. Film of John Lumpkin Jr. Funeral. London Museum, New London, TX.
New London disaster. King Features newsreel. 1937.
New London disaster. Universal newsreel. 1937.

**Newspapers**
The authors relied on information from dozens of newspapers and three major wire services that provided real-time accounts of the New London school explosion and its aftermath. Although journalists at the scene made a few glaring mistakes, the news coverage as a whole was correct, insightful, and vivid. This book could not have been written with as much historically accurate detail without those sources, including the following: *Henderson Daily News, Overton Press, Kilgore Daily News, Kilgore Herald, Tyler Courier-Times, Tyler Morning Telegraph, Rusk County News, Longview Morning-Journal, Longview News, Shreveport Journal, Dallas Morning News, Dallas Daily Times-Herald* (which later became the *Dallas Times Herald*, dropping *Daily* and the hyphen), *Fort Worth Star-Telegram, Houston Chronicle, Houston Post, Daily Oklahoman, New York Times,* and *Herald-Examiner* (Chicago).

# Index

# About the Authors

**David M. Brown** is a journalist with more than two decades of experience as a reporter, feature writer, and political analyst for newspapers and magazines. He worked as a staff writer for United Press International, the *Memphis Commercial Appeal*, the *South Mississippi Sun*, the Biloxi-Gulfport *Daily Herald*, and, most recently, the *Pittsburgh Tribune-Review*. During a fourteen-year career with the *Tribune-Review*, his work was distinguished by awards from local, state, and national organizations. He graduated from Mississippi State University with a degree in English literature. He lives with his wife, Mary, and their cat, Mia Bella, in South Fayette, a suburb of Pittsburgh, Pennsylvania.

**Michael Wereschagin** is a reporter at the *Pittsburgh Tribune-Review* covering metropolitan, state, and national news. He has been dispatched to the scene of national disasters, including the deadly 2006 Sago Mine explosion in West Virginia, the execution of five Amish girls in a one-room schoolhouse in Pennsylvania later that year, the Virginia Tech massacre, and the I-35W bridge collapse in Minneapolis. He was part of the reporting teams that covered the shooting deaths of three Pittsburgh police officers in April 2009 and the shooting spree at a Pittsburgh health club in August of that year in which four died. His reporting has received awards from local, state, and national organizations. He lives with his wife, Neva, on the North Side of Pittsburgh, Pennsylvania.

Together, Brown and Wereschagin covered local, state, and national politics, including the 2008 presidential race.